Happy birthday

Ruth.

D1346180

NEW BAYREUTH

Other books by Penelope Turing:

TRAVEL
  Your Guide to Sicily (Alvin Redman)
AUTOBIOGRAPHY
  Lance Free (Michael Joseph)

1 Wolfgang Wagner

New Bayreuth

by

PENELOPE TURING

JERSEY ARTISTS

Distributed by

NEVILLE SPEARMAN

Made and printed in Great Britain
at the St Ann's Press, Park Road, Altrincham
for Jersey Artists Ltd.,
Mon Contour, St Martin, Jersey, C.I.,
and distributed by Neville Spearman Ltd.,
112 Whitfield Street, London W.1

To the Mitwirkenden of the
Bayreuth Festivals

*This book is dedicated in gratitude to all the
artists, technicians, workers seen and unseen,
to whom we owe the glory of these festivals*

Contents

LIST OF ILLUSTRATIONS

Plate No.

Author's Note

THE opinions and enthusiasms expressed in this book are of course my own. The facts are, I hope, accurate. Space has not permitted me to mention every singer, and not always even the leading singers in alternative casts, in the text, but complete cast lists are given in Appendix A.

I should like to record here my most grateful thanks to Herr Wolfgang Wagner for his sympathetic interest, for allowing me to consult official records, and for giving me permission to reproduce Bayreuth Festival photographs (plates 1, 2, 4-10, 12-24a, 26-48, 50-80). My warmest thanks also to Herr Herbert Barth, Press Officer, for his unfailing help and patience, and to Frl. Armann of the Press Office; to Frau Schuster of the Richard-Wagner-Gedenkstätte, Bayreuth; and to Herr W. Bronnenmeyer of the *Nordbayerischer Kurier*. Without their help, and that of many other friends in Bayreuth, this book could not have been written. I also acknowledge with thanks permission granted by the Editor of the *Sunday Times* to reprint excerpts from articles by the late Ernest Newman which appear in Chapter I. Permission to reprint photographs which appear here as plates 11, 24b, 25 has been granted by the Fremdenverkehrsverein, Bayreuth; plate 3 is by Lammel, Bayreuth, and plate 49 by Deutsche Grammophon, and for these pictures I am also most grateful.

London, December 1968   PENELOPE TURING

So widespread and keen is the interest in Bayreuth Festivals, and so encouraging the reception given to this personal record of them, that it has been decided to bring out a second impression of the book as soon as possible. This volume contains chapters and cast lists on the seasons of 1969 and 1970, and so is completely up to date. It has not been possible, however, to adjust the writing standpoint in time of the earlier chapters, so that where references are made to a span of time such as "seventeen years ago" it must be remembered that this was written for 1969.

London, January 1971   PENELOPE TURING

Introduction

ACROSS the post-war world of opera the style of production known as New Bayreuth has cast a searchlight beam extraordinary in its intensity. Extraordinary in several ways. Wagner's operas have always had a strong even impassioned following, but Wagner lovers form only a minority group among operagoers. Yet the new methods of staging inaugurated at the Wagner festival centre of Bayreuth in 1951 have profoundly affected opera production of all kinds all over the world.

Naturally the influence of this Bayreuth style is seen most strongly in productions of Richard Wagner's own works, or reactions to them. Any operahouse putting on a new production of one of the operas is judged, acclaimed or condemned, according to its apparent conformity to the Bayreuth conception. Occasionally, depending on the personal taste of the observer, they may be praised for being unlike Bayreuth, but it remains the universal yardstick.

Given artistic vision sometimes amounting to genius—and such has been the special quality of Bayreuth—this supremacy in the world of the Wagner canon is understandable. But the simplified sets, muted lighting, and a minimum of histrionics which are the basic ingredients of the Bayreuth style have spread to the works of many other composers, ancient and modern. Sometimes the results are singularly unsuitable, but the inspiration stems from Wagner's Festspielhaus on its green hill in Northern Bavaria, and is acknowledged to it. People who have never been there, and probably never will, talk glibly about New Bayreuth. It has become part of the operatic vocabulary.

Two men are responsible for the inspiration and initiative which created this phenomenon. Several hundred people have been vitally concerned in making it a tangible reality: conductors, singers, instrumentalists, and all the unsung workers without whom no stage performance—least of all opera—can reach its public.

The brothers Wieland and Wolfgang Wagner, grandsons of the composer, were these two men. They had a unique heritage, and faced a unique challenge in revealing it to the changed world which followed the Second World War. To describe something of the way in which they have achieved their aim is the purpose of this book.

Wieland's tragically early death in 1966 marked the end of the first phase in the development of New Bayreuth. But it was only the first phase, though being the initial period it was the most vital one. His brother continues as director of the festivals, and the inspiration which both possessed is very much alive. Obviously it will take different forms as the years pass. The very essence of Wieland Wagner's work was its fluidity, its rethinking and development from year to year. His own variations in his work did not always result in improvement, but they prevented stagnation, they engendered excitement. He would have been the last person to wish his productions to become mummified.

After an inevitable interim festival in 1967, the pattern of Wolfgang Wagner's plans for the future is beginning to show. He is himself a gifted producer and designer, less startling and in some ways more subtle than his brother. His productions at Bayreuth have maintained a consistently good standard, and sometimes have been outstanding. But they have never attracted the publicity and excitement of Wieland's work. When Wieland succeeded he did so magnificently. When he failed—and despite the enthusiasts' blind devotion there were several failures in later years—the results were monumental errors which echoed round the world as partisans and critics crossed swords. It is almost certainly true that without Wieland Wagner's special gifts New Bayreuth would not hold its unique place in the world today, but time may well prove that Wolfgang Wagner is the man best fitted now to steer this richly-laden argosy on the sea of European festivals.

The history of the Bayreuth Festivals is known, in outline, to most Wagnerites. Richard Wagner, after a heartbreaking series of problems and disappointments, mostly financial, opened his new and indeed unfinished Festspielhaus at Bayreuth on August 13, 1876 with a performance of *Das Rheingold*. The other operas of *Der Ring des Nibelungen* followed, and three cycles formed the first festival.

Owing to lack of funds the theatre remained closed for the next six years. Then in 1882 it was reopened for the first performance of *Parsifal*, Wagner's last opera and the work which was designed especially to be given in the Festspielhaus. Only *Parsifal* was performed that year, but it was given sixteen times, and proved to be his swan song if not his Nunc Dimittis. He himself conducted the final scene at the last performance. Six months later he died in Venice.

Between 1883 and 1906 there were fifteen festivals, all directed by Richard Wagner's widow Cosima. In 1907 she handed over control to their son Siegfried, then thirty-eight years old, and he held the reins—and sometimes the baton, being a conductor and composer in his own right—until his death, which took place during the festival of 1930. His mother Cosima had died only a few months earlier. Once more the direction of the festivals devolved upon a Wagner widow, this time Siegfried's British wife Winifred. From 1931 until 1944 she was in sole control. Then the final phases of the war and its aftermath closed the Festspielhaus. When the new day dawned for Bayreuth in 1951 Winifred Wagner handed over to her two sons Wieland and Wolfgang.

That is the bare framework of the Bayreuth heritage as it came to these two young men, but to understand even dimly the task with which they were faced some flesh must be added to these bones.

The early years of the festivals had created a veneration for them among Wagner lovers all over the world. A pilgrimage to Bayreuth became the aim of the true enthusiast. At the same time veneration for Wagner's own wishes and stage directions was very naturally Cosima's guiding principle. Conductors such as Hans Richter, Felix Mottl, and Karl Muck and many of the great Wagnerian singers of the time appeared at Bayreuth during her reign. Under Siegfried Wagner much the same pattern continued, though later he began to introduce some new ideas in staging. Nonetheless right through the years to 1930 Bayreuth was the Wagnerian Establishment in the modern sense.

This Winifred Wagner inherited, at a time which proved to be the beginning of the most unhappy period in Germany's history, and with which Bayreuth was all too closely associated. Much has been said and written of Winifred Wagner's admiration for Adolf Hitler. The practical reasons which made an alliance between Bayreuth and the Nazi regime desirable on both sides are not always seen objectively. Hitler was clearly enthralled by the heady quality in Wagner's music, and hitched his political wagon to the star of Wagner's operas, several of which could be slanted to glorify German nationalism. Also the great artistic prestige of Bayreuth was an asset to the Nazis. Winifred Wagner apparently really believed in Hitler's ideas, and of course his patronage enabled her to carry on the festivals with considerable success. Without that patronage they would presumably have died; certainly if there had been any hint of anti-Nazi sentiments in or round the Festspielhaus. With it, the Bayreuth festivals were continued almost to the end of the war, but the stigma which attached to them from that time was very nearly fatal afterwards.

Fortunately music is the most international of all the arts. In itself it knows no boundaries of language, race or creed, and even when harnessed, as in the form of opera, it gives the drama an extra dimension, a plane on which the experience of beauty can be shared by all. The taint of Hitlerism clung to Wagner's operas, and especially to

B

Bayreuth, for a time. There are still some people, and they are mostly Germans of the older generation, who turn aside from Wagner's music with a shudder of remembered evils. But the majority knew that Wagner's works are for all time and all peoples, and cannot permanently be held captive to any political ideology. They wanted the operas, and they wanted them at Bayreuth. The way was open for a fresh start.

Because of the past, Winifred Wagner was debarred from administration of the festivals in a new Germany, but the Festspielhaus remained her property. She herself chose the solution of making over control completely to her two sons.

In 1951 Wieland Wagner was only thirty-four and his brother Wolfgang two years younger. Wieland had married in 1941 the choreographer Gertrud Reissinger, who later was responsible for ballet arrangements in many of his productions, and they had one son, Wolf-Siegfried, and three daughters, Iris, Nike and Daphne. Wolfgang's wedding to Ellen Drexel followed in 1943, and their children were Eva and Gottfried.

Both brothers had done some years' practical work in other opera-houses; Wieland in the small, former court theatre at Altenburg, where he had produced a number of the repertory operas and also the *Ring;* Wolfgang, after being invalided out of the army following a serious wound, as assistant to Heinz Tietjen at the Berlin State Opera. Tietjen was in charge of productions at Bayreuth from 1933 until 1944, and both the Wagner grandsons took part in the last few festivals. Wolfgang was production assistant in 1942, 1943 and 1944. In 1943 and 1944 Wieland assisted with decor and costumes; he had also designed *Parsifal* sets in 1937, at the age of twenty.

With this experience the two brothers tackled the mammoth task of restarting the festivals virtually from scratch. The Festspielhaus building was intact, but its contents—costumes, properties and so on— had been disposed of or looted. Money was limited. Despite enthusiastic support from musicians and other well-wishers the response of the public was still non-proven. Faith in the abiding greatness of Richard Wagner's work, unremitting hard work, and perhaps almost a sense of desperation drove them on to a resounding success.

Since Wieland was primarily an artist and designer, while Wolfgang had a good business head, labour was divided; Wolfgang became the administrator of the festival, leaving Wieland free to carry out most of the productions. Wolfgang's first Bayreuth production was *Lohengrin* in 1953, and up to the time of his brother's death he had produced only seven of the operas, compared with Wieland's seventeen.

Necessity is often a fine spur to art. Here there was a double one:

first the need to blot out the Nazi stain, and therefore to make a clean break with the traditional methods of presenting the operas which had been used through the '30s and the '40s. Secondly money was none too plentiful, and there were six operas to be mounted afresh. To meet these practical requirements and release their own ideas of Wagner production they evolved the simplified designs which have won them fame.

It was, of course, the right time for new ideas. Europe and much of the world was dragging itself out of the grim single-mindedness of war and its immediate aftermath. Pre-war operagoers were thirsting for a return to the joys they had known, and although many of these wanted to see Wagner's operas given in the old way and were therefore opposed—sometimes violently—to Bayreuth's new forms, an extraordinary number of them accepted the changes with enthusiasm. But it was naturally the new young public who embraced New Bayreuth with whole-hearted fervour. Nor were all these so very young. Twelve years had passed since the outbreak of war in 1939. Few people under thirty had any clear recollection of peacetime Bayreuth, and outside Germany there had been little enough Wagner during the war for obvious reasons. The operas themselves, even the music, were a novelty to many, and in the modern form young listeners felt Wagner belonged to their own generation.

Moreover they did not need to be familiar with the accepted practices of tradition. It is not always realized that one of the reasons why young people reject established forms is that they feel at a disadvantage among others who know the rules. This is particularly true of opera, where the same works are performed over and over again in different cities and by a limited number of international artists.

Wherever the "inner ring" of opera addicts meet they are apt to behave like a society of initiates, discussing minutiae of individual performances or variations of production detail to their own delight and the intense boredom of everyone else. New young outsiders are completely at sea, and since modern youth is nothing if not voluble about its opinions, they do not like it.

In the early days of New Bayreuth there was none of this. Young and old, experienced operagoers and the newest recruit to the army of music lovers were all on an equality; all voyaging together over unknown seas of dramatic experience and into the dream world of Wieland Wagner's creation. This is no longer true. After eighteen years Bayreuth audiences are once more divided into the regulars and the novices. But we who now bore the newcomers with our tales of past glory can remember those days. Then we too were young.

By leaping into the public consciousness as a new artistic movement

Bayreuth was also in the forefront of the post-war fashion for music and drama festivals. In fact Bayreuth is almost the oldest of them all. It cannot compare with the English Three Choirs Festival which dates from 1717, but it is the oldest stage festival of our time, and in the tradition of classical Greek theatre. When Richard Wagner gave those first *Ring* performances in his Festspielhaus in 1876 he was founding something more than a centre for the performance of his own music dramas. Even the original Shakespeare Memorial Theatre at Stratford-on-Avon was not opened until 1879. The Three Choirs Festival has always pursued its own quiet way. It was Bayreuth and Stratford which quickly achieved national and then international fame, and they are the true progenitors of the whole host of modern festivals.

The two have many things in common. Each is dedicated to the work of one great artist. It is true that over the years non-Shakespearean plays are performed occasionally during Stratford festivals, but they only serve to accentuate the fact that Shakespeare reigns there supreme. Beethoven's Ninth Symphony is performed from time to time in the Festspielhaus, but only because of the special place which this particular work held in Wagner's life. Both remain one-man festivals.

Again Bayreuth and Stratford are provincial towns, and in the early days each was ridiculed for the temerity of attempting to establish a world art centre in such humble surroundings, instead of in the intellectual atmosphere of a large city. Time has proved that the small town setting is the right one.

The one major difference between the two is that the Wagner Festivals at Bayreuth are a family affair. More than two hundred and fifty years elapsed between Shakespeare's death and the beginning of regular festival seasons of his plays in the town of his birth. So little historical fact about his life exists undisputed, so much theory and conjecture has been woven round him, that it is quite impossible to know for certain how he would have liked to see his plays performed in the mid-twentieth century. Richard Wagner, on the other hand, created his festival centre himself, built his own Festpielhaus, and produced those first performances in it of the *Ring* and *Parsifal*. Moreover, as everyone knows, he left copious stage directions for the performance of all his works, and also wrote extensively not only about the operas but about his ideas and views on most subjects.

Add to this the "master's wishes" handed on by Cosima, and the total experience of hereditary festival control through seventy-five years, and the result is a formidable total of directions beside which David's catalogue of the mastersingers' rules would be the veriest child's play. The Shakespeare producer knows too little of his author's wishes; he must interpret from the plays alone, but if he has a real understanding of them the result will be—as far as we can tell by instinct—true Shakespeare. The Wagnarian producer is in a fair way to know too much.

Someone had to break the chains of tradition, and since the Wagner family remain active in the operatic world, only they could do it with authority. Most people feel tenderly towards traditions that are familiar to them personally, but even the most dedicated follower of the old ways would probably admit that it would not be possible to carry out all the original instructions to the letter in modern conditions.

The personal Wagner character of Bayreuth is one of its charms to devotees. They can walk where he walked, look at his grave, see the square plain face of Haus Wahnfried where he lived, study manuscripts and treasures in the memorial museum, and altogether steep themselves in the atmosphere which Richard Wagner chose for his home and theatre. Until a couple of years ago they could even read the daily paper which he read, but now the *Bayreuther Tagblatt* has been absorbed in the *Nordbayerischer Kurier*.

It is this unhurried pursuit of associations, of atmosphere, and the chance to discuss performances with like-minded listeners which makes a festival holiday so enjoyable. Especially now, when most people allow their lives to become one frantic, diabolic race against time. A visit to operahouse, concert or theatre must be fitted in between the demands of profession and home. Before the curtain falls eyes are straining to read a watch-face, thoughts on the time of a last train or the impossible place in which the car is parked. By the following day the magic of the performance has evaporated, in a week it is forgotten. Very often one simply cannot help this kind of approach to a great work of art, and it is better than going without altogether. But it is hardly fair to the artists concerned.

This is why the festival habit has grown in proportion to the increase in tempo of everyday life. The vast majority of festival audiences are on holiday. They can sit up at night discussing the performance, and sleep late in the morning. They can relax, study scores or libretti, eat, drink, talk, wander among the attractive surroundings possessed by most festival centres, and if they indulge in hero-worship for the composer or the artists who interpret him—well, it is a harmless passion, and adds greatly to the excitement of the holiday.

There are now well over one hunded festivals all over Europe and beyond, and Bayreuth is among those at the head of the list.

The Bayreuth public, however, is not typical of most festival audiences. Those whose tastes in music range widely choose a centre with a variety of programmes. Others who are only moderately interested in music go to places where there is additional social life. Bayreuth is Wagner first, last and all the time, and only those who really enjoy his operas come here, though there are always a few globe trotters "doing" one or two performances at Bayreuth as part of the itinerary. They are easily recognizable from their slightly bewildered manner.

Bayreuth audiences are a study in themselves, for considering that all are linked by a common love of Wagner's music they are amazingly diverse. There are the true fanatics, for Wagner attracts a considerable number of eccentrics to whom his works are a way of life. There are the escapists, for to some people this music acts like a drug. There are the old dreamers and the young intellectuals, the musical snobs and the booing exhibitionists. But the majority are people of all ages, races and classes who genuinely find joy in hearing and seeing Wagner's operas: wealthy or impoverished, diplomat or student.

Having come once, a surprisingly high proportion come again—and again. Thus they form the annual hard core of the Bayreuth public, together with a number of Bayreuth inhabitants who are also confirmed Wagnerites. This continuity means that they come to know the ten operas performed regularly at Bayreuth very well. A mixed operahouse audience may see two or three Wagner works in a year interspersed with Verdi, Mozart, Puccini, Strauss and the rest of the general repertory. The Bayreuth regulars not only see the performances here year after year, but will attend Wagner performances in their home cities, London, New York, Vienna, Munich, Berlin, and may also travel about to any or all of these places during the year, simply following Wagner. On points of musical performance they are a body to be reckoned with: a late vocal entry, a lapse of memory, a cut in the score will seldom pass unnoted. Sometimes they are unreasonable, often biased, but there are few indeed who have not the saving grace of enthusiasm.

Without Richard Wagner the Bayreuth Festivals would never have been founded, without his grandsons they would not have their present form, but without musicians they could not continue to exist. It is the conductors and singers, the orchestra and chorus who uphold the real reputation of the festivals, and it is the selection and direction of the artists which counts for more than the staging, however brilliant this may be. In opera music must come first, and the drama be so welded to it that the two become one: the whole inspiration of Wagner's music dramas. There were times when Wieland did not seem to hold this view, when production was superimposed upon the music, but in his unqualified successes music and decor were in harmony.

Wagnerian singers of the first quality are always in short supply. Bayreuth has had its ups and downs, but those who come and prove their worth usually return again and again—like the audiences. To sing at Bayreuth is an accolade for any young singer, and once famous, loyalty brings many of them back. In 1951 only a few of the company were known internationally, but they were well chosen and in the next few years the Wagners gathered together the finest voices of the time. In the mid '50s they were affectionately known to the cricket-minded English as the Wagnerian First Eleven.

The late Hans Knappertsbusch must stand out among the many fine conductors who have appeared at New Bayreuth, for in many ways he *was* Bayreuth, and his death has left a gap that will not be filled.

There are, however, several conductors at each festival. There is only one chorus master, and the chorus is, perhaps, Bayreuth's most perfect feature. Individual artists and conductors come and go, productions fluctuate, his work has continued unbroken since 1951, and he has made the Bayreuth chorus famous throughout the world. A man who will stand with the Wagner brothers as one of the founders of New Bayreuth—Wilhelm Pitz.

CHAPTER I

1951—The Great Venture

LOOKING back over eighteen years, Wolfgang Wagner says that his most vivid memory of 1951 is of the atmosphere which pervaded that festival and all who worked to give it being. No subsequent year has known quite the same spirit. Naturally so, for a great new enterprise unites all those concerned in it with a common aim and devotion. So much hung in the balance, and only complete dedication on the part of everyone could have achieved the result which placed Bayreuth and its festivals in the forefront of post-war musical life.

The two directors were young, and so were many of their fellow workers; inspired with fresh ideas, endowed with the determined strength to put them into practice. Young artists rightly saw a chance to help create what was virtually a new festival and, if it succeeded, to win personal laurels at the same time. Those who had served earlier festivals in various ways must have been overjoyed to see the flame rekindled. The town was excited at the prospect of retrieved artistic prestige and—an even more important consideration—the trade which it would bring. To all, new life on the Festspielhügel meant far more than a few weeks of opera performances that year: it was a talisman for the future of Germany's music and musicians.

Financial help was needed, and it came, too. The Bayreuth Festivals were, and remain, a private organization, but they receive some assistance from country, state and town. That first year grants were made by the State of Bavaria, the city of Bayreuth and also by the Society of the Friends of Bayreuth. This last was a newly formed organization of Wagner lovers who banded themselves together to give practical aid at that crucial time. Their numbers have grown steadily with the years, and the Wagner family have always paid tribute to the loyal support which the Society continues to give. In every audience a number of people will be seen wearing a tiny gold circle as a lapel badge. This is the Society's insignia. It is an outcome of the festivals' success that today many people join not from altruistic motives, but simply because membership gives a priority status for the booking of seats for the performances.

There were no half measures about the 1951 season, no question of a short trial run to test public response. The festival opened on July

29 and lasted until August 26. Two cycles of *Der Ring des Nibelungen* were given, and several performances each of *Parsifal* and *Die Meistersinger von Nürnberg.*

Six operas, all in new productions, all to be launched in the space of a week or so. The immensity of this undertaking may not be apparent to some operagoers, so—consider for a moment. In the world today few leading operahouses mount as many as six new productions in a whole year, and if they do these will be spaced out through a season lasting ten months. Each will have several weeks' rehearsal time allotted to it, and conductor, producer and cast will certainly declare that the time allowed was hopelessly inadequate.

Wagner's *Ring* is always a vast, unwieldy problem from the production point of view wherever it is staged, for it is four separate operas constituting one single work. Several operahouses (including Covent Garden) have adopted the system of producing one opera a year, thus taking four years to achieve the complete cycle. Bayreuth's three post-war *Ring* productions in 1951, 1960 and 1965 have each been launched in a single year. For a lengthy festival such as Bayreuth this is virtually essential: the public are not going to travel from all over the world to hear the *Ring* in fragments. True, Herbert von Karajan is at present producing his *Ring* at Salzburg on the sectional system, but that is a brief Easter festival, and closely linked with the recording of each opera.

Festivals, because of their short span and gathering together of personnel from many different centres, always demand intensive work of a kind which could not be continued at the same pressure throughout the year. It may be argued that many festivals put on three or even more new productions each summer. Yes—but these are usually each handled by a different conductor-producer team. The four operas of the *Ring* must of necessity be conducted and produced by the same men, and most of the leading singers will appear in two or more of the operas.

To judge by reports, the *Ring* was by no means perfect that year. Each time a new *Ring* production has been put on there during the past eighteen years it has creaked at the joints during the first season, but it is better that the public should be able to see Wagner's magnum opus complete, if imperfect, than as dismembered limbs—especially since some of the audiences come from places where they cannot see the operas at other times. By the second year the whole thing will have settled down, and can fairly be judged.

The amazing feat is that Wieland Wagner, for the first time in control of the heterogeneous collection of people which make up a festival ensemble, succeeded in producing the *Ring* at all. In fact he did more, not content with producing the four *Ring* operas he also designed and produced an entirely new *Parsifal*. It was this which was the real revelation of New Bayreuth. Its beauty had a mysterious, spiritual quality which made *Parsifal* a unique experience to many of those who had known it in older forms. Wieland Wagner was acknowledged as a great operatic producer.

There remained the sixth opera, *Die Meistersinger*. The programme for the opening year had been carefully and wisely chosen. The *Ring* and *Parsifal* had always formed the heart of Bayreuth festivals; it was obvious that they should reappear. Wagner's other important operas had been performed in rotation, and *Die Meistersinger* was the most popular with the public, especially in Germany. Moreover the warm humanity of this work makes it an ideal foil to the mighty themes of *Parsifal* and the Nibelung saga. Clearly Wieland Wagner could not have undertaken another production that year, and his brother's hands were full with getting the whole complicated organization under way. An outside producer, Rudolf Otto Hartmann who was later to become well known as the General Administrator of the Munich State Opera, was invited to produce this *Meistersinger* with decor and costumes by Hans Reissinger. Together they staged it in the traditional manner. (Plate 4b.)

Because of the novelty and impact of Wieland Wagner's innovations this *Meistersinger* received scant attention; probably an unjust reaction, but almost inevitable under the circumstances. However, it is important in the history of New Bayreuth for two reasons. First because Wieland is reported to have said that *Meistersinger* could not be treated in a symbolic way: an interesting remark in view of his revolutionary approaches to it in 1956 and 1963. Secondly because no other producer from the outside world was responsible for a Bayreuth opera until after Wieland's death in 1966.

This, then, was the fare offered to those first post-war pilgrims who journeyed to Northern Bavaria at the end of July 1951 and in the following weeks, but what kind of place did they find at the end of the journey?

Bayreuth was then a simple provincial town of some 60,000 inhabitants. (It is rather larger now.) Its old character as seat of the Margraves of Bayreuth, and later the Margraves of Ansbach, gives it a certain patrician grace, and the broad-faced gabled houses and cobbled streets in the old part of the town are picturesque and typical of Bavaria. The little Roter Main flows through it, and north of the river a newer district is gathered round the railway station. Here and there were gaping bomb scars.

North again lies the *Gartenstadt*—the garden town, and rightly so-called, for it consists of houses of varying degrees of modernity set among trees and flowers, where birds sing and there is a restful parochial silence after nightfall. Above this rises the 'green hill' on which stands the Wagner pilgrim's temple—the Festspielhaus.

This building in itself is one of the wonders of Bayreuth, and the most indispensable feature of the festivals. It was Richard Wagner's own creation, built largely of wood owing to lack of funds and, as he hoped, to be replaced later by a more worthy permanent building. But time proved that the heart of it must never be altered, for it is acoustically perfect, producing a quality of sound which is unique in the world. The building as it stands now is sheathed in brickwork, broad, solid, with a squat tower rising above the stage. In front is a terrace where the audience meet and talk before performances or during the intervals, and look down between the trees to a glimpse of the spires and roofs of the old town. A fair view, and one in the tradition of Hans Sach's Nuremberg. The Festspielhaus cannot be said to be fair at all. It is functional with a touch of 19th century grandiloquence. But those who know it well see it with the eyes of love.

Inside are stone-paved foyers—all too limited of space in wet weather—and flights of steep steps leading into the auditorium. Guides, taking the sightseer round the building, describe this as being built like a violin, and the simile is quite apt. It is shaped like a half-opened fan with stalls seats on a tremendously steep rake. The panels of the flat wooden ceiling are painted in blue and gold, on white which has long ago matured to a gentle nullity. The side walls are broken by apparent stone buttresses and pillars, but these too are wood. Everything is wood, and from this comes the quality of the sound.

Only in the boxes and galleries at the back is there any upholstery. The old stalls seats were all cane with wooden frames They were without arms, but wide enough to accommodate people of generous proportions, and less uncomfortable than the hard, imitation wood seating which was installed in 1968.

Below, between audience and stage, is Wagner's invention: the covered orchestra. The pit is tremendously deep, and behind the conductor rises a shell-like screen, curving forward towards the stage. Neither conductor nor players are visible to the audience, and the purpose of the screen is to throw the orchestral sound on to the stage, where it blends with the voices instead of rising as a direct orchestral barrier between stage and listener. It is hard to describe this musical conjuring trick, but the effect is quite extraordinary and provides a unique quality in operatic balance.

It was Beethoven's music, not Wagner's, that rang majestically through the Festspielhaus for that opening performance on July 29, 1951. The great Choral Symphony—Beethoven's Ninth—was chosen for the occasion because Richard Wagner himself regarded it as one of the most powerful musical influences in his life. He had conducted a performance of it in the old Margraves' operahouse in Bayreuth when the foundation stone of the Festspielhaus was laid in 1872. Now, when the life of his festivals was being reborn, it was given upon his own stage.

There was another link with earlier days. The conductor was Wilhelm Furtwängler, who had conducted at a number of festivals during Winifred Wagner's reign. The soloists were Elisabeth Schwarzkopf, Elisabeth Höngen, Hans Hopf and Otto Edelmann. Wilhelm Pitz had trained the chorus.

Among the audience that day and at the subsequent opera performances was one man whose presence there was to have a great influence on the English operagoers who hurried to Bayreuth during the next few years. This was the late Ernest Newman, then the doyen of British music critics, biographer of Richard Wagner, and one of the leading world authorities on Wagner's music. He was already an old man, and one who had seen and heard much of the greatest Wagnerian interpretation during many years. He might reasonably have been expected to prefer the ways of earlier days. Yet he came to Bayreuth with that combination of wisdom and receptivity which should be the aim of all critics, and hailed Wieland Wagner as a young genius who had faithfully and with inspiration released Wagner's music from traditional bonds, to its greater glory.

Newman was the music critic of the *Sunday Times* and he wrote four articles on Bayreuth which appeared on successive Sundays throughout August 1951. Many operagoers and Wagner lovers in England read avidly what he had written. I was one of them, and Newman's enthusiasm was one of the main reasons which made me decide to come to Bayreuth the following year. I know that I am only one of many who followed his lead.

He praised not only the new style of timeless, unlocated settings, but also the new school of acting which Wieland developed: a minimum of gesture, the authority of stillness. And he perceived the potentialities in several artists who were to become famous names in Bayreuth during the next few years.

"The Brynhilde of Astrid Varnay had many excellent features. The voice is not enormous, but there is always a reserve of power to be drawn upon when the drama calls for it, for Miss Varnay is not only a sensitive musician but has an exceptional intellectual control in whatever she does. The one reproach I have to bring against her is that some of the details of her miming seem to be overstudied and too apt to force themselves on our attention." (*Sunday Times* August 12, 1951.)

But it was *Parsifal* which won him completely. In his first article he had written:

"About the musical part of the performance I can hardly bring myself to speak, so ravishingly, heart-breakingly beautiful was it. This was not ony the best *Parsifal* I have ever seen and heard but one of the three or four most moving spiritual experiences of my life. The exquisiteness of the orchestral playing was beyond the power of words to describe. Hans Knappertsbusch conducted, and in a style that calls for the highest praise; but I understand that the rehearsals (extending over several weeks) have been taken by the greatly gifted Karajan. On the stage we had, for the first time in my experience, the combination of beauty of singing tone and dramatic insight that the subtle work demands.

"Ludwig Weber's Gurnemanz was an incomparable creation that dominated the whole drama; and the Parsifal of Wolfgang Windgassen, the Kundry of Martha Mödl, the Klingsor of Hermann Uhde and the Amfortas of George London were all first-rate. No one who heard this performance will ever forget it." (*Sunday Times* August 5, 1951.)

When he had had time to reflect on the background of this supreme experience he attempted to describe the *Parsifal* staging:

"The new settings and general treatment of *Parsifal* and the *Ring* have been remarkable not only for their technical ingenuity but for the way in which they have liberated our imagination for the things that really matter, and so increased the impressiveness of the works. We received our first surprise when the curtain rose on the opening scene of *Parsifal*. According to the score, the scene is a glade in a solemn, shady forest in the domain of the Grail, with Gurnemanz and the two young Esquires lying under a tree: the time is daybreak. In what we saw, however, there was no forest definable, nor even a tree.

"But it took us only a few minutes to realize that this dark, imprecise setting was the ideal one for the action. The eye was not outraged or amused by botanical curiosities of the customary stage kind; we felt the forest rather than saw it, a legendary forest that was of no time and no place, and one, moreover, over which mystery and sorrow and pain seemed to have brooded long. The result of it all was that we were conscious, for the first time, of the characters as Wagner must have seen them in his creative imagination, and the music, with nothing intruding now between it and us, spoke to us with a poignancy beyond the power of words to express." (*Sunday Times* August 19, 1951.)

And yet we still do not have a very clear impression of what the new wonder was. That has always been the problem in conveying Wieland Wagner's work to those who have not seen it, for it was, especially in those early days, a negation of the concrete for which he substituted visual moods. In later chapters, however, I shall try to establish something of the effect. Ernest Newman was hampered by the limitations on space which newspaper criticism imposes.

From a number of accounts of the 1951 festival one point emerges which is of particular interest in relation to later years. While both *Parsifal* and the *Ring* exemplified Wieland Wagner's new conception, *Parsifal* was the more extreme in its adoption of the revolutionary style, and it was by far the more popular with the public. (Plate 6.)

As I said earlier the *Ring* was not entirely successful. Some critics described it as a halfway stage between the familiar traditional settings and the new order as shown in *Parsifal*. The photographs bear this out (plates 5 and 6). There were walls and steps leading to the Gibichungs' hall in Act II of *Götterdämmerung*. A solitary pine—of a sort—presided over the barren hilltop where Wotan left Brünnhilde in her flame-girt solitude. There was still a whole tree for Siegfried's Woodbird. In fact these sets were much what we are now accustomed to find on other stages, where they are considered a diluted form of New Bayreuth.

Now did Wieland Wagner deliberately choose to stage the *Ring* and *Parsifal* in two different degrees of his new idea in order to ascertain public opinion? Or to test his own judgement?

One thing is certain. Whatever the reason, he very quickly decided to dispense with compromise. When I saw the *Ring* in the following season a number of major changes had been made, all simplifying the designs. Whereas *Parsifal* has never changed in basic conception. It was an inherent part of Wieland's work to vary every production a little from year to year: in lighting, or grouping, or the design of one of the few essential seats. But beyond this he seemed content to leave *Parsifal* in its own ethereal dignity, and there are many people who will always consider it his greatest work.

Two very famous conductors shared the operas that year, Hans Knappertsbusch and Herbert von Karajan. Karajan conducted *Meistersinger* and one *Ring* cycle, and returned the following year for *Tristan und Isolde*. After that, alas, he came no more.

Hans Knappertsbusch became a bulwark of Bayreuth. There were always countless anecdotes about him—told with an affectionate smile, for "Kna" was much loved. Till the end of his life the Bayreuth

Parsifal remained almost his sole prerogative, and he conducted several *Ring* cycles.

Certain names stand out among the leading singers, because they were to become a part of the Bayreuth ensemble for many years. Astrid Varnay, the Swedish-American dramatic soprano who had leaped to fame at the Metropolitan New York ten years before (Brünnhilde). Martha Mödl of the Hamburg State Opera, a mezzo-soprano who later sang many of the higher dramatic soprano roles (Kundry and Gutrune). Leonie Rysanek, dramatic soprano (Sieglinde). Wolfgang Windgassen, a leading heldentenor of the Stuttgart Opera (Parsifal, Froh). Hans Hopf, heldentenor (Walther von Stolzing). George London, bass-baritone (Amfortas), Hermann Uhde, baritone (Klingsor, Günther), Gerhard Stolze, tenor, who was later to become a fine Mime and David, made a first appearance as Augustin Moser in *Meistersinger*.

Ludwig Weber was, of course, already a very famous singer and had one of the most beautiful bass voices ever heard at Bayreuth in post-war festivals. That year he sang Gurnemanz, Fasolt and Hagen. He came back many times. Otto Edelmann, bass-baritone (Hans Sachs), returned to sing again in Hartmann's *Meistersinger* the following year, but was not seen at Bayreuth again. Elisabeth Schwarzkopf (Eva, Woglinde) and Sigurd Björling (Wotan) were seen at Bayreuth only in 1951.

CHAPTER II

1952—Face to Face with Bayreuth

ANYONE who believes that music critics are all hardened cynics satiated with a continual feast of what is only a rare and precious dessert to other mortals, is very far from the truth. Critics and those who write on various aspects of music or theatre are essentially human beings, which is why their judgements are sometimes biased, or cloaked with a display of experience. They are all, at heart, enthusiasts; otherwise they would choose another less exacting form of profession, since continual attendance at performances curtails very considerably the spare time which most people enjoy.

When I made my first visit to Bayreuth in July 1952 I was still a very ingénue critic, but brimming over with enthusiasm for the splendour of Wagner's music and the excitement of foreign travel. Seventeen years later I am a middle aged critic, but the enthusiasm remains. I suspect it will still be burning brightly—and unsuitably—when I am pushed up to the Festspielhaus in a bath-chair.

I travelled by night boat from Harwich to the Hook of Holland, and from there through Holland and right across Germany by train. Through Cologne, where we shunted to and fro on the Rhine bridge for a time, under the lofty dignity of the cathedral spires. Up the east bank of the Rhine, where the track clings to the steep valley side, poised between river and vineyards, while improbable little castles peer down at it, and smiling wine-making towns and villages spread out their terraces and gay umbrellas, and you can almost hear the musical clink of glasses. On to Mainz, where the Main joins the Rhine, and up the Main valley to Frankfurt, Aschaffenburg and so over the shoulder of the Spessart hills. This is some of the loveliest country in Germany, though little enough is written of it: bright green fields by shining water, and the great peaceful majesty of the forests.

After the line enters Bavaria the mood changes. We are in flatter country now, wide and sunlit, and burnished with cornfields. And so to Würzburg, patrician eighteenth-century city of the prince-bishops. This is vineyard country again, home of the *Frankenwein*—the Franconian or Main wines which are almost invariably bottled in a squat flagon known as a *Bocksbeutel*. These are white wines, dry and fragrant, and one drinks them habitually—and with great pleasure—in Bayreuth.

C

Nuremburg of *Meistersinger* fame comes next, and then the railway skirts the wooded hilly district called the Franconian Switzerland and comes, by way of little towns and village halts, to Bayreuth at last.

As far as the British visitor is concerned it is of course quicker to fly to Nuremburg and have only the final ninety minutes rail connection from there, or to fly to Munich, from which the train journey takes three-and-a-half hours. There are also other railway possibilities, but the old Hook of Holland route is still my favourite. It is comfortable, especially by the new T.E.E. Rheingold/Rheinpfeil express to Nuremburg, and somehow it sets the scene for Bayreuth. In 1952 we did not arrive until about 10 o'clock at night, but now you get there several hours earlier, and therefore in daylight. Bayreuth habitués stand at the windows for the last mile or so, knowing exactly where to look for the broad gable which surmounts the Festspielhaus tower. Even critics are known to glance nonchalantly at it. Just to make sure it is still there.

At the end of that first journey I was so deathly tired that I tumbled into bed wondering why in the world I had worked so hard to come to Bayreuth. There is a certain point at which enthusiasm evaporates, and the place seemed dark and composed of long weary roads full of trees, where a few sentinel lamp posts only illuminated the shadows.

By day I saw Bayreuth not only in sunlight but in the perspective of a good night's rest, and breakfast. And all was fair.

Nonetheless it is a spreading place. As mentioned earlier, the railway station lies between the old town and the Festspielhaus; it is in fact about the halfway mark. Fifteen minutes' brisk walk takes you from the station to the Festspielhaus by way of the *Gartenstadt* and the Siegfried Wagner Allee, which is the graceful tree-lined avenue leading up the hill to the theatre itself. Fifteen minutes' walk in the other direction leads through the administrative centre of the town, the quarter of banks, tourist offices, cafés, the elegant old Margraves' Operahouse, and so to the main shopping street Maximilianstrasse. Beyond this lie the cobbled byways of the middle ages, the Wagner family home Wahnfried (not open to the public) and the Hofgarten park where all visitors go to see Wagner's grave (plate 10).

There are buses, but in my experience most newcomers to a town are much too frightened to trust themselves to such vehicles, which have a diabolical habit of following their own routes, and not those which the stranger hopes they will take. Actually, Bayreuth has now an excellent and entertaining bus service, but my appreciation of it belongs to a later chapter. In those early days I walked or took an occasional taxi of which Bayreuth has an admirable and extensive fleet. Fortunately Bayreuth is a pleasant place in which to walk, and when you spend some five hours of each day in an operahouse, a certain amount of exercise is advisable for both physical and musical digestion.

For the opening week of the 1952 season the sun shone and I learned the easy, leisurely routine of life at this particular festival. Leisurely, that is, for the public which includes those who come to write about it. For the people whose job it is to make the wheels of the whole organization turn conditions are nearer to those of a maelstrom. Art is at least equalled by gruelling hard work.

But from the outside there is time to live in the company of music. One of the particular characteristics of Bayreuth is that most visitors stay in private houses. There were not in 1952, and there never will be, enough hotels to accommodate all the festival guests, for the simple reason that a five-week season cannot support a large number of hotels throughout the year. Therefore it had become a tradition in pre-war days that the people of the town took in paying guests for the festival period. Lawyers, local government officials, shopkeepers, postmen—a cross-section of the whole Bayreuth population do this. Accommodation is registered and graded, and visitors staying in the top grade houses are often in very much more luxurious surroundings than the hotels can offer.

In that first season I was lucky enough to stay with a family in the vicinity of the Festspielhaus to whom I have returned many times in later years. A large number of Bayreuth "regulars" do this: coming back faithfully year after year to the same house, the welcoming faces, the familiar coffee pot at breakfast time, and the delightful little chats about local news and gossip. Bayreuth hostesses are wonderfully kind and thoughtful, sometimes even embarrassingly so. I remember one case of a gentleman returning to change for the opera in rather a hurry, who found that the trousers of his dress suit had completely disappeared. In a state of deshabille and limited German vocabulary he sought his landlady through house and garden. When he had finally managed to explain the problem, it turned out that she had put the trousers to press under his mattress.

In the mornings most people gravitate to the Festspielhaus where, especially in those early days, the space outside the stage door constituted a sort of club where artists, writers, and general public mixed and chatted. It was a happy hunting ground for the autograph collector, and a wonderful place for fans to watch their idols, noting the registration numbers of their cars and other important data.

After circumnavigating the Festspielhaus once or twice—a roadway circles the building, and this is the regular promenade during intervals of the performance—one strolled down to the town for a beer, lunch at one of the hotels or restaurants, and more talk. Then back to one's room to rest or study, change, and set off for the real business of the day.

Since 1953 all the operas have begun at 4.00 p.m. with the exception of the two short ones—*Das Rheingold* and *Der Fliegende Holländer*—which start two or three hours later. In 1952 the starting time for all public performances was 5.00 p.m. but even that was fairly early. It meant that one sallied forth in full evening dress at a time when friends in England were stirring the sugar in their first cup of tea and hesitating over the momentous choice between cucumber and pâté sandwiches.

But experience soon proved that this was the proper thing to do. Bayreuth has always had a well-dressed audience. Then as now at least half the women wear full length evening dresses, often extremely elaborate and beautiful. More than half the men seem to wear dinner jackets and the balance the continental formal dark suit. A tweed jacket is so noticeable that it suggests that the wearer must be demonstrating about something.

The ritual of arrival at the Festspielhaus was a fascinating new experience to me. From every road and almost every house little knots of well-dressed people appear, sometimes with a rapt, reverential expression on their faces, and turn their steps towards the operatic temple. At the same time, large, sleek, wealthy cars follow each other up the hill, nose to tail. Police, with careful experience, control the traffic, guide the pedestrians across the road, and keep the onlookers from mixing with the élite bound for the performance. For the townspeople turned out in their hundreds (and still do, to a lesser extent) to watch the celebrities and the *grandes toilettes*. They brought their babies in prams, their toddlers and their dogs, and lined the route, watching with smiling, friendly faces. It made the youngest of festivalgoers, struggling with a long skirt, feel like royalty.

Fifteen minutes before the performance a group of brass players who belong to the orchestra but are not of it—being the stage and interval musicians—appear on the balcony above the Festspielhaus terrace. They play the first fanfare—a single motif from the first act of the opera which is about to be performed. Then they go round to the back of the building and repeat it there. Five minutes later two fanfares are given, and when there are only five minutes left before curtain up, come the final three fanfares. The whole is repeated at the beginning of each act, and one of the most haunting of all Bayreuth memories is the sound of a last act *Parsifal* or *Tristan* fanfare sounding out across the valley through the darkness of a summer's night.

For me, the first experience of this amazing building was that 1952 *Rheingold* conducted by Joseph Keilberth. The music welled up and out from the stage, catching the hearer unawares from all sides, engulfing him, making him something that is carried on the stream of music. There is perfect balance, the building makes the most delicate pianissimo audible and undistorted. A newcomer in 1968 described part of the *Parsifal* playing as "like a chamber orchestra".

Actually that *Ring* was not really very exciting from the orchestral point of view; Keilberth did much finer things in later years, but I was enthralled by the Bayreuth sound.

In that *Rheingold* the opening Rhine scene was immensely dark. The Rhinemaidens, seductive in skin-tight satin swimsuits, were spotlit at different points in the gloom. Alberich, splendidly sung by Gustav Neidlinger, brought evil into this primeval world with fine effect. On the heights where Wotan views his new Valhalla Wieland Wagner's passion for geometric balance in design became apparent. Throughout the early years of his productions visual symmetry was almost his hallmark. Here the stage platform was marked by four corner blocks low enough to be used as seats. Valhalla was an insubstantial projection on the cyclorama dead centre. The rainbow bridge at the end was a perfect arc extending right across the stage. (Plate 12a.) The most effective scene was the rocky cavern of Nibelheim, with the fierce glow of the forge fires.

Rheingold is always the most difficult part of the *Ring* in performance. It has not the great musical climaxes of the later operas, nor the heights and depths of emotion. It has some of the finest music, but it is subtle, and the opera depends for success on its drama, the interplay of character, the unfolding of the results of Wotan's fatal decision to achieve his ends by expediency. There are three key characters: Wotan himself, centre of the whole *Ring* story, Alberich, personification of evil, but yet with a certain dignity, and Loge, impersonal spirit of fire, serving yet mocking the perplexity of the gods. In this production there was an excellent Alberich, and no less admirable Loge, Erich Witte. The opera was unbalanced because Hermann Uhde was miscast as Wotan. The voice was too light, and he never appeared wholly at home in the part.

Die Walküre had a large austere room for Hunding's hut where Siegmund was not allowed to sit at table with his hosts, but recounted his story from another part of the stage. The second act had one of the finest settings in the whole cycle: a narrow pass between two mighty walls of rock. (Plate 12b.) For the final act the Valkyries arrived with their warrior cries, and cowered before Wotan's wrath on a bare circular platform, while clouds scudded over the cyclorama,

and the sky changed to sorrowful peace and finally to the flames of
Loge's fire, as Wotan left Brünnhilde in her magic sleep.

Here the drama and the singing were in different hands. Hans
Hotter was in 1952 already the outstanding world Wotan. His mastery
of the role, vocally and in the interpretation of this complex character,
was complete, and he carried the evening with this magnificent
performance. Astrid Varnay was the Brünnhilde, dramatic and well
sung, though the top of her voice was hard. Inge Borkh was a
passionate, musical Sieglinde, Günther Treptow a strong, unsubtle
Siegmund. As Hunding I heard, for the first time, Josef Greindl.
What a voice, and what a magnificent actor! He and Erich Witte
had both sung at the Bayreuth Festival of 1943 (Greindl as Pogner,
Witte as David). On his return nine years later Greindl was beginning
an association with New Bayreuth which has continued unbroken
ever since.

Scenically *Siegfried* and *Götterdämmerung* followed the pattern
of the earlier operas: symmetrical square rocks and platforms, wonderful colour effects on the cyclorama—the exquisite transition through
rose and aquamarine to the real blue of heaven when Siegfried awakes
Brünnhilde is something which no one who saw it will ever forget.
The Woodbird's tree had gone from *Siegfried*, but there was a really
splendid Wurm: a green scaly dragon with glittering eyes and a vast
maw emitting steam to the deep hollow tones of Kurt Böhme. (Plate
13a.) The *Götterdämmerung* second act was another superb bit of
staging with the Gibichung vassals grouped on a low circular wall (and
there are a lot of them at Bayreuth) to form an intense human rampart
round the arena on which the drama of Brünnhilde, Gunther, Siegfried
and Gutrune unfolds, swayed by Hagen. (Plate 13b.)

Varnay sang Brünnhilde right through the cycle. Hotter was
Wotan/Wanderer in Siegfried, magnificent of voice and bearing.
Greindl was even more impressive as Hagen than he has been in the
role of Hunding. In *Siegfried* the name part was sung by Bernd
Aldenhoff, a heldentenor of harsh voice and no great acting ability.
In *Götterdämmerung* the Siegfried was Max Lorenz, who took over
the part at short notice. Lorenz had been one of Germany's most
famous tenors in earlier years. By 1952 his voice was probably little
more than a shadow of its former quality. But he possessed such
musicianship and was so fine an actor, that his performance lingers
in the mind. He even made that irritating young man Siegfried a
likeable character, which only a few artists are able to do.

Paul Kuen's Mime was overplayed to the distortion of his singing,
but Hermann Uhde was a most admirable Gunther. There are several
ways of playing this unfortunate Gibichung chief who gets caught up

in the great tragic pattern of gods and heroes. Uhde, while showing the character's weakness and vanity, made one distinctly sorry for him. Martha Mödl was less successful with Gutrune.

All newcomers to post-war Bayreuth have been struck by the lack of light in Wieland's productions. Later one has come to accept this as part of his stage vision—though it is distinctly tiring to the eyes. In 1952 I felt when entering the Festspielhaus from the sunlit hillside without that I had stumbled into a London fog; the gauze curtains which, inevitably, separate the singers from the audience ofter. irritated me. And yet the magic was there. Perfection was within reach. A little more light, a willingness to incorporate the best of the past in his own artistic vision, and he might have reached it.

That year there were revivals of *Meistersinger* and *Parsifal,* both conducted by Knappertsbusch, and a new Wieland production of *Tristan und Isolde* with Karajan as musical director. Mödl sang Isolde and Ramon Vinay Tristan. (Plate 16b.) I was not able to see any of these, my first visit being limited to the *Ring.*

My memories of my last night (*Götterdämmerung*) are of a noisy and dramatically well-timed thunderstorm which blew up during the performance. Also of an important event in my education regarding German food.

As you face the Festspielhaus from the terrace the large detached Festspielrestaurant is on your right. Opposite, on the left, is the small restaurant (now self-service), and behind the Festspielhaus is the canteen. Therefore there is a fairly wide choice—and price range— in places to eat and drink during the two long intervals which occur in every opera except *Rheingold,* and *Der Fliegende Holländer* which usually has one. The canteen is, of course, only meant for the artists and Festspielhaus workers, but a good many others seem to drift in.

On that particular evening two friends and I had decided to treat ourselves to dinner in the main restaurant during the second interval, but at the end of the trip money was not too plentiful. My small stock of German amounted to rather more than theirs (which was nil) so I was deputed to study the *Speisekarte.* The cheapest item was sausages, but we had had enough of them. The second cheapest was "Tartar Steak mit Ei." We had no idea what it was. "Shall we?" I asked, and they agreed. With a lordly air I ordered Tartar Steak— "dreimal". In due course a waiter arrived bearing three plates on which were three mounds of raw minced beef, each surmounted by a completely raw egg. Round the sides were a few olives. It all looked very, very naked, and as I like both meat and eggs well cooked it struck me as particularly nasty. We looked wildly at each other. Then we ate it, for there was nothing else to do. You learn that way.

CHAPTER III

1953—Enter Wolfgang Wagner

THERE was a special stir of excitement for the 1953 festival, for this was Wolfgang Wagner's debut as producer in New Bayreuth. Very few members of the present audiences could have seen his work during the war in Berlin. (A production of his father Siegfried Wagner's opera *Schwarzschwanenreich*, in 1944.) We knew him only as administrator and co-ordinator of the festivals, and as a handsome smiling personality who could be seen hurrying in and out of the Festspielhaus or talking and laughing with guests in the Festspielrestaurant. His elder brother Wieland had carried all production responsibility for the first two years (apart from Hartmann's *Meistersinger*), and won all the artistic laurels.

Now we had *Lohengrin*, seen through Wolfgang's eyes. Immediately the curtain rose both the similarities and differences between the two brothers' styles were apparent. Here was the same spacious simplicity, the same feeling for symmetry, though not to Wieland's extent. But where Wieland made his effects with misty colour, half tones and sombre costumes, his brother used light as a positive quality, and the performers were dressed in bright, clear colours. The first act, with chorus massed on either side of a bare circular platform, Lohengrin arriving with swan at the back centre, was as austere in its own way as any of Wieland's *Ring* settings, but it was clearly a different way. (Plate 17a.) For the fortress of Antwerp—the second act scene set in the square between the palace and the minster—he dispensed with symmetry of design and provided a towering realistic set which served the opera well. (Plate 17b.)

Already Bayreuth had begun to establish its own style in acting, which can be summed up briefly as the art of stillness. Wolfgang also achieved this in training his cast. A minimum of gesture, combined with the power to express mood or character simply by stance is the acting counterpart of New Bayreuth's austere, unencumbered decor. The two have become virtually one art through the years.

First let it be said that this kind of acting is not new. There is nothing revolutionary about it in the way that Bayreuth introduced a new kind of stage spectacle. It has become a part of the Bayreuth style simply because it was adopted by the Wagner brothers as the most suitable method of carrying out their aim that the music should be left free to express all but the simplest actions of the story.

Every great actor knows the importance of stillness and economy of gesture; knows it partly by the instinct of his talent and partly from hard work and experience. "Suit the action to the word, the word to the action; with this special observance, that you o'er step not the modesty of nature", said Hamlet to the players. Shakespeare knew all about acting three hundred and fifty years ago. Operatic acting, however, has its own problems.

In the straight theatre an actor or actress is seldom cast for a leading role unless they can act. They may be endowed with good looks or a beautiful speaking voice, but their primary qualification is acting ability. Singers, on the other hand, become famous through the quality of their voice and their musicianship in using it. Sometimes they are not even good musicians. Given the musical qualifications they must then learn to act—if they are going to suceed in opera. Occasionally a singer is also a very great dramatic artist—Maria Callas and Hans Hotter are two outstanding examples—but the majority need all the help and drilling which a producer can give them.

New Bayreuth has helped to make great opera stars out of some of the artists who came there in their formative years. With others it failed dismally, reducing them to little more than puppets.

Wolfgang Windgassen is one of those who has achieved greatness. It would be wrong to claim that this is simply due to Bayreuth. The son of a well-known heldentenor Fritz Windgassen, he had been a member of the Stuttgart Opera since 1945. But seventeen years ago when I first saw him at Bayreuth he had much to learn about acting. That he did learn, and was to become one of the outstanding interpretive artists of the present-day operatic world is due to his own gifts, but certainly these were aided and developed by the work of the Wagners.

Windgassen was the Lohengrin in Wolfgang Wagner's production. Still a little wooden from the dramatic point of view, the beautiful quality of his voice was ideal for the role, and he sang with the dignity and tenderness which is needed for this knightly hero. Eleanor Steber was not more than an adequate Elsa. It is a difficult part, requiring a voice of great beauty and purity. If the singer is not an outstanding actress the voice must convey Elsa's innocence and lack of commonsense. Eleanor Steber had good looks, but the voice was inclined to be edgy in the upper register.

On the whole, however, Wolfgang Wagner was well served by his artists. Hermann Uhde was a suitably craven Telramund, Astrid Varnay a fiercely dramatic Ortrud, weaving the web of destruction round the unsuspecting Elsa. Joseph Keilberth conducted, and the orchestra like the chorus acquitted themselves finely.

It was fascinating to compare this *Lohengrin* with Wieland's productions, especially *Parsifal* and *Tristan und Isolde,* both of which I was seeing for the first time.

In common with most of those who have seen it, I was completely entranced with *Parsifal.* The shadowy suggestion of trees surrounding the simple, circular platform of the first scene, where the figures were superbly directed and grouped. The mighty columns implying the vastness of the Hall of Grail. The elliptical, claustrophobic, projected background, half well shaft, half spider's web, from which Klingsor lured his victim and commanded Kundry. The dream disc of the magic garden, with its rose and blue lighting and fairy dancers. And above all the Good Friday scene with its return to the simplicity of the first set—with the addition of a central rocky seat—yet subtly touched with the spirit of redemption by inspired lighting.

No wonder Ernest Newman bestowed on it the accolade of genius. No wonder, year by year, fresh visitors to Bayreuth have come away conscious of a rare spiritual revelation. The wonder lies, of course in Richard Wagner's music, but this presentation of it in his own theatre is certainly Wieland Wagner's masterpiece. In those early years he used spotlights on the characters both in *Parsifal* and the *Ring.* Some people criticized this, and later he discontinued it, leaving the figures in the embracing shadows, and the public to strain their eyes in an effort to follow facial expression. For me this—very artistic—form of spotlighting was one of the chief beauties of the 1953 *Parsifal.* The figures were illuminated clearly yet softly, and in the Good Friday scene Gurnemanz and Parsifal in their stone-coloured costumes stood out with the quality of sculpture.

Clemens Krauss conducted *Parsifal* that year, and with great beauty. Ludwig Weber continued his famous Gurnemanz. Weber was a great artist with a great voice—the two do not invariably go together. By a great voice I do not mean simply one of enormous volume, though he certainly had plenty of that, too. There are good voices and beautiful voices which give us immmense pleasure; there are also very ordinary voices which when combined with fine musicianship can produce memorable singing. Very occasionally there are great voices which are beautiful, belong to a fine musician, and still have something more—a unique quality which makes them instantly recognizable and sets them apart from all other sopranos, contraltos, tenors, basses, as the case may be.

Ludwig Weber had such a bass voice, and I would describe its special quality as one of loving kindness: warm, rich, beautiful, fatherly

—infinitely kind. It limited the roles for which he was really suited. Although he was a well-known Hagen his impersonation of this hybrid Nibelung-mortal did not sound right to me. Even his Fasolt was rather too sympathetic, but as King Marke, Pogner, above all Gurnemanz, he was quite superb.

The Amfortas was George London, and it was a role with which he was identified at Bayreuth for many years. His voice had a hard grain, a roughness which I could never wholly admire, but he was a good singer and a fine dramatic actor, and his portrayal of the master of the Grail's knightly order, tortured by remorse and seeking only death, was very harrowing. Martha Mödl was a most moving Kundry, and Ramon Vinay brought his own particular gifts to the role of Parsifal.

He was also the Tristan in Wieland's production carried over from 1952, and since the chief protagonists in *Tristan und Isolde* are always infinitely more important than any scenic devices on the part of the producer, let him come first.

Ramon Vinay is an unusual singer, and the public has always been divided between those who admire him very much and those who actively dislike his voice. I belong to the first group. He was born in Chile and educated in France. By 1953 he had already sung in Milan, Rome, San Francisco, at Covent Garden, Salzburg and the Metropolitan in New York. I believe he started his musical career as a baritone, but he made his name as a dramatic tenor, and he will long be remembered for his magnificent portrayal of Verdi's Otello. Later, after a vocal crisis, he started a new career as a baritone in 1962.

As a tenor his voice had an unusually dark quality, was sometimes harsh, and his enunciation of German was not always very good. But he is an artist in the fullest sense of the word and used his voice in several of the great Wagnerian tenor roles to tremendous and intelligent effect. Lyric passages were not his strong point, but where the music requires passionate, intense feeling, or the expression of suffering he was hard to equal. Strikingly handsome, he was well equipped to play romantic heroes, but he was never merely a matinee idol.

Tristan was one of his greatest roles, and it was the kind of performance which remains vividly imprinted on the memory. I never see or hear another Tristan without the agony of Vinay's performance in the third act living again in the theatre of my mind. It was absolutely electrifying. His Parsifal at this same festival well displayed his range in characterization: Tristan the tortured lover, Parsifal the pure fool, learning compassionate wisdom on the hard road of temptation. Both gave the hearer new understanding of the characters. That year he also sang Siegmund for the first time. He was, therefore, only growing into a role which suited his voice and acting ability admirably, and which he was to sing again several times at Bayreuth as well as at other operahouses, and to great effect.

Astrid Varnay was the Isolde whom I heard (Mödl sang it at some performances). Varnay is a first-class actress, and a sound well trained singer who has used a not very beautiful voice to superb effect in the service of Wagner's music. She is what the English theatre of the old days would have caled a "real trouper " with all the affection and admiration which that implies. Throughout some seventeen years whenever a leading soprano at Bayreuth fell ill, or was prevented from appearing for some reason, Astrid Varnay would stand in, or "spring in" to use the graphic German expression. No one was better fitted, for she knew all the Wagnerian soprano leads, and all the Bayreuth productions.

Varnay's special gift is portraying a positive radiance in love, a real joy in living—and in the case of Isolde no less joy in dying, in the mood of Wagner's spiritual exaltations. Musically there have been far more beautiful Isoldes; dramatically others have touched and wrung the heart more deeply. I have never seen an Isolde who was more *exciting* than Varnay, and this is true of most of her impersonations.

It was a strong cast, Weber's King Marke, Gustav Neidlinger's sturdy, true-hearted Kurwenal, and Ira Malaniuk as Brangäne: a singer with a mezzo voice of unusual beauty, and face and figure to match. Two small parts were taken by singers who were to become famous at Bayreuth in later years: Gerhard Stolze sang the shepherd and Theo Adam the steersman.

Eugen Jochum was the conductor, and with the orchestra he wove all the passionate beauty and longing of the score into a very splendid performance.

Wieland Wagner continued his habit of architecturally balanced design; what was seen on the left must have its counterpart—preferably identical—on the right. The first act was played in a huge tent, with an opening, centre back, which revealed the stern of the ship, Tristan peering out to sea, and Kurweral crouching at his feet. The tent was absurdly large quarters for Isolde and Brangäne, though sparsely furnished with only a day-bed and a chest for the potions, but it was very effective. The second act was even more austere: a bare sloping circular platform, sky of changing moods, and a seat for the lovers. Tristan's castle was much the same: side ramps indicated walls girdling the central disc, and there was a very hard couch for the wounded knight. No more, but again Wieland's artistic instinct won, and the music and the acting came over with amazing impact.

To my delight the *Ring* was appreciably more brightly lit that year, Keilberth had found a new inspiration for his conducting, and most people I think shared the feeling that it was within measurable distance of being an ideal cycle. Martha Mödl sang and acted beautifully as Brünnhilde. Hotter sang Wotan throughout and thereby there was consistency of casting and strength in the central character. Wolfgang Windgassen sang his first Bayreuth Siegfried in both operas (he had done a trial run at Naples in the spring), and though still tentative it was a young musical performance full of promise. Only Regina Resnik's Sieglinde was not a success. Her voice spread, and gave no indication of possessing the power, warmth and beauty of which great Sieglinde voices are made.

The season included another performance of Beethoven's Ninth Symphony this time conducted by Paul Hindemith. The list of soloists —Ira Malaniuk, Anton Dermota, Ludwig Weber—was headed by a name new to Bayreuth—that of Birgit Nilsson.

CHAPTER IV

1954—The First *Tannhäuser*

BAYREUTH'S weather is, all too often, an uncertain goddess. At the beginning of the 1954 festival it was damp and cool with tantalizing spells of sunshine, and I believe it had been worse during the rehearsal period. A friend who met me on arrival said, "Everyone has had colds—except the Swedish girl." This was no doubt an exaggeration, but certainly several artists had been ill, Ramon Vinay and Ludwig Weber among them, while Birgit Nilsson made her operatic debut at Bayreuth in perfect vocal form as Elsa. She was one of the sensations of the season, and the public hailed her as a great new Wagnerian.

There were other excitements too. Though the weather was chilly, controversy about Wieland Wagner's *Tannhäuser* raised the critical temperature. This was really the first time that any serious adverse criticism had been voiced about Wieland's work. There had, of course, been some who deplored the ignoring of Richard Wagner's stage directions, and many who found the darkness of the staging irksome, but on the whole *Parsifal,* the *Ring* and *Tristan und Isolde* had all been intensely musical productions. Those who were not hidebound to the old traditions found a new dimension in the Bayreuth productions, and hailed them as the outward and visible form of Richard Wagner's music. They accepted the innovations and omissions because the Wagnerian heart of the works beat strong and true.

With *Tannhäuser* Wieland carried his symbolic ideas a step farther, and where they did not entirely fit the music, he superimposed them upon it. There was for many people a clash between the magic of Richard Wagner's inspiration which for all its timeless greatness is rooted in the nineteenth century, and the strictly twentieth-century thinking of his grandson.

The opening Venusberg scene was played in the setting of a slanted elliptical cavern. In front of this the ballet (choreography by Gertrud Wagner) writhed, with static miming of erotic passion. From the centre of her claustrophobic domain Venus tried to hold Tannhäuser's allegiance, while he, downstage in the foreground, struggled for spiritual freedom. It was all cold; coldly sterile, utterly futile. There is certainly a case for depicting loveless sex thus, cold as the hand of death, and within this conception it was cleverly done. But it simply does not belong to the fiery passion of Wagner's Venusberg music. For him the devils of temptation are still very much alive, throbbing, titillating, enticing the sinner to forget the thorny path of remorse.

As Venus' world was depicted by curves, the virtuous surroundings of Elisabeth were all straight lines. The minstrels' hall in the Wartburg had a chequered floor with blocks of seats for the chorus in straight lines on either side. At the back were some pairs of arches planted here and there like giant croquet hoops. (Plate 19a.) The chorus entered in small blocks, each moving to their places with the measured precision of a military display. Even the principal characters moved with mathematical exactitude, and in this chessboard setting the drama of Tannhäuser's hopeful return, his fall from grace, and Elisabeth's intercession for him, were played out as in a game where head, not heart, controls the moves.

For the last act a huge cross symbolized redemption at the front of the stage (and served as the shrine for Elisabeth's prayer), the concentric caverns of the Venusberg appeared again, faintly, during Tannhäuser's final temptation (plate 19b), and the closing procession of pilgrims was only a blur behind a gauze curtain in the background.

Added to all this Wieland Wagner did some daring things on the strictly musical side. A mixture of the Dresden and Paris versions was used. The original overture was played followed by the Venusberg music and not the later combined overture and Venusberg music. The performance followed the Paris form until halfway through the Venusberg scenes where it went back to Dresden. Several of Wagner's later revisions and alterations were ignored. Unfortunately I did not make detailed notes of exactly how the balance lay between the two versions, but Andrew Porter wrote fairly fully about them in *Opera* (September 1954) and I agree with him that Richard Wagner knew what he was doing when he made the alterations. However, Wieland Wagner was here seeking to obtain the most effective presentation of his own ideas.

Nonetheless the production was clever and striking in its rather perverse way. It would have had even more success if the first performances had not been dogged by ill luck. Igor Markevitch was to have conducted this opera, and the announcement that owing to illness he could not do so, meant that Joseph Keilberth was called in at a late stage. Ramon Vinay was obviously suffering from throat trouble, and on the first night was able to do little more than indicate his notes, though it was a fine dramatic performance on the acting side. Such problems are always liable to affect the other singers, but in fact they did extremely well considering the handicaps of this particular production, and the fact that it was quite new. Gré Brouwenstijn was more than a well-sung Elisabeth. She was graceful (even when pacing backwards diagonally across the stage) and beautiful, and possessed the spiritual quality which is essential for the part, but which only a few Elisabeths are able to convey. Josef Greindl was a fine Landgrave, noble of voice and bearing. But the real vocal joy of the evening was Dietrich Fischer-Dieskau's Wolfram von Eschenbach.

This was his Bayreuth debut, and although even Fischer-Dieskau was not at his best on that occasion, it was a beautiful and memorable performance. His is another of the voices which possesses a special quality of beauty, and it is an ideal quality for this particular role. Wolfram is considerably more than a Don Ottavio. And he is not just one of the blameless men who fail to win the heroine's love as much because of their own lack of personality as because the sinner is so much more attractive. He is a strong man: only a great love and real strength of character combined can produce the renunciation of his own hopes, and the devotion which made him strive to rescue Tannhäuser from despair for Elisabeth's sake. Wolfram is one of the noblest of all Wagner's characters, but many singers make him little more than a saintly bore. Fischer-Dieskau succeeded in showing us a complete Wolfram, vocally moving and dramatically wise and understanding. It was a beautiful performance.

In the revival of *Lohengrin* Birgit Nilsson succeeded for other reasons. Hers was not, at that stage anyway, an outstanding interpretation of the part, but it was gloriously sung. Her voice conveyed exactly the quality of purity: true, cool, innocent, almost sexless, which can make the plight of this poor princess—so ignorant of worldly wisdom —touch the heart. Windgassen had developed his interpretation of the knightly champion, and sang it beautifully. Astrid Varnay and Hermann Uhde repeated their well-matched, sinister Ortrud and Telramund. Fischer-Dieskau was a fine sonorous Herald, and Josef Greindl was again the strong, well-sung King Heinrich.

Owing to the illness of Ludwig Weber, Greindl performed a vocal marathon during the first week of the 1954 festival which I do not think I have ever heard equalled. In eight days he sang seven leading Wagnerian roles: Landgrave (*Tannhäuser*), King Heinrich (*Lohengrin*), Fafner (*Rheingold*), Hunding (*Die Walküre*), Fafner (*Siegfried*), Hagen (*Götterdämmerung*) and Gurnemanz (*Parsifal*). If his voice was rather tired by the end of it one could hardly be surprised, but every performance was that of an artist and musician.

That was the first time I heard him sing Gurnemanz. After Ludwig

Weber it seemed to lack warmth of tone and the finer points of characterization, both of which Greindl developed in later years, but it was a sound sketch of the part. Knappertsbusch returned to the conductor's desk, proving that this was especially his opera, though even he did not efface memories of Clemens Krauss' beautful *Parsifal* the year before. Alas, Krauss died before the 1954 festival. Windgassen was the Parsifal, singing more beautifully, but less identified with the part than Vinay, and therefore less compelling. Mödl repeated her Kundry, and year by year was developing it into one of the finest performances of the part I have seen. Much the same could be said of Gustav Neidlinger's Klingsor. Neidlinger is one of those excellent artists who can take a character part and give full value to acting without sacrificing the vocal line.

Lastly we had Hans Hotter as Amfortas, a role which he had sung at Bayreuth the previous year, but not at the performance I attended. Hotter, as most people know, is as great an actor as he is a singer. In fact he might very well win in a contest with straight actors on their home ground—the stage of the spoken word. Therefore one knew that his portrayal of the self-tortured knight would be something outstanding. It was: the agony of the ascetic leader, the spiritual man who had surrendered to temptation, and felt forever defiled, as symbolized by the unhealed wound, all this was here. Also the selfish side of his own bitter remorse which in itself brought suffering upon his father Titurel and the other knights by withholding from them the sacrament, and placed him beyond its redemptive power. I do not think I have seen a more anguished Amfortas before or since. Vocally it was not his best role, partly perhaps because it already lay rather high for his voice, which was growing larger and darker, and was to become far more bass than baritone. But more, I think, because he acted Amfortas with such itensity that the singing of it was afflicted with some unsteadiness. No one who saw that performance is likely to forget its embodiment of suffering; it was an El Greco painting in musical form.

As always, Wieland Wagner made minor changes in production. The first act of *Parsifal* remained as beautiful as before, the second act was even better, thanks to improved lighting, but at the end of the third act in the hall of the Grail he introduced a circular motive— "It shall be moon or star or what I list" as Petruchio would have said. Whatever it was, the effect was wholly inappropriate to *Parsifal*. Fortunately it vanished again in later seasons, but at that time the idea seemed to have a particular appeal for Wieland Wagner. He used a rather similar effect for the final moments of *Götterdämmerung*.

This was something of a vintage year for the *Ring*. Keilberth's

D

mastery of the score grew with the years. Hotter was in magnificent form as Wotan/Wanderer throughout the cycle, with the sure, artistic balance of Greindl in each opera, and Gustav Neidlinger as Alberich. Smaller roles were filled by different singers with varying success, but these with Hermann Uhde were stalwarts of the First Eleven, and so—with increasing brilliance—were Astrid Varnay and Wolfgang Windgassen.

Newman found that Varnay overacted in 1951. That was an interim stage. By the time I saw her the following year she had overcome the difficulties of acquiring the particular acting technique which Wieland required, and also the vocal problems which had ruined her London singing in 1951 with a disastrous wobble. By 1954 her interpretation of Brünnhilde was already a complete character, and one recognizably distinct from other readings. She was essentially the warrior maid, and when the Valkyrie immortality was changed to human womanhood there was still laughter, courage—and of course later a fierce retribution—in her love.

It was exciting to watch Wolfgang Windgassen developing his Siegfried. All the great roles in Wagner's operas require years of study before even the most gifted singer can give anything like a full interpretation. On the musical side alone these parts are a vast undertaking, and the most that can be expected at first is that the artist will sing the role accurately. The finer points of phrasing and expression, vocal understanding of the character—these things come gradually to those who become great interpreters. Some never achieve more than a superficial command of the part. But a too hasty judgement of the singer's potentialities only betrays the listener's ignorance of what is involved. Windgassen, already a successful artist in the more lyric Wagnerian roles, accepted a tremendous challenge with Siegfried. He was not an obvious champion as the *Ring* hero since his voice was never a particularly large one, but he has succeeded by sheer artistry, by his ever deepening understanding of Siegfried, and his ability to portray in voice and acting the gay, unthinking confidence of unsmirched youth. Already in 1954 his Siegfried was becoming a personality. Later it was to develop into the definitive interpretation for a whole generation of operagoers.

All non-Wagnerites are amazed, even appalled, at the staying-power of Bayreuth audiences. To see seven different operas (which is the usual programme) in nine days is undoubtedly a gargantuan musical feast, and I would not recommend anyone to undertake the whole set unless they really are devoted to Wagner's music. For the addict, of course, this only whets the appetite for more. Many would like to stay on—and some of them do—to see repeat performances, and some managed to attend the performance of Beethoven's Ninth Symphony which was conducted by Furtwängler.

But it must not be thought that we do nothing else except listen to music. Every five or six days there is a "spielfrei" day without a performance when all the singers, orchestra, technicians, office personnel, vanish thankfully from public view. Each season there are also at least two "closed" performances, specially organized for trade union groups or others. On these days the ordinary festival guests must find other interests. Some potter in the town, eat and drink and sleep off the effects of a surfeit of music. Others go out into the surrounding country. The local tourist office always has information about coach trips on "spielfrei" days, but the Bayreuth regulars usually take a train or local bus to the place of their choice—there are excellent local services. Motorists of course have no need to consider public transport.

One of my own favourite haunts is the Fränkische Schweiz or Franconian Switzerland. The name suggests twentieth-century tourist nomenclature, but apparently has been used for hundreds of years. The whole length of Bavaria and the width of the Bodensee separate it from Switzerland, but it has something of the mood of Swiss foothills without the guardianship of giant mountains.

There are three principal towns in this eastern part of Northern Bavaria: Nuremberg, Bamberg and Bayreuth, and the Fränkische Schweiz lies in the triangle between them. Most of it can be explored comfortably by car in a day's outing, or on one of the coach tours. It is a land of small, steep-sided valleys, clothed in woods. On the hilltops are little castles, old and unpretentious, and great outcrops of rock. Below are the rivers, fed by miniature streams which skip and chatter down among the rocks to the narrow bright green fields along the valleys. The Wiesent, one of Bavaria's best trout streams, is the principal river, and there is fishing to be had here by ticket and also in some of the tributaries.

Even now when the tides of tourism have swept over so many lovely districts, carrying away much of their native charm, the Fränkische Schweiz remains almost untouched. There have been some changes. In the early 1950s almost all the farm carts and ploughs were drawn by calm-eyed golden oxen. Now the ubiquitous tractor has taken over. But the villages of broad timbered houses with high gabled roofs are the same. Fowls scutter happily in the straw and midden of the farmyard. One still sees women working in the fields with their menfolk, and children minding a flock of geese. Beside the roads are little Calvaries, sometimes with a bunch of wildflowers offered by a passing villager.

During the rich flowering of German baroque and rococo architecture in the eighteenth century, the bishops of Bamberg built a summer palace close to the pilgrimage church designed by Balthasar Neumann at Gössweinstein, in the centre of the Fränkische Schweiz. This is a charming little town well worth a visit, and two other superb examples of baroque architecture are on the northern fringe of the district—the Church of the Fourteen Saints—Vierzehnheiligen—and the Monastery of Banz.

It was no doubt from one of the castles which watch over this countryside that the Walther von Stolzing of Wagner's imagination set off to the burghers' town of Nuremberg to lose his heart to Eva and his temper over the petty bureaucracies of the mastersingers—and to learn wisdom from Hans Sachs. It is pleasant to stop at a wayside gasthof and drink beer or wine or even coffee, and dream of Stolzing studying Walther von der Vogelweide, and listening to the birds, running waters, and the country's spring song. A bottle of Franconian wine does wonders in producing this romantic mood.

CHAPTER V

1955—The Coming of the Begum

THE opening of the 1955 festival marked a great event—though a non-operatic one—in the history of New Bayreuth. This was the first visit of the Begum Aga Khan, wife of the (now) late Aga Khan. Bayreuth has always been accustomed to famous visitors. The President of the West German Federal Republic, Ministers of State, kings, princes, film stars, many of the glittering figures of the world as well as musical celebrities come from time to time. They are entertained royally, photographed and fêted and their names inscribed in the Golden Book. But "die Prinzessin Aga Khan" or "die Begum", as she is affectionately known to the whole of Bayreuth, immediately established herself in the hearts of the townspeople in a very special sense.

This French lady who had married the Aga Khan and shared with him his place in the international worlds of society and sport, came to see and hear the operas, not merely to make a formal visit. Very tall and strikingly beautiful, she wears the brilliant graceful saris which are the dress of women of her husband's race. Wears them thus by right, and with a flair which very few Europeans possess. This beautiful figure with her oriental draperies, her jewels, and her personal charm electrified the Bayreuthians, and most of the festival visitors too. They lined the streets where she was to pass, flocked round her car, watched her walking from the Festspielhaus to the restaurant, begged for her autograph.

But what has really endeared the Begum to local people and to the regular festival-goers is that she too is a devotee of New Bayreuth. Since 1955 she has attended every festival except that of 1957—the year of the Aga Khan's death. Like most of us she always stays in a private house: with Herr and Frau Hirschmann at 5, Rheingold-strasse. The house is quite famous, and a small knot of onlookers is always gathered round the gate, waiting for her departure for the Festspielhaus.

Her presence adds glamour to the Festspielrestaurant where she dines in the second interval. In 1955 it still had a great deal of operatic glamour also. The usual gastronomic programme is that one drinks coffee, tea or an aperitif in the first interval, and dines in the second

(each lasts for an hour). However, some people prefer a meal afterwards. In the early years of New Bayreuth many visitors went to
the main restaurant after the opera, either for dinner or just to drink
a bottle of wine and discuss the performance. The great attraction was
that, following a pre-war tradition, a number of the leading singers
usually came to eat there too.

The restaurant is a large one, on two levels, the main entrance
being from a terrace opposite the south-east corner of the Festspielhaus.
This leads into a large room accommodating several hundred people,
across which is a kind of highway which takes you to the top of a
flight of steps and thence to the even larger restaurant below. There
the singers would have their reserved tables. At one time there was
a single long artists' table running right along the centre of the room.
The experienced Bayreuth regulars hurried into the restaurant
immediately after the performance and got themselves a table in this
lower section, choosing one with a good view of the stairs. As soon as
the first singer arrived the applause would start near the entrance,
spread like wildfire through the tables on the upper level, and then
rise to a climax in the lower restaurant as the artist walked down the
steps. It was a wonderful opportunity for adorers to see their idols
carrying their bouquets and looking beautiful or handsome as the case
might be, in evening dress. In those days, too, tradition still maintained
a "no applause" rule for performances of *Parsifal* (a tradition, by the
way, maintained by the audience, not the Wagner grandsons; Wolfgang
Wagner has now succeeded in breaking it) so this was the only chance
of paying tribute to singers in that opera.

Afterwards, of course, came the autograph hunters, sidling
ingratiatingly up with programmes, photographs, souvenir books,
even menu cards to be signed. Fame is a demanding business. It
requires great unselfishness to sing a long and exacting role and then,
tired and hungry, to sign autographs and be charming to a horde of
admirers, especially if the soup is getting cold. It is probably no wonder
that this particular tradition has almost completely died out. A pity
though; it was a harmless and very pleasant part of the Bayreuth
life.

The Eule, on the other hand, has certainly not lost its old character.
I went there often in the early 1950s, and in 1968 it was just as
crowded, as noisy, as "gemütlich". This is far away in the old town,
in one of the little cobbled streets leading off the farther side of
Maximilianstrasse. (plate 24b.) It is a good half hour's walk from
the Festspielhaus, so those who go there after the performance take
a taxi if they have no car: it will almost certainly be full by the time
a walker arrives.

A picturesque old corner house, the Eule is one of the typical German restaurants where one small room leads to another and the whole can accommodate a surprising number of people. The name translated is Owl and there is a number of stuffed owls in the different rooms. Also, because it is an artists' pub—"Künstlerlokal"—the walls are covered with signed photographs of singers, going far back into Bayreuth's past.

The tables are clean bare wood, the chairs and settles are wood. If you see a table with eight chairs round it at noon that same table will take twelve people by ten o'clock, and sixteen at midnight. Chairs appear as if by magic. Hot, smiling humanity moves up to eke out a few inches of space, and you squeeze in, to eat and drink with your elbows pinned to your sides, to bawl at your companions above the general hubbub—and to enjoy it. The Eule has a camaraderie all of its own. Here too there is applause when any of the artists come in.

Talk, talk—whenever the music stops in Bayreuth a buzz of conversation starts anywhere and everywhere, and in at least three languages. German of course; English with many different intonations from the British, American, Canadian, Australian, South African music lovers who gather here; and also French, for there is a tremendously keen body of French Wagnerites. In 1955 the verbal bees buzzed chiefly round the honey pot of the new production—*Der Fliegende Holländer*.

This was Wolfgang Wagner's second Bayreuth production. A certain aura of superstition hung about this opera as far as Bayreuth was concerned. It had been given in the festival of 1914, and because the rotation of operas was not so methodical in the inter-war years as it has been during New Bayreuth, the *Holländer* was not seen again for twenty-five years—until 1939. After that it was revived in 1940, 1941 and 1942, and then vanished until this new appearance in 1955. Much as *Macbeth* has the reputation of bringing bad luck in the theatre, there were half-serious forebodings about the ill-fated Holländer setting foot in the Festspielhaus once more. Fortunately that year broke this particular superstition, and the later production of 1959 and revivals have been carried out without precipitating another world war!

It was a good, sound production in the now accepted form of Bayreuth staging. Not so beautiful or so effective as Wolfgang's *Lohengrin* of two years earlier, and much of it was quite as dark as his brother's productions. In the first act the sea heaved and surged on the cyclorama, bluish-green under great dark clouds. The phantom ship was a phantom indeed—a ghostly projection of spars and sails and rigging which sailed across the cyclorama and was gone before the watcher had time to question its composition. As such, it was one of the most effective ships I have seen in any *Holländer* production. (Plate 20.)

Daland's home was a bleak, square room where the girls sat spinning in neat rows round the walls. Finally for the last scene the ship was there again, anchored this time as background to the stage, but straining like a live thing to take to the seas again, now showing sails, now bare rigging, eerily handled by an invisible crew.

The chorus moves were arranged as a corporate body, not quite so geometrically as Wieland Wagner's *Tannhäuser*, but on much the same principle. In the first act, it is true, the sailors' chorus did not appear onstage; in the third they were a conglomerate mass, reeling in formation. The spinning girls were, as I have said, also regimented into lines. At this stage in their artistic work both brothers chose to use the chorus as a single entity reflecting or expressing only one reaction at a time. The result was a powerful, highly formalized effect. I own I enjoyed this *Holländer* very much, but there was some justification for the criticism that Wolfgang had here imposed his own conception upon an opera which is meant to have a far more human and realistic setting. After all the real drama of the story lies in the entry of the unearthly, accursed Holländer upon the very ordinary life of a little Norwegian seaport. The Holländer with his burden of guilt, and Senta, fey and inspired to his redemption, are the only extraordinary characters. The rest are fully occupied with their own lives, working or wenching, drinking, spinning, gossiping. It is really more effective if they react as a crowd of individuals would.

Musically this was a very fine *Holländer*. Knappertsbusch conducted with the feeling which he always had for the heart of Wagner's music: the doubt and longing of the Holländer himself, Senta's spiritual strength, and the supernatural consummation above and beyond the rollicking earthiness of Daland's home port.

Hermann Uhde sang the Holländer at the first performance (Hotter also sang it during the season). It was, I think, one of Uhde's best roles, even though his voice had not the richness to convey all the emotional depth of the character. His tall slim figure looked suitably haunted, and he acted the agony and longing to great effect. Astrid Varnay's Senta was brilliantly if not always beautifully sung, and her dramatic gifts were well used in the service of the part. This was a Senta who would certainly be capable of casting off the shackles of home to carry out her mission; who had no part in the giggling, gossiping lives of other girls, and who could welcome death to achieve her hero's redemption.

As Daland, Ludwig Weber's beautiful voice and warmly human

acting made the old captain a kindly father, according to his lights. He was not one of the Dalands who sell their daughter simply for the stranger's treasure. The two tenor parts were admirably taken too. Wolfgang Windgassen's Erik was well sung, and acted with real feeling for this unfortunate and bewildered lover reject. Josef Traxel had one of the most beautful lyric tenor voices heard at Bayreuth in all the post-war years. His singing of the brief but exquisite little part of the steersman remains for me the ideal. I have never heard it bettered.

Wieland's *Tannhäuser* was this year conducted by André Cluytens and on almost all counts it had improved enormously. Windgassen sang and acted the title role extremely well, bringing to it dignity as well as passion. Gré Brouwenstijn was a very moving Elisabeth, though at times she forced her voice to the detriment of its quality. Dietrich Fischer-Dieskau repeated and enriched his beautiful Wolfram. Again Greindl sang a masterly Langrave, but the Venus of Hetra Wilfert was a mistake as it had been in 1954; altogether too light a voice for the part. Josef Traxel and Toni Blankenheim both provided good singing as Walther von der Vogelweide and Biterolf.

Scenically Wieland had made a number of modifications, although the Venusberg Bacchanale remained as chill and static as before. The valley of the Wartburg had grown some trees, formal ones to be sure, but trees nonetheless, and the minstrels' hall had in place of its croquet hoops a new design of round Romanesque arches poised—without aid of pillars—above and behind the acting area. On balance the production gained a good deal by these alterations: the final result had a more medieval quality. But the chief laurels went to Cluytens and Fischer-Dieskau.

Parsifal was a disappointment, at least at the performance which I saw. Knappertsbusch lacked inspiration that night, and his slow tempi seemed ponderous and dull, instead of dedicated and mystical as they usually did. The three leading artists—Weber as Gurnemanz, Vinay as Parsifal and Martha Mödl as Kundry—were all in poor voice. The last scene was still framed in a strange circle of light thrown on to the gauze curtain. It may have been a halo. To me the effect was of peering into the Hall of the Grail through a porthole. However, the chorus sang superbly, and there was one fine new contribution— Fischer-Dieskau's Amfortas. This was a poignant, very artistic performance, not so moving as some but well sung. Gustav Neidlinger was the excellent Klingsor and there was some beautiful singing by the flower maidens.

Josef Keilberth again conducted the *Ring* and had now found the full measure both of the orchestra and the Festspielhaus acoustics. There was some magnificent playing in the first cycle which I saw, and the *Götterdämmerung* was superb. In *Rheingold* Rudolf Lustig was a disappointing Loge. He had sung the role also in 1954, but lacked the graceful, mocking, quicksilver quality of Erich Witte. But there was Hans Hotter's magnificent Wotan, matched with Neidlinger's Alberich.

Die Walküre was an outstanding evening, with Hotter, Greindl's Hunding, a warmly human Sieglinde by Gré Brouwenstijn, and Ramon Vinay as Siegmund. Vinay was not in good voice, but he made a wonderfully strong tragic character of the unfortunate Volsung. And Astrid Varnay sang Brünnhilde with deep understanding and brilliant musicianship.

Siegfried had again Windgassen in the name part, singing well, and also using his voice with intelligence. Most Wagner enthusiasts have probably heard other singers, some of whom have a larger voice than Windgassen, but who use it with such prodigal recklessness in the first act of *Siegfried* that by the time they come to awaken Brünnhilde at the end of a long evening of gruelling singing there is only the shadow of a voice left. Windgassen has never fallen into this particular trap. Already critics were saying that his musicianship and style made him the best Siegfried since Max Lorenz in his prime.

Paul Kuen's Mime was a clever performance which always tended to be overacted and vocally distorted. Maria von Ilosvay was Erda; why is a mystery, for the part lay uncomfortably low for her.

That *Götterdämmerung* is one which stands out in memory, from the Norns—Maria von Ilosvay, Georgine von Milinkovic, and Mina Bolotine—to the final inundation of the Rhine. Varnay and Windgassen radiant of voice. Uhde's Gunther, a brilliant study in weakness. Greindl's dark implacable strength as Hagen. Maria von Ilosvay as a moving Waltraute. Gré Brouwenstijn, a pretty, bewildered Gutrune.

Above all Greindl and the chorus in the second act. Astrid Varnay was always at her best in the drama of that act too: the fury with which she seized Hagen's spear from Siegfried's hand to make her own oath—and the sense of tragedy. All of which vanished before the mystic strength and splendour with which she sang the final Immolation scene.

Bayreuth had already taken Madame Varnay very much to its heart and that year there was an added affection and sympathy, for her husband, Hermann Weigert had died three months earlier. As her musical coach, and a general musical assistant at Bayreuth, he was much respected and greatly missed that season. Following the death of Wilhelm Furtwängler in November 1954 and Clemens Krauss some months earlier, there were shadows of sorrow mixed with the enjoyment of the 1955 festival.

CHAPTER VI

1956—"Die Meistersinger ohne Nürnberg"

WALTER PANOFSKY, writing in the *Süddeutsche Zeitung*, said that Wieland Wagner had administered a wholesome shock with each of his Bayreuth productions, "This is the hardest, the most painful". He was describing the 1956 *Die Meistersinger von Nürnberg*. Certainly it was a shock, and not unwholesome in our sense of the word, but whether it was a justified one is quite another matter.

"Die Meistersinger ohne Nürnberg"—the Mastersingers without Nuremberg—became the catch-phrase of the season. For there was no Nuremberg. The town had vanished, and the story became a disembodied one in the realms of fantasy. The decor was not symbolic in the form of some of Wieland's later work; its effects were impressionistic, suggesting a scene rather than showing it. For an opera such as *Meistersinger* where the characters, romance, humour and philosophy are essentially human and firmly rooted in the place and period—a prosperous middle-class German town of the sixteenth century—this style threw away much of its meaning. It distilled a fine full-blooded wine into a rather thin spirit, while the music of course remained rich and complete. The *Meistersinger* score is one of Wagner's most miraculous works, in which one discovers some new magic at every hearing. But Wieland Wagner's theory of letting the music speak for itself was not justified by this particular treatment, for the music spoke of many things which were ignored, almost denied by the stage pictures.

All the same, those stage pictures were in themselves extremely beautiful—with the exception of the final scene. Many people were enchanted by the fairy beauty of Acts I and II. Within its own conception this production was wholly successful, and it divided the public sharply. Here it was mainly the young and those who had had no previous experience of *Meistersinger* who were carried away by Wieland's scenic alchemy. Fewer experienced operagoers accepted it without reservations; some condemned it outright. The Press were divided too, but the revolutionary approach was news value. The fame of Bayreuth spread more widely than ever.

The first act setting was another example of Wieland's passion for exact balance in design. Above a screen at the centre back was a three-sided carved Gothic frieze, surmounted by Adam and Eve in niches. Below were carved stalls. This was St Katharine's church. The chorus of worshippers, all dressed alike, stood in symmetrically arranged groups in the centre of the stage facing the audience, with Eva and Magdalene on the right-hand side and Walther gazing at Eva across the heads of the congregation from the extreme left. (Plate 26.) It was a very effective picture, and one which did less violence to the mood of the opera than the later scenes, but it was still too formalized.

It was the second act, however, which really set the critical storm raging. Here Richard Wagner decided on a street scene, with the house of Pogner, well-to-do goldsmith, on the right, shaded by a lime tree. Opposite is Hans Sachs' home and workshop, simpler but certainly comfortable and well kept. An elder tree grows beside it, shading the roof with its branches in the pleasant way in which growing things have place in a country town. Other houses along the street and the alley which leads off from the centre back, have shutters—which the apprentices are closing when the scene opens. This is one of the better quarters of Nuremberg, a street where respectable burghers and their wives come and go, where 'prentices frolic when their masters' backs are turned, and where at night the watchman patrols to see that those same burghers can sleep quietly in their beds, safe from thieves, brawls or fire. That is the scene which Richard Wagner sketched verbally in his stage directions, and which the music conveys no less strongly while the comedy of errors, of which this act consists, takes place.

In Wieland's staging the curtain rose upon a blue, poetic nothingness. In the centre of the stage was a kidney-shaped platform with a tracery of cobbles on it. A seat stood on either side, one for Sachs' home and the other for Pogner's, because you cannot soliloquize, philosophize, converse and mend shoes standing up all the time. Sachs' cobbler's bench appeared from space at the appropriate moment, adding a rather incongruous touch of realism. For there were no houses at all: not a door, or a window, no street, no town. A giant floral globe, made like a cowslip ball, represented the elder tree on Sachs' side of the platform. The lime tree had dwindled to a bush behind Pogner's bench. (Plate 27a.)

Therefore there was no window for Beckmesser to serenade, no apparent reason for the nightwatchman to make his rounds here, and no homes from which the neighbours could sally forth to join in the final fray. It was a pretty setting for a midsummer night's dream, which ended with a nightmare when the crowd performed a rhythmic riot. The trouble lay in the fact that the second act of *Meistersinger* is not a dream: it is a lively and important part of the opera's action.

In the last act Sachs' workshop was transformed to a bare monastic room decorated with the top of a rood-screen (plate 27b), and the festival meadows by the Pegnitz had given place to the inside of a circus tent. The chorus of citizens sat primly in serried ranks and identical costumes watching a tumbler's act until the mastersingers arrived. (Plate 28.)

This metamorphosis of the opera made things very difficult for the singers, and the conductor too. The latter was André Cluytens, and his interpretation of this wonderful score was frankly uninspired, though the chorus sang superbly. Their placing—in the first act in the centre of the stage, and in the last scene in a complete semicircle of tiered seats like the Albert Hall—gave them a wonderful opportunity. The attack and precision, together with an overwhelming beauty of tone which Wilhelm Pitz achieves with his choirs, were superbly displayed. But frankly the true meaning and balance of the story should not be sacrificed to choral excellence!

Hans Sachs is, and must always be, the central figure of *Meistersinger*. He is by far the greatest human character Wagner ever created. It would not, I think, be going too far to say that Sachs is the finest complete character in any opera. He is an ordinary man who had learned wisdom and philosophy in the everyday work and sorrows of life (he had lost wife and children). He has a sense of humour and an unsentimental but kindly understanding of men and their weaknesses. He is human enough to have moments of irritation, and a mischievous enjoyment in outwitting the bombastic, conceited Beckmesser. He loves Eva, but knows that her youth is not for him, and he is able to find real happiness in smoothing the path of her romance with the young Franconian knight.

Any interpretation which lays too much stress on Sachs as the humble shoemaker is wrong. He is a power in Nuremberg, respected and admired as a man and a poet by the townspeople, envied by Beckmesser, a trusted friend of Pogner. Wagner has given him some glorious music to sing—and provided the artist who plays him with a considerable challenge. Musically and dramatically this is a very long and very taxing role. Quite a number of singers make a reasonably good job of it. Very very few have all the qualifications to make a really great Hans Sachs.

Hans Hotter is one of those few, and he sang the part in the 1956 production at Bayreuth. Wise and understanding, tender, and robustly humorous of his own weaknesses and those of others, his was as near the ideal Sachs as we are ever likely to see and hear it. And yet the production made his performance seem in a way insulated, cut off from its proper human world. Those of us who had seen Hotter's Sachs in London in 1951 (when Sir Thomas Beecham conducted *Meistersinger* at Covent Garden) mourned Bayreuth's missed opportunity.

If Walther von Stolzing can act, so much the better, but the main thing is that he should have a beautiful voice. Windgassen sang the part most beautifully, though his acting was rather wooden. Gré Brouwenstijn, on the other hand, was a charming Eva: graceful, winning without being the determined young schemer which some singers have chosen to make her. It was easy to accept her as the prize desired by many hearts. Her singing did not quite match her performance as a whole, but this was a happy Eva.

Josef Greindl was a kindly Pogner, and Dietrich Fischer-Dieskau a personable, self-important Kothner. This was a memorable performance of the chairman of the guild. Well sung and acted with a real undertsanding of character, Kothner stood out as a leading personality of Nuremberg in a way that is rare among most *Meistersinger* productions.

The Beckmesser was Karl Schmitt-Walter, an artist who is a real musician, and one with a thorough understanding of Wagner. His Beckmesser was a brilliant performance in a subtle way, but it suffered from the production; it is impossible to bring out all the comic facets of the part without more stage business. The same was true of Gerhard Stolze's David.

Joseph Keilberth conducted the revival of Wolfgang Wagner's *Der Fliegende Holländer* (he had been responsible for some performances the previous year). Here he seemed completely in his element, and the orchestra played splendidly for him, carrying us along on the great tide of emotion and excitement as a first-class performance of this opera does. George London was the Holländer. His dramatic gifts made it an important, strong performance, though his rough-grained voice prevented him from being an ideal exponent of this role, at least for me. There must be beauty as well as anguish in the singing, for this is, after all, a romantic opera. Astrid Varnay repeated her vivid Senta.

Arnold van Mill was Daland. He had not the fatherly quality of Ludwig Weber, nor the rollicking seaman's character of Josef Greindl who sang the part at Bayreuth in later years. Van Mill's Daland was not a complete impersonation in the way of these other two, but he had a beautiful ringing bass voice, and vocally it was a fine performance.

Josef Traxel exchanged the steersman for Erik, and again sang superbly. The new steersman was a young tenor, then unknown in

Bayreuth—Jean Cox. In 1967 and 1968 Cox has won laurels as Lohengrin and Parsifal. Those who study operatic form and forecast future winners should always watch for success in certain of Wagner's small roles: a fine Froh or *Holländer* steersman today will often prove a Tannhäuser, a Tristan, even perhaps a Siegfried in ten years' time.

I wrote of the 1956 *Parsifal*, "This year *Parsifal* was extremely beautiful, and a few bits of unnecessary symbolism which have marred its simplicity in recent years were removed." These included the final telescope lens effect. The amazing quality of visual spirituality had returned, and we bowed before it. Knappertsbusch conducted with his own measured, dedicated fervour. Apart from one or two performances in 1961, this was the last year that Ludwig Weber sang Gurnemanz at Bayreuth. His voice no longer had the heart-breaking beauty of a few years before, but as happens with great singers his interpretation continued to develop. It was a wonderfully moving performance.

Much is spoken and written about the delight of having young, fresh voices. Of course they are a joy; of course they are tremendously important, because these are the artists who can give us all our opera-going tomorrows. But for sheer, selfish enjoyment of the moment, I would always rather have the mastery and art of the great singer, even when his or her voice has lost its bloom, than the inexperienced artist who may at the time have a potentially far more beautiful vocal instrument. Between the two lies the precious time of a singer's prime, but the really great often become even finer artists after this meridian is passed.

Ramon Vinay, in excellent voice, was a noble Parsifal. Gustav Neidlinger repeated his menacing Klingsor, and Martha Mödl her dramatic Kundry. Fischer-Dieskau's Amfortas was even finer than before. Altogether this was one of the *Parsifals* after which the audience wakes slowly to reality, as from a trance. The mystery, and beauty, and sense of having shared in a rare spiritual experience was strong upon us. At such times ordinary conversation seems to profane the vision; the trees and night sky, even the dim lamps in the garden below the Festspielhaus were better companions than one's fellow creatures. I think most people share this feeling after a fine *Parsifal;* as the crowds move down the hill there is less chatter than on other nights.

For the *Ring* we had a brand new Valhalla. It was still an insubstantial palace projected on to the cyclorama, but a rather splendid pile, flushed with the rosy light of sunrise and far more effective than the former ivory tower. However, no Bayreuth Valhalla has been wholly successful, which is a pity. After all, Wotan's palace was the beginning of all the trouble. One feels that it should look to the audience, as it seemed to him at the opening of *Das Rheingold*'s second scene, a castle fit for gods.

Wieland Wagner was still changing each production, little by little, from year to year. Sometimes the variations were scarcely perceptible, but the overall effect was to simplify the scene still further. The new Valhalla was an exception, since it was more impressive, more obvious than the old one, but otherwise ramps or blocks became smaller, the whole picture more bare, concentrating attention on the naked disc which was the acting area of the stage. In *Die Walküre* the two almost vertical walls of rock between which Brünnhilde made her first entrance in Act II had gone. The same effect was obtained—but not so dramatically—entirely by projections. In the second act of *Siegfried* the disc which was hung above the centre stage (rather like a sounding board), and presumably represented the leafy roof of the forest, had gone too, and with it the side ramps. Siegfried now sat on a few shallow steps nearer the front of the stage, and the swaying green and gold world of the treetops was conveyed simply by dappled patterns of light behind and on the ground. Even in the vassals' scene of *Götterdämmerung* the last vestiges of steps and walls had vanished. Wieland built his effects with the tiered ranks of the chorus themselves.

Not all these particular changes were made in 1956. Some had been introduced in previous years, but the *Ring* had, by 1956, become different in many respects from that I had seen four years earlier. There was more light, too, in all four operas. Personal taste must always influence opinion on when and how Wieland Wagner's productions were at their best. I am inclined to think that 1956 was the peak year of his first *Ring*, from the scenic point of view. It was simple, strong, with some remarkably beautiful lighting effects and fine grouping.

For the four years 1953-56 Martha Mödl and Astrid Varnay each sang Brünnhilde in one complete *Ring* every season, alternating as to who appeared in the first cycle. In 1956 it was Mödl. The contrast between these two artists is complete, and therefore it was particularly interesting to follow their work year by year. Certain qualities they share: both are good musicians, and highly intelligent, gifted actresses. Their stage personalities and their voices were always entirely different.

Martha Mödl is very feminine, with a round-faced large-eyed beauty. Her voice, of definite mezzo quality, had at that time a warm timbre, human, emotional. At its best it was a much lovelier voice than Varnay's diamond-hard tone, but it was always prone to troubles of voice production. Often, alas, Mödl's voice sounded tired or worn, breath support was inadequate or pitch uncertain. Yet at her best

2   Wieland Wagner, 1966

3 Waiting for the fanfares—the audience gathers on the
Festspielhaus terrace

4 (a)   Above.   Festspielhaus
4 (b)   Below.   The last traditional production: Hartmann's *Meistersinger*, 1951

5 The *Ring*, 1951. (a) *Siegfried*, Act III

5 (b) *Götterdämmerung*, Act II

6 *Parsifal,* Act I Scene 2, 1951–69

7   Ludwig Weber as Gurnemanz, 1951

8 The orchestra pit

9   Wilhelm Pitz

10 Richard Wagner's grave

11   Old houses in the town

12 The *Ring*, 1952. (a) *Das Rheingold*, last scene

12 (b) *Die Walküre*, Act II

13 The *Ring*, 1952. (a) *Siegfried*, Act II

13 (b) *Götterdämmerung*, Act II

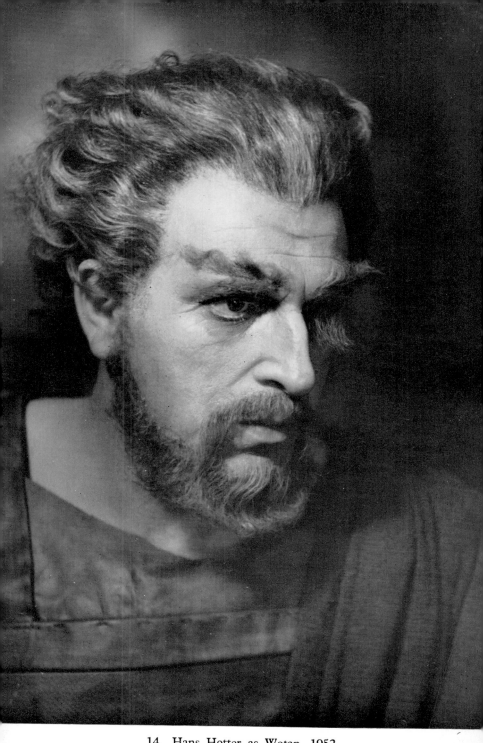

14 Hans Hotter as Wotan, 1952

15　Erich Witte at Loge, 1952

16 (a)   *Parsifal,* Act I Scene 1, 1952

b)   *Tristan und Isolde,* 1953, Gustav Neidlinger as Kurwenal, Ramon Vinay as Tristan

17   *Lohengrin,* 1953   (a)   Act I

17 (b)   Act II

she was for a number of years one of the most beautiful and moving singers on the Wagnerian stage.

I remember that *Ring* as being one of the times when she was at her best—except in *Siegfried*. She was, naturally, among the more human Brünnhildes. There was more of the loving daughter and Siegfried's radiant bride than of the Amazon Valkyrie. But she was a god's daughter too, touched with an elemental spirit. Her soft singing could be extraordinarily beautiful—tender and passionate, or the chaste voice of the untouched Valkyrie. Moreover her acting, even when she had nothing to sing, was always exactly right. During Wotan's narration in the second act of *Walküre* Brünnhilde has only an occasional line to sing while her father unfolds the tragic history of his long struggle to right the wrong that he had committed in his pride. The whole scene is virtually a monologue, yet Brünnhilde's reactions to the story are vitally important to the scene, and of course to the singer who is playing Wotan. No other Brünnhilde I have ever seen has played that particular scene so beautifully as Mödl. Her tender concern as she knelt beside him, "Ich bin dir treu; Sieh', Brünnhilde bittet!" and her expression as his unhappiness is revealed, all were quite outstanding. Many of us will, I think, always remember Martha Mödl and Hans Hotter together in that scene (plate 23), and in the agonizingly beautiful Abschied at the end of *Walküre*. Such moments are the real glories of all operagoing.

Windgassen was not in good form as Siegfried, in this cycle, but the rest of the leading singers—Greindl as Hunding and Hagen, Neidlinger's Alberich, Vinay's Siegmund—were all memorable, and there was a lovely Sieglinde by Gré Brouwenstijn. Keilberth's conducting was exciting and even sumptuous.

E

CHAPTER VII

1957—Wolfgang Wagner's Way with *Tristan*

IN July 1957 the Aga Khan died, and the Begum naturally did not come to Bayreuth that year. Festival and town missed her colourful presence. The weather was uncertain during the first week, and after the previous year's violent reactions over *Meistersinger* there was less general excitement, though the season was a very good one musically.

The new production was by Wolfgang Wagner and it was *Tristan und Isolde*. This formed another milestone on the road of New Bayreuth, because it was the first time one of the operas already produced by one brother was given new staging by the other, so that a direct comparison of their styles could be made.

Scenically there were not really any vast differences. Wolfgang's first act was also played in a big tent extending right across the stage, and without any of the rich tapestries which Wagner stipulated and no doubt thought fitting for the pavilion of a royal bride. (Plate 30b.) It was bare and functional but, like Wieland's, did not distract from the music. For the second act garden a curved wall extending halfway across the stage from the left provided a hint of the mundane world, though it hardly suggested a building in which Isolde lived. Wieland's garden had been a dream world with no touch of reality save a seat for the lovers. Tristan's castle in the third act was far more effectively conveyed in the new production by bold curving walls and a flight of steps leading to a symbolic form of battlements.

Broadly speaking the difference in approach was that Wieland's *Tristan* lifted the opera out of the harness of time and place: the great exaltation of love and death was in some half-world between earth and heaven, whereas Wolfgang Wagner indicated with a few modern theatrical touches the local habitation which his grandfather had chosen.

Wolfgang Sawallisch conducted. He too approached the opera from a modern viewpoint, spare, restrained, shorn of overt emotionalism. It was beautifully balanced, clear in texture, even perhaps more spiritual than is usual. But one missed some of the voluptuous glories of the score.

The singing also was transitional rather than complete. This was Birgit Nilsson's first Bayreuth Isolde. Her voice with its rare blend of purity and strength already showed her to be one of the great Isoldes of the century, but although she sang superbly the characterization was still only partly formed. She was at her best in the first act; in the great love duet and in the Liebestod she was still rather cold, lacking the splendour of love's passion. Wolfgang Windgassen's Tristan was unimpressive at the beginning, but got steadily better, and he was very fine in the great music of the last act.

Gustav Neidlinger made a strong, warm-hearted Kurwenal, though his acting in the third act was hampered by having to stand staring at Tristan throughout most of the act. Grace Hoffman sang Brangäne's part with beauty and understanding. The King Marke was Arnold van Mill, rich and fine of voice, but otherwise unremarkable. It has been said that life is made up of the things that come off and the things that do not. Wagnarian bass singers may be divided between those who can touch the heart as King Marke and those who merely make him rather a dull old man. It has little to do with the voice; a considerable gift for acting is required to convey the tragedy of this unhappy and very human king who loses his friend and his hope of married joy at one stroke.

Without sensational *coups de théâtre* this was a successful *Tristan und Isolde,* though not a particularly memorable one. There was, however, one exceptionally beautiful production effect. At the ending a silvery light spread over the scene as though the frosts of winter had descended on the stricken castle when the fire of a great love was withdrawn.

Wieland Wagner's *Die Meistersinger von Nürnberg* had undergone a number of changes, and most of them for the better. Most noticeable was the second-act setting, for Nuremberg had appeared. Not in the substantial traditional form of timbered houses with doors through which people could walk, windows for serenading. No, this act remained a dream, but the dream included a vista of narrow gabled roofs stretching away into the distance on either side of the kidney-shaped segment of cobbled street. The street was bordered with fencing. A shoemaker's sign hung out from the left-hand side of the stage to mark where Sachs' house stood, and a goldsmith's device on the opposite side indicated Pogner's dwelling. The elder tree was no longer a floral sphere suspended in mid-air; it had put down a trunk and taken root in the stage, but Wieland was evidently too much enamoured with the original idea to forgo it altogether, so a succession of flowery globes hung above the line of the street receding into the background. (Plate 30a.) The whole effect was lovely, an enchanting fairy-tale picture. As a setting for the second act of *Meistersinger* it was a distinct improvement on the first version, but still far from supplying the true background for the events of the opera.

There were several changes among the leading singers also. Otto Wiener sang Hans Sachs (Gustav Neidlinger sang the role at some performances, and had also shared it with Hotter in 1956). Wiener was an effective, satisfactory Sachs, though not a great one. His voice, a fine musical baritone, was of the right quality for the part and stayed the course well. He gave beauty and expression to the musical highlights of the role: the Fliedermonolog, the Wahnmonolog, and the eulogy of sacred German art which, coming right at the end, is such a cruel test for any singer. He was a handsome, kindly, humorous and believeable shoemaker-poet. What was lacking was the inner spark which gives greatness to a performance. Wiener's acting remained acting, applied, like the costume, to the outside of the character. One did not feel that it was generated by a deep inward understanding. For this reason his Sachs did not hold attention until the second act.

In the first act of *Meistersinger* Hans Sachs has little to do except hold a watching brief, and yet his presence and his influence are immensely important. He fails to bring the thinking of the other master-singers into line with his own tolerant commonsense, but they are all well aware of his proved wisdom. Only an outstanding artist can show all this without trying to steal the scene from others who have most of the singing to do. It is a parallel case to that of Wotan in *Das Rheingold*. The artist who can be a great Wotan in the prologue to the *Ring*, or show as a great Sachs in the first act of the *Meistersinger*, will undoubtedly triumph in the mightier musical and dramatic opportunities which come later in each case. Otto Wiener did not pass the first act test, but he was a very good Sachs nonetheless.

Gottlob Frick made his Bayreuth debut as Veit Pogner. Over the years Bayreuth has been rich in fine bass voices, but Frick's is among the most individual of them all. "Granite" is a word often used to describe his voice, and hard as rock it can be, when the part requires it. Black, black, powerful, steady, and absolutely true—I cannot remember ever hearing Gottlob Frick sing off-pitch. It is an amazing instrument, and he is a fine actor too. Wagnergoers who had seen the London *Ring* in 1951 were already familiar with his Hagen there. As the Bayreuth Pogner he sang with great beauty, revealing a tenderness in the great voice which always surprises those who have heard him only in villainous roles.

Elisabeth Grümmer was the Eva. Temperamentally hers was an ideal performance. This was the gay, warm-hearted loving girl who won and held all hearts—her father's, Sachs', probably many of the neighbours' too, and most of all of course that of the impressionable young nobleman from the hills. Vocally this performance fell somewhat short of perfection, but as a whole it gave enormous pleasure. I did not see Sena Jurinac who also sang Eva during the season. There were no less than three Walther von Stolzings: Windgassen, Josef Traxel and Walter Geisler. I saw the last named, who sang reasonably well but made little of the part. André Cluytens conducted, with much greater feeling for the opera than in 1956.

It was another vintage year for *Parsifal*. Knappertsbusch and André Cluytens shared this opera, Cluytens conducting the performance I saw. He seemed to have far more instinctive sympathy for *Parsifal* than for *Meistersinger*, or perhaps it was due to the productions. At any rate Cluytens' *Parsifal* had real inspiration. The orchestra played beautifully for him, and it was deeply moving.

All the leading singers had grown into their parts with the experience of previous years. Josef Greindl's Gurnemanz in particular had developed tremendously in understanding and tenderness. As I said earlier, all great voices have an individual quality of their own. Greindl's possesses a tragic ring which touches the heart with a sense of pain distilled into beauty by hard-won wisdom. In certain roles where this quality is in character Greindl uses his gift superbly: here, one feels, is a man who has achieved peace out of great suffering. Gurnemanz is such a role, and his 1957 performances were among the outstanding characterizations of the season.

Ramon Vinay's Parsifal, too, was memorable for a sense of identification which lifted his performance out of the range of mere singing and acting. This *was* Parsifal, and the audience lived with him a lifetime of harsh experience in the course of the opera's three acts. George London's Amfortas, though it had not the musical quality of the other two, was a fine and—as it should be—a harrowing performance. Astrid Varnay, whom I was hearing as Kundry for the first time, seemed less happily cast. She sang the seductive music of the second act very well, as was to be expected, but some of this seductive mood was carried over into her acting in the Good Friday scene, which is completely wrong. It may have been unintentional, or it may have been the outcome of some instructions of Wieland Wagner's which did not work out well in practice. Astrid Varnay is too good an actress to make this kind of psychological mistake, so it was all the more noticeable, but she did not repeat it in later years.

Hans Knappertsbusch conducted both *Ring* cycles. Year by year the *Ring* has its ups and downs everywhere. It is almost impossible to keep four operas all on a consistently high level. One or another may sag as singers change or are not at the top of their form. In the 1957 first cycle neither Astrid Varnay as Brünnhilde nor Wolfgang Wind-

gassen as Siegfried were at their best, but otherwise all four operas
were given very fine performances, especially *Rheingold* and *Walküre*.
Hotter's Wotan held three of them with the mastery of a great
performance. Neidlinger was again the Alberich, strong, evil, with
ringing voice. Gerhard Stolze was the new Mime in *Rheingold,*
finicking, but dramatic and well contrasted with his Nibelung big
brother. Georgine von Milinkovic was a sound if not outstanding
Fricka; she had sung the part regularly since 1954. Elsabeth Grümmer
made an attractive Freia. The giants, Arnold van Mill as Fasolt and
Greindl as Fafner, were a fine pair with voices of heroic proportions.
Ludwig Suthaus sang Loge, a part he had taken over in 1956. His was
a dark, sinister spirit of fire, but an effective one. Dorothea Siebert,
Paula Lenchner and Elisabeth Schärtel sang beautifully as the Rhinemaidens.

It was a joy to hear Birgit Nilsson as Sieglinde. She sang exquisitely
and was an unusually seductive sister to the rather ineffective Siegmund
of Suthaus. One felt that Greindl's grim Hunding would have been
more than a match for him without Wotan's intervention.

In the later operas most of the casting remained constant to that
of preceding years. Paul Kuën was the *Siegfried* Mime, Stolze singing
only the smaller part in *Rheingold.*

There was, however, a new Gutrune—Elisabeth Grümmer. Of all
Wagner's soprano roles Gutrune is about the least rewarding. She has
little to sing, and what there is provides more problems than rewards.
The character is really a study in empty-headedness, glossed over with
a primitive desire to get a husband, and preferably a notable one.
Cynics may say that Gutrune is not the less true to life for this.
Certainly as far as outward appearances are concerned the world is
full of Gutrunes, but this does not make the part any more interesting
to play. No one can be a great Gutrune, because there is no greatness,
good or bad, in the role. The best any artist may hope to achieve is
to be hailed, with rather patronizing surprise, as "an extraordinarily
good Gutrune". More often the verdict is failure. It cannot be said
that Elisabeth Grümmer won laurels for her performance on this
occasion, but any and every Gutrune has my sympathy.

Gunther is a very different matter. He is a weakling, but there is
plenty of scope for character drawing in both his music and the acting
of the part, and it allows of variations in interpretation. Hermann
Uhde repeated his self-tortured, craven Gunther with great effect.

There was also a beautifully sung Waltraute by Maria von Ilosvay,
who had appeared in this role at Bayreuth for several years. Waltraute
is the only Valkyrie, apart from Brünnhilde herself, who has any
individual personality in the *Ring*. This stems from her one interview

with Brünnhilde in the first act of *Götterdämmerung* when she comes
to plead for the return of the ring to redeem the heartbroken Wotan,
waiting in the stricken halls of Valhalla. The first few times I saw the
opera I barely noticed Waltraute, and other operagoers may have had
the same experience. The part must be superbly sung (it contains
some of *Götterdämmerung*'s most glorious music) and acted with real
perception of its importance, for from this tragic messenger we have
our last glimpse of the gods in their suffering. Years later I was to
hear the finest Waltraute I have ever known—Josephine Veasey in
London's Covent Garden *Ring*—but Maria von Ilosvay was a very
moving Valkyrie.

During the festival I went to a lieder recital given by Josef Traxel—
Schubert's cycle *Die Schöne Müllerin*. It is rare for a tenor voice to
possess both power and lyrical beauty, but Traxel had this happy blend
of qualities. It was an evening of most lovely sound.

Their lieder recitals are a regular part of Bayreuth festival life. In
case the visitor should feel starved of music on "spielfrei" days, when
the Festspielhaus closes its doors and takes a holiday, there are usually
some musical events in the town. An organ recital in the principal
church and, at least once or twice during the festival, a lieder recital.
Occasionally it is a pianist or a chamber-music ensemble, but more
often one of the leading singers in the festival gives a programme of
Schubert, Schumann, Wolf—any of the great song composers. Wagner's
Wesendonck lieder make their appearance from time to time—Martha
Mödl sang them in 1952—but usually one is glad of a contrast in
composers.

The idyllic plan is to spend one of these free days idling among
sunlit woods in the Fränkische Schweitz or elsewhere, returning to
Bayreuth in time for an early dinner, and then to stroll into the
town for an evening of lieder. I have often known this to work out
as hope prescribed it, but not always. The day of Traxel's recital was
wet and miserable; the kind of day when you shelter damply in one
museum, exhibition, office, shop, after another. Therefore the evening's music was all the more welcome.

Whatever the quality of the performance, however, one good reason
for attending these recitals is that they are held in the old Margraves'
Operahouse. This is one of Bavaria's famous examples of baroque
and rococo art. It was built between 1745 and 1748 for the Margravine
Wilhelmine by Joseph Saint-Pierre, who had come from Paris to
take up the appointment of Court Inspector of Buildings. (Plate 34.)

The small courts of many of the German princelings and nobles
were extremely lavish in magnificence, as well as strict in observance
of protocol and etiquette. Margravine Wilhelmine's operahouse is one

which any sovereign might envy. The interior was decorated by the great theatrical architect Giuseppe Galli da Bibiena, and his son Carlo, and it is often called the Bibiena Operahouse. Tier upon tier of boxes rise to the ceiling, with the great royal box in the centre, and all are encrusted with carving and moulding, gilded scrollwork, cupids, Grecian beauties. There are pillars and balustrades of simulated marble, golden urns, and over the royal or Margraves' box a gold pelmet and a very splendid crown.

This was the operahouse which first attracted Richard Wagner's interest to Bayreuth. It was here that he conducted that performance of Beethoven's Ninth Symphony in 1872 which celebrated the laying of the Festspielhaus foundation stone. Gay and graceful, prinked out with all the finery of an eighteenth-century *grande dame*, the Bibiena house stands dreaming in the heart of the town, while the big, blunt-featured, masculine Festspielhaus on the hill enshrines greater fame than any margrave brought to Bayreuth.

CHAPTER VIII

1958—Farewell to the First *Ring*

WHEN the fanfares sounded for the opening of the 1958 festival it was to greet a new *Lohengrin*—Wieland's *Lohengrin*. Wolfgang had produced it first, and the interest centred on how his elder brother would rethink the staging after Wolfgang's very successful version in 1953-54. The result was not really so very different. The New Bayreuth style was formed, and both brothers adhered to its basic principles in all their productions until Wieland branched out into new, expressly symbolic forms with his *Tristan und Isolde* in 1962. But this *Lohengrin* was more ethereal, more timeless. It was Wieland's way to seek a universal plane of interpretation for all his grandfather's works.

To me this *Lohengrin* will always remain the most beautiful of all Wieland's Bayreuth productions. Not beautiful in the same way as *Parsifal*, which was his greater work, but as a series of stage pictures which entranced the eye and mind. *Parsifal*'s beauty is not only, or even primarily, visual. It is often too dark; it is a succession of misty visions, a symphony of subtle half-tones in colour and mood where the music is always paramount. *Lohengrin* on the other hand was clear and bright, very simple in its effects. Seeing these two productions in a single season gave one an insight into where Wieland Wagner's genius really lay, and how great it was when he did not allow himself to be led away into "fancy" experimental productions which were not rooted in the music. Here he pointed the difference perfectly between the early work which still has links with the generality of grand opera, and the late music drama which is in a class, in a musical world, of its own. Despite the fact that the stories are linked by the knightly world of the Grail, *Parsifal* is a parable; *Lohengrin* is an allegorical fairly tale.

It was a surprise and a joy to find that Wieland had, like his brother, adopted colours for this production. And what colours! The opening scene was set on a virtually bare stage. Behind, the cyclorama was bathed in a wonderful sapphire blue light, and above hung a lacy wreath circling a spray of oak leaves. (Plate 37a.) This device could have been maddening, instead it subtly suggested the decoration of an illuminated missal. A broad flight of steps led downwards from the centre back to a shallow circular platform which served as the main acting area. At the sides were tiered platforms for the chorus. On this

Wieland set his living pictures with beautifully grouped figures in magnificent mediaeval costumes, red and blue, green and violet, brilliant as jewels. At the crucial moment a glittering swan appeared beyond the steps, and then Lohengrin himself, all in gold. Here indeed was a knight of old romance—*sans tache et sans reproche*. It was a brilliant stroke of production.

Throughout there was the same absence of scenery. For the minster square a broad festal carpet was laid down the steps and right up to the front of the stage. Two huge seven-branched candlesticks stood on either side at the top of the steps. Behind was a dim suggestion of stained glass windows. Above, hung a great frieze formed by the tops of gothic arches, and this device which seemed so alien in the homely atmosphere of Nuremberg was entirely justified in fairy-tale Brabant. There was nothing else. A graceful little cabinet with damasked walls and a gilt mirror formed the bridal chamber. At the end Lohengrin departed into the same mystic blue world as the first act.

André Cluytens was the conductor, and his reading was a happy one. The orchestra brought out the warmth and the shimmering beauty of the music, and of course the chorus was in splendid form.

A well-balanced cast also gave the new production every chance to succeed. Leonie Rysanek sang well as Elsa. Astrid Varnay was a splendidly dramatic Ortrud, well partnered by the French baritone Ernest Blanc whom I remember as one of the best Telramunds I have seen. He conveyed a fine knightly presence flawed by a streak of evil, and had an exciting, dark, well-focused voice. This was a potentially noble Telramund who had gone wrong. Eberhard Waechter was a fine Herald, Kieth Engen a young and vocally rather light-weight King Heinrich.

But however good the rest of the cast everything really depends on the Lohengrin. It was Sándor Kónya, and his share in the great success of this production was second only to Wieland Wagner's. This Hungarian tenor was already well known in Germany for his singing in Italian as well as German operas, and the lyric quality of his voice made him an ideal exponent of the role. The voice was powerful though not enormous, of great beauty, and used with real musicianship. Added to this he looked the part. Not tall, but graceful and well proportioned, Kónya's good looks are sensitive and romantic, and he is an admirable actor. He was exactly right for the knightly hero. Lohengrin is no passionate lover. His love for Elsa is tender and idealistic, and would no doubt have been quite unsuited to the humdrum realities of marriage. Just as Hamlet would never have made a good King of Denmark, so it is impossible to imagine Lohengrin and

Elsa settling down to any ordinary home life. Ecstasy and renunciation marked the path of Parsifal's son, and this other-worldly love is exactly what Kónya conveyed so brilliantly. I have never seen or heard a more complete Lohengrin.

Wieland Wagner's *Ring* had been in the Bayreuth repertory continuously since 1951, and although each year saw its minor changes in production with a cumulative effect of whittling away the few links with traditional staging, in principle it remained the original production. Now it was decided that Wolfgang Wagner should have his turn with the Nibelung saga, launching an entirely new production in 1960. More, the *Ring* would not be given at all in 1959 (the only year of New Bayreuth when this has happened). Therefore 1958 saw the final appearances of Wieland's first, epoch-making *Ring*.

In performance the first cycle was rather uneven, despite Knappertsbusch's conducting. *Rheingold* failed to come alive completely; *Die Walküre* was extremely fine; *Siegfried* good in parts; but the *Ring* ended with a glorious *Götterdämmerung* accompanied by a spectacular thunderstorm echoing round the Bayreuth hills. The elements here are very conscious of their Wagnerian cues. There is often a thunderstorm on *Götterdämmerung* nights.

It would be pleasant to say that all the Bayreuth stars gave of their best, but unfortunately this was not true, at least in the first performances. It may have been quite otherwise in the second cycle (and from the reports of other writers I believe it was). This is a point to remember. Productions as a rule remain constant throughout the season, but musical performance is a very ephemeral thing, and the opera which you find a complete disaster on Monday may be given a superb rendering on the following Friday. Herein lies the cause of much disagreement with critics and, I would hasten to add, a basic injustice of printed criticism, but one which is virtually unavoidable. The critic is not concerned with intentions, he can only write of how the performance he attends impresses him.

In the *Ring* which I saw, Astrid Varnay was not up to her usual standard as Brünnhilde, nor was Windgassen's Siegfried worthy of him in the opera of that name, though his *Götterdämmerung* performance was fine. The new Fricka, Rita Gorr, made her dramatic effects by harsh, strident tone. Frans Andersson, also new in the role of Alberich, was a disappointment. By a mysterious vagary of casting Maria von Ilosvay, an admirable Waltraute, was still singing Erda, a part much of which lay too low for her voice. Leonie Rysanek seemed oddly cold as Sieglinde.

However, there was much on the credit side, too: Greindl's Hunding and Hagen, an effective Loge by Fritz Uhl, Kónya's Froh, Gerhard

Stolze's fascinatingly dramatic Mime—though it was achieved at some
sacrifice of the musical line—and Jon Vickers' Bayreuth debut as
Siegmund. This last was a very fine performance, splendidly sung and
acted with deep feeling for the ill-fated Volsung. It created a definite
sensation among the Bayreuth public and the Press. Above all, towering
physically, musically, dramatically over the dwellers of earth and
heaven as the god should was the Wotan of Hans Hotter. He was in
glorious voice, and at the height of his career.

To the generation of post-war Wagnerites all over the operatic
world Hotter has been *the* Wotan in a very special sense. Few artists
become so closely identified with one particular role. Apart from
Sigurd Björling in 1951 and some performances of Uhde's in 1952 he
had been the sole Wotan of New Bayreuth. If New Bayreuth has
been the yardstick by which modern Wagnerian productions are
measured, during the same period Hotter's interpretation of the chief
god has been the definitive one by which other Wotans are judged.
During the past year or two he has sung the part less often, turning to
other, less taxing roles. New and interesting Wotans have taken the
stage, and a young generation of operagoers is growing up who have
not seen this great performance. For them, I will attempt to describe
what is so familiar to many of us, an operatic experience which always
left one with a sense of wonder, humble in the presence of a very
rare creative art.

Nature had endowed Hans Hotter with nobility of face and figure.
A height of six feet four, and features not only classical but expressive
—a very important gift for any actor or singer. It had also given him
one of the rare truly great voices: a bass-baritone of exceptional beauty
and enormous reserves of power. But these gifts alone do not constitute
a passport to greatness of the kind which Hotter possesses. He is a
sensitive, versatile musician (witness his lieder singing), and an actor
who would be outstanding in the straight theatre, without help of
music. He also has a ready sense of humour, and though this may not
appear a necessary qualification for singing Wotan it is as important
here as for most things in life. He began to sing Wotan while in his
twenties before the Second World War, and by the time he came to
Bayreuth it was a fully formed characterization—though like Wieland
with his productions, Hotter's Wotan grew and developed from year
to year, possessing thus the breath of life.

In *Rheingold* he was the young god, imperious, patrician, impatient
of criticism or remonstrance, proud with the pride of an extremely
sensitive nature and intellect. This was a facet of the character which
few other singers succeed in showing—Hotter's Wotan was a thinker
and a visionary, and his suffering when it came was so much the

deeper. As I have said elsewhere, Wotan's part in *Rheingold* is dramatically more difficult than in the later operas. I have not yet heard another singer who has Hotter's perfect command in it, maintaining the balance of the story without eclipsing the other singers. All the same, it was in *Walküre* that he won his greatest fame. Every trial and emotion was expressed in face and stance and voice. The narration, begun in a whisper floated on a pianissimo of that great voice, came to a terrifying climax with "Das Ende"! Here was a god, a man, recounting the story of his life, his error and its bitter consequences; speaking both to himself and to his Valkyrie daughter who is the embodiment of the finer side of his own nature. His mighty anger in the last act, sweeping Brünnhilde and the other Valkyries, and ending with the infinite tenderness of a father's love, had a poignancy which sent his hearers out into the night spellbound in an agonizing glory. And this not once, but year after year.

Humour and philosophy came in *Siegfried* with the Wanderer's exchanges with Mime and Alberich, then the great scene with Erda, and the final breaking of his power by the hero grandson. "Zieh' hin! ich kann dich nicht halten." And Hotter bowed his head and leaving the stage carried with him the tragedy and splendour of one of Wagner's greatest creations.

Wotan is the most important character in the *Ring* for it is he who has caused the whole chain of events which forms its story. Also he is the only person who understands what is happening, and understands it all more clearly because he is powerless to control the outcome. He is, when well played, the one who can touch the heart most deeply because there is no human being who has not at some time made an unworthy decision, and learned how hard it is to right the wrong. This human bond of error was a very important part of Hotter's reading of the part, but he was also, and more strongly than many other artists, the god. Wagner's Wotan is, like a king, set on a pinnacle above the aid of friend or counsellor. Hotter's Wotan was forever alone with his suffering.

In *Parsifal* the winds of change were already felt in the casting, though Knappertsbusch in the year of his seventieth birthday again conducted, to the opera's greater glory. The new Gurnemanz was the American bass-baritone Jerome Hines. Tall and handsome, he had a fine presence and a noble voice for the part. His interpretation was quite different from that of most other artists. Gurnemanz is usually the wise, fatherly old man. Hines was ascetic, rather withdrawn, and more the monk than a former knight, but it was an interesting performance. As Parsifal Hans Beirer was not more than adequate. Régine Crespin, the French soprano, was a tiny, dramatic and well-sung Kundry. Some of the most beautiful singing came from the new Amfortas, Eberhard Waechter. Toni Blankenheim, a sound but not outstanding Klingsor, was the only leading singer who had appeared in the same role in previous years.

Of the other two operas, *Meistersinger* remained a controversial production. Otto Wiener was less successful as Sachs than in 1957. Toni Blankenheim was an excellent Beckmesser, Gerhard Stolze rather too boisterous as David. Unexpectedly, Josef Traxel's Walther was disappointing. Hampered by a disastrous make-up he made little attempt to act, and used his lovely voice to poor effect. Hans Hotter, changing to the bass role of Pogner, gave us a new reading of Eva's father, less tender and more intellectual than is usual. Like Hines' Gurnemanz it was interesting but failed to touch the heart. Cluytens conducted.

Wolfgang Wagner's *Tristan und Isolde* went from strength to strength. Sawallisch had now found the real splendour of the score, and Birgit Nilsson the warmth and passion which make her Isolde such a glorious experience. Windgassen, after a subdued start, gave us a magnificent Tristan, Greindl was a very moving King Marke and Grace Hoffman proved herself an ideal Brangäne. Only the new Kurwenal, Erik Saedén was less than good.

CHAPTER IX

1959—No *Ring*

IT seemed very odd indeed to have a Bayreuth festival with no *Ring*. After 1876 there had been no further performances of the *Ring* until 1896 but after that every festival except those of 1943 and 1944 had included the great cycle. New Bayreuth had immediately established its pattern of two cycles each year.

Theoretically it was a sound idea to rest the *Ring* in 1959 before Wolfgang Wagner's new production the following year. It looked a good idea to present a programme made up of five of Wagner's other operas: a new *Fliegende Holländer, Parsifal, Tristan und Isolde, Die Meistersinger, Lohengrin*. Quite enough, you might think, to keep any Wagnerite happy. But it was unsettling, and the fact that the *Ring* was not dropped before the later new production in 1965 suggests that the *Ring* is an essential part of the festival.

Those who have never been to Bayreuth may not realize how important the accepted pattern of the festival is to the regular visitor. The Wagnerite is a creature of habit. He or she expects, even demands, new productions and some variety among the singers, but they like their holiday to follow the familiar form which they have enjoyed and learned to expect. The first *Ring* is given within a few days of the opening of the festival. The second comes towards the end, followed by several performances of other operas. Between the two there are about two weeks when these other operas are each given a few performances in turn.

Those people who attend only two or three operas come, therefore, at the beginning, in the middle, or at the end. There are a few who are genuinely not keen on the *Ring*, but there are probably more who are solely interested in it to the exclusion of all the other performances. The wholly dedicated Wagnerite comes to see everything at least once, and therefore books for one *Ring* plus the single operas either before or after his chosen cycle. A surprisingly large number of people do this, and there would be even more of them if it were not for the high cost of tickets, personal limitations of time, and the ever-growing problem of getting seats at all.

In several seasons there have even been three *Ring* cycles. From the visitor's point of view the whole season could be extended with advantage. This would save a great deal of heartbreaking disappointment, for the demand for seats far extends the supply, and has done for a number of years. Nor is there any real solution. More and more people join the Society of the Friends of Bayreuth, as I mentioned earlier, because this gives them priority booking. Otherwise the only way is to apply to the Festspielhaus box office or to certain travel agents in different countries which have allocations of seats, at the beginning of the previous November when booking opens. Even then some are disappointed.

Obviously, therefore, it would be a splendid thing if there were three *Rings* every year, and a proportionate increase in the number of performances of the other operas. Economically this would be good for Bayreuth, and psychologically also: no festival is happy about turning away large numbers of disappointed customers, or about being pestered by them for returned tickets. I have no doubt that Wolfgang Wagner would be delighted if the festivals could be extended. But even the most superficial consideration shows that this is virtually impossible.

Bayreuth's conductors, singers, and most members of the orchestra and chorus are drawn from operahouses all over Europe or beyond. The regular opera season at most European houses closes in the middle or at the end of June, and opens again in September. Bayreuth starts rehearsals in mid-June, which allows only some five weeks' preparation to get seven or eight operas ready for performance by the time the festival opens in the fourth week of July. The season runs from then until almost the end of August. There literally is no margin for expansion. Add to this the fact that the Salzburg summer festival is almost exactly concurrent with Bayreuth, and the Munich opera festival runs from mid-July to mid-August, and that many of the leading artists commute between all three, and it is clear that it would be extremely difficult to cast extra performances.

I wish that I could show prospective visitors an infallible way of getting the tickets they want. Alas, I cannot—apart from joining the Friends of Bayreuth. But those who apply at the beginning have the best chance, and there are usually a few returns at the last moment.

Since each year some people fail to get *Ring* seats perhaps it was good for all of us to practise an enforced abstinence in 1959, but, as I have said, it felt very odd. Not only the lack of the operas themselves, but one simply could not find the familiar personalities of the audience.

Some people always come to the first *Ring*, some always to the second. Nothing short of death really seems to prevent the hard core of Bayreuth habitués returning year after year, and at the same time. Socially the first ten days of the season form the most important

18   Astrid   Varnay   as   Isolde

19   *Tannhäuser*, 1954.   (a)   Act II

19   (b)   Act III

20 *Der Fliegende Holländer*, 1955, the phantom ship.

21   Hermann Uhde as the Holländer, 1955

22   Martha Mödl as Brünnhilde, 1955

23 *Die Walküre,* Act II, narration, 1955. Hans Hotter as Wotan, Martha Mödl as Brünnhilde

24 (a) *Götterdämmerung*, Act II, 1955, Josef Greindl as Hagen

24 (b) The restaurant "Eule"

25 Narrow streets in the old heart of Bayreuth

26 *Die Meistersinger von Nürnberg*, 1956. Act I

27 *Die Meistersinger*, 1956. (a) Act II

27 (b) Act III Scene 1

28   *Die Meistersinger,* 1956, Act III Scene 2

29   Hans Hotter as Hans Sachs, 1956

30 (a) *Die Meistersinger*, Act II—as transformed in 1957

30 (b) *Tristan und Isolde*, Act 1, 1957. Wolfgang Windgassen
as Tristan, Birgit Nilsson as Isolde

31 Wolfgang Windgassen as Tristan, Birgit Nilsson as Isolde, 1957

32   Ramon Vinay as Parsifal, 1957

33 Josef Greindl as Gurnemanz, 1957

time, as do "first nights" anywhere, but by no means all the first *Ring*
audiences come then because of snob value. Far from it. They are
simply first *Ring* people. Others are just as devoted to the second, and
some hold that the second cycle of the *Ring* is often better because it
has had time to settle down. This is not always the case on account of
the many other imponderable circumstances which affect a musical
performance, but it is an understandable assumption.

Most people, I think, simply return at the same time from habit.
Therefore you can always rely on finding them there at their own
season. Many friendships are made at Bayreuth, and these people for-
gather at each festival. Some of them come from the same country,
Britain for example, and yet never meet at home. They may not even
correspond during the year, but they know that they will meet again in
Bayreuth, probably in the same café or under the same tree in the
gardens. This gives them an added happy sense of continuity.

This rather endearing delight in habit is not apparent to the newcomer, or the passerby who comes once to add Bayreuth to his
collection of experiences, but it is a most characteristic part of the
festivals. During seventeen years I have become part of the Bayreuth
furniture myself, and am quick to notice the absence of another land-
mark. Often one does not know these people personally, but year
after year one sees them: the hair a little greyer, the step a little
slower, but enthusiasm burning as brightly as ever. Perhaps all this
may sound a trifle depressing to the outsider, but it is not so—for
they enjoy themselves to the full. And every year there are more young
people to balance the old guard. Youth which comes again too, with
its own delight and outspoken comment. One of Bayreuth's great
services to the world is that it captures the young and initiates them
into the splendour and the brotherhood of great music. In an age
when many of the distractions of youth are harsh and even desperate
this would, in itself, be justification enough for the Bayreuth festivals.

In 1959 the *Ring* addicts did not come at all. Others were scattered
through the season, seeing the five operas at different times.

Most people naturally made a point of seeing Wieland Wagner's
Der Fliegende Holländer. This was his first Bayreuth *Holländer* (the
1955-6 performances being Wolfgang's production), and with this
he completed his own "first round," as it were, of all the ten operas
regularly given at Bayreuth: the four parts of the *Ring* (1951), *Parsifal*
(1951), *Tristan* (1952), *Tannhäuser* (1954), *Meistersinger* (1956),
Lohengrin (1958), *Holländer* (1959).

It was one of his most successful productions, and instead of
vanishing after one further year, as was the usual production pattern,
it has been revived in 1960, 1961 and 1965.

F

Wieland decided to accentuate the contrast between the haunted, mystical Holländer and his inspired Senta, and the mundane world of Daland and his home port, by stressing the earthiness of the latter. Perhaps earthiness is hardly the right description for fisherfolk. When someone commented on the huge-bosomed girls of the spinning chorus he is reported to have said "They ought to look dreadful—they should smell of cod-liver oil!"

This contrast was another of Wieland Wagner's "shocks". It was in fact overdone; this was not really Richard Wagner's *Holländer,* but it was brilliantly clever and the result justified the means, at least for most people.

Most of Wieland's chosen methods of staging were in evidence. The first scene had a central, symmetrical platform as acting area, in this case the deck at the stern of Daland's ship. The Holländer's vessel loomed behind it, and was shown not by a silhouette of masts and spars, as in Wolfgang's production, but as a vast hull which towered above Daland's ship. (Plate 37b.) Daland himself was a greedy, drunken figure of fun in a stovepipe hat and striped trousers. The sailors' chorus formed a double circle swaying to the storm, and later stamped and reeled rhythmically backwards and forwards across the deck. How such a tipsy master and crew could have weathered the northern seas was a matter of wonder, but it was immensely effective, and when the Holländer himself appeared, a tall lonely figure, the chill of tragedy fell upon the scene. He stood in front of the bows of his own ship, bare-headed, cloaked with a curious kind of netting, and with arms outstretched as though crucified on the hull he sang "Die Frist ist um".

The second act in Daland's house was a great square room, bare and bleak. Round this the hoydenish Norwegian girls sat with their spinning-wheels, dressed for the northern winter with thick, long, homespun skirts and tight-fitting bodices bulging with their generous curves. Wieland chose to make Mary, Senta's former nurse, very decrepit, and the girls trundled her about the stage in a tall chair on wheels. Again the contrast between these noisy, empty-headed women and the dreamy, visionary Senta singing passionately of her tragic hero was arresting, memorable. To anyone who knows Norway the room was also a very clever, impressionistic version of the kind of homes now preserved in folk museums.

The last scene was the least satisfactory. What had been the deck of Daland's ship was now a pier, with steps and wooden galleries on either side. It was a good setting for the chorus—and one of the greatest joys of this production was the choral singing—and the appearance of the Holländer's ghostly crew in the background, masked with skulls, was eerily effective. But at the end the set was cramping. Senta had to run up the steps to sacrifice herself in the sea, and the Holländer died on the pier itself. There was nothing to suggest their union in death.

Musically this was also a really fine production. Wolfgang Sawallisch was the conductor, and the orchestral playing was almost faultless: exciting, romantic, riotous, tragic—all the moods of the score welded into a glowing whole. As the Holländer George London was strong, dramatic, and well conveyed the haunted unhappiness of the character, but vocal beauty was lacking. Leonie Rysanek's Senta, on the other hand, sounded ideal as well as looking the part. Dainty, golden-haired, she sang with purity of tone, power and warmth.

Josef Greindl as Daland was required by this production to make Senta's father a two-dimensional comic character. Within this hampering conception he gave an effective performance and sang well. Georg Paskuda as the steersman and Fritz Uhl as Erik both sang well. Res Fischer acted rather than sang Mary, and made a clever little character study of the part on the lines Wieland had chosen.

Lohengrin had, for some reason, lost a little of the enchantment of the previous year. Lovro von Matacic conducted (Heinz Tietjen at some performances) and did not reveal the spiritual beauty which Cluytens had done. However, Sándor Kónya repeated his beautiful Lohengrin and there was a promising King Heinrich by Franz Crass. Elisabeth Grümmer's voice lacked the crystal clarity needed for Elsa, and Rita Gorr was a shrill Ortrud. Ernest Blanc's excellent Telramund was less secure vocally than it had been in 1958.

Year by year from 1957 Wolfgang Sawallisch had discovered greater beauty and magic in *Tristan und Isolde*. He gave an inspired performance on the evening when I saw it, and Wolfgang Wagner's simple, effective settings continued to serve the opera well. *Tristan* relies less on staging than any of Wagner's other works. Provided the scenery does not distract or irritate, the music will carry the whole performance.

Birgit Nilsson and Wolfgang Windgassen certainly carried the vocal side. Her Isolde was by now world famous, and like all great performances it develops new beauty and insight with each season. The same is true of Windgassen. There are some artists who have the knack of giving an effective portrayal of a role almost from the start, but who never seem able to progress farther, to go deeper into the character. Very often even the reverse happens, they lose interest or become careless and repetition produces a routine performance. With a really serious artist this is never the case. Vocal quality may vary, indeed it is bound to do so, but the depth of understanding and grasp of a great operatic role grows steadily, and even at the end of twenty years of singing one particular part the singer will still find some new and fascinating aspect to reveal. Windgassen is of this calibre. Intelligence is a word which one uses with caution, because a singer is often described as intelligent when there is little else to praise, but Windgassen's intelligence is combined with a beautiful voice, a fine stage presence and real musicianship.

Grace Hoffman repeated her moving Brangäne, Frans Andersson was a good, sound Kurwenal, and there was a new King Marke— Jerome Hines. A tall, kingly figure and a noble bass voice should have made Hines an ideal Marke, but like many another he failed to make the character interesting or to touch the heart.

Die Meistersinger returned for the fourth year, but this time Erich Leinsdorf was the conductor, and not Cluytens. His way with the orchestra gave scant consideration to the singers, and the new Walther von Stolzing suffered most. This was Rudolf Schock, who made Eva's suitor a handsome, romantic-looking young man, but had too small a a voice to succeed vocally. Elisabeth Grümmer repeated her charming Eva, and Otto Wiener his strong Sachs, at his best in the third act.

With no *Ring*, *Parsifal* was the crown of the season, the heart of the festival. Wieland's production was not marked by any notable changes in 1959: the misty beauties, the sense of spiritual dedication worked their magic as before. So did Hans Knappertsbusch in the pit. Josef Greindl and Hines shared the part of Gurnemanz that season, and it was Greindl whom I heard: wise and fatherly and deeply moving. Voice and acting were irradiated by compassion in the long monologues, which are never too long when delivered with singing of this quality. Hans Beirer was not a memorable Parsifal, but Régine Crespin had grown into the part of Kundry. It was now a really fine performance. Toni Blankenheim was Klingsor.

For many people the outstanding performance of this *Parsifal* was Eberhard Waechter's Amfortas, as it had been the previous year. It was superbly sung, beautiful and poignant, touching heart and mind with its anguish. Waechter's acting matched his voice. This was a very fine Amfortas. And yet . . . Waechter was not to me the real, the whole character. The essence of Amfortas' suffering is that he is a man, a good man, even a saintly man, and that he had succumbed to temptation. His shame, his torture, his despair stem from the fact that he had fallen a victim to Kundry's powers of seduction. The weakness which caused him to fall and thus to be Wagner's example of an unwilling sinner, but a sinner none the less, is also the weakness which prevents him from putting the needs of the other knights of the Grail and of his father Titurel before his own suffering. Had he been able to do so he would have found his own redemption in their blessing. As he could only writhe in his personal torment of guilt, he had to wait for the absolution brought at last by Parsifal and the sacred spear.

There are many personal interpretations of the story of *Parsifal*, but this is Amfortas as I have always understood him. And Waechter did not convey this character to me at all. His Amfortas was too pure ever to have fallen to Kundry's kiss. He was too ascetic, and though the suffering was most poignantly conveyed I simply did not believe in it. Many people will disagree, but to me this was not Amfortas.

CHAPTER X

1960—The *Ring* According to Wolfgang Wagner

EXCITEMENT was rife before the opening of the 1960 festival. A new *Ring*. The tremendous impact of Wieland Wagner's 1951 staging had ceased to be a shock some years before, except to newcomers. Regular visitors noted the minor changes in the production introduced between one season and another, but were primarily interested in the performances of individual singers or conductors. The whole conception had become simply "the Bayreuth *Ring*", known and admired, with or without reservations, through eight years.

Now, after one year without the cycle, we were to see an entirely new production by Wolfgang Wagner. What would he do? Would he revert to earlier traditions, or would he attempt to take Wieland's principles still farther? Gossip eddied round the Festspielhaus, ebbed and flowed in the restaurants and cafés. The *Ring* fanatics returned to Bayreuth in force, ready to enthuse or condemn, and above all thirsting for their beloved music.

The result, as far as the first cycle was concerned, proved an anticlimax. It was almost bound to do so; expectations ran too high. Added to this there were technical difficulties beforehand which resulted in the four operas being under-rehearsed. As I have said earlier, to mount the entire *Ring* at one time is a gargantuan task. No one should fail to realize this when assessing merits and shortcomings. On the other hand, neither critics nor public can be expected to judge a stage performance on its intentions. The actual effect, the joint creation of music and drama as transmitted by artists and orchestra, is the only test as far as success is concerned. Later performances are another matter, they will be better or worse, and will almost certainly come closer to the producer's intentions. But as far as that first *Ring* of 1960 was concerned the total result was ineffective because as a whole, it was still in embryo. The parts had not grown into a living whole.

Some of the parts, however, were brilliant. Such as Wolfgang Wagner's basic idea for the decor and staging. He had certainly not returned to the old traditions of the *Ring*. Nor had he attempted further to develop Wieland's mystic touch which—in the *Ring*—had gradually dismissed most solid forms of scenery. This was New Bayreuth going off at a tangent into a new, bold, and very effective form of simplicity.

acted it better than any other Alberich I have seen. His cry when Wotan seizes the ring from him, and his curse afterwards are among the most electrifying experiences of the Wagnerian stage in my time. It is when actors like Otakar Kraus are on stage that one particularly regrets the prevailing darkness of Bayreuth productions, because it is very difficult to follow facial expression—except with powerful opera-glasses—if you are farther back than about the eighteenth row. Wolfgang's *Ring,* though clearer and on the whole brighter than his brother's, still had some very dark scenes.

One of the weaknesses of the 1960 *Ring* lay in the fact that the part of Wotan was divided between two singers. It is sometimes necessary to do this with several of the great roles of the *Ring.* I have seen at least one cycle with three different Brünnhildes. In many operahouses there are two Wotans, two Brünnhildes, or two Siegfrieds in the same cycle. Usually this is due to the fact that a singer has not yet been able to study the part in all the operas concerned. Sometimes it is caused by illness. In an imperfect world one has to accept the fact that this multiple casting is unavoidable from time to time, but no one pretends that it is a good thing. In this case the new Wotan was Jerome Hines but he sang only in *Walküre,* presumably because he had not studied the role in the other two operas. Hermann Uhde, a practised Wotan, sang in *Rheingold* and *Siegfried.*

Any artist following Hotter in this part was bound to be at a disadvantage; it was equally hard for a young Brünnhilde to follow Flagstad. Yet it was natural that Bayreuth should have a different Wotan at this point. Unfortunately Uhde, excellent Wagnarian artist as he was, had never been an ideal choice for the chief god. His voice and his stage personality in this part were not big enough, though he sang very well in *Siegfried.* Hines, on the other hand, had a beautiful Wotan voice, but had not yet the experience to provide more than a two-dimensional character, though it was well modelled, and sometimes moving.

The new Siegfried (in both operas) was Hans Hopf. Already an experienced Wagnerian, he had a bigger, more heroic voice than Windgassen. He made Siegfried a bouncing, rather endearing young man, but again he had a difficult task to follow his predecessor. Windgassen *is* Siegfried, the character unfolds by expression and inflection from the artist's mind. Hopf was, and remained in subsequent years, a professional heldentenor giving an adequate performance.

In this *Ring* Windgassen appeared as a fine Siegmund, partnered by the beautifully sung Sieglinde of the Norwegian soprano Aase Nordmo-Loevberg. They made an exciting pair. Herold Kraus was an effective Mime. Another singer who was to become a famous name at Bayreuth appeared in the *Ring* as Donner and Gunther—Thomas Stewart.

Finally, but in many ways most important of all, there was the conductor: Rudolf Kempe, making his first appearance at Bayreuth. Kempe is, without any doubt, one of the great Wagner conductors of our time. London operagoers in particular were familiar with Kempe's *Ring*: his supremely artistic overall conception of the work, his exquisite feeling for string tone, his consideration for the singers, and withal the majesty and fire which he could unleash in the orchestra. They came expecting him to perform the same magic in Bayreuth, but unhappily the magic was absent. Perhaps this was due to his unfamiliarity with the unusual acoustics of the Festspielhaus; perhaps the rehearsal time was too short. There were many beauties in the playing of that first *Ring*, but they did not add up to greatness. As on the stage, it never coalesced into a whole. Things got better with each opera of the cycle, but it had started with one of the dullest *Rheingold*s I have ever seen.

All the other four operas given that summer had the advantage of one or more year's polish and experience. One of these revivals also witnessed the season's most exciting debut. This was Anja Silja's Senta in *Der Fliegende Holländer*.

Anja Silja is one of those artists who are bound to create a sensation. She was extremely young, just twenty, tall and very slender with a mop of red-gold hair, and possessed an enormous voice of extraordinary ringing quality. She is of Finnish descent, born in Berlin, and had started her vocal training in childhood. From the age of ten she had sung at concerts. Later she sang regularly at several German opera-houses, and had made guest appearances at Vienna and Hamburg. Thus when most singers of her age are still in their very early stages Silja was already an experienced artist with a highly developed voice. In later years one has had cause to wish that this had not led her to sing the heavy dramatic soprano Wagnerian roles when so young. Her voice has suffered. But in 1960 it had the full bloom and beauty of youth combined with phenomenal power and range.

Wieland Wagner rightly saw in Anja Silja an ideal Senta. She is a fine actress and possesses a special gift for this particular heroine. Senta is ethereal, inspired, impassioned, and above all young. Silja swept the opera to an emotional glory, and operagoers, old and young, came away completely bowled over by her performance.

Opposite her was a new Holländer, Franz Crass who brought a most beautiful voice to the part and gave a dignified and promising performance, though he looked rather young for the unhappy Vanderdecken. Sawallisch conducted again, and there was a forceful Erik by Windgassen. Greindl repeated his rollicking Daland. Res Fischer and Georg Paskuda sang Mary and the steersman, as in 1959.

Parsifal was in very good form in 1960. Under the baton of Hans Knappertsbusch the orchestra played magnificently. Wieland Wagner's production pursued its mystic way, and was not hampered by untoward innovations. Greindl sang Gurnemanz beautifully. Hans Beirer had deepened his understanding of the name part considerably, and made a dignified and moving Parsifal. Régine Crespin had developed her Kundry into a real characterization. Gustav Neidlinger made a welcome return as Klingsor, one of the roles which he has made especially his own at Bayreuth.

All these were very much a part of New Bayreuth's traditional *Parsifal*—New Bayreuth was a counterblast to tradition, but with the recurring *Parsifal* production it had already established an almost sacrosanct one of its own. But there were two new voices. One was Great Britain's David Ward, sonorous but unseen in the part of Titurel. The other was Thomas Stewart in the major role of Amfortas. This American baritone from Texas had been singing in Germany for three years when he came to Bayreuth in 1960, and he was already a regular member of the West Berlin opera. In recent years he has become one of Bayreuth's leading artists. That first Amfortas was a memorable performance. Stewart is essentially a dramatic singer, and he found and expressed in voice and bearing the harrowing remorse, the restless agony of the wounded master of the Grail.

There were some *Meistersinger* performances in 1960 which I was unable to see. They were conducted by Knappertsbusch. Josef Greindl was the new Hans Sachs. Most of the rest of the cast had sung their roles here before: Elisabeth Grümmer as Eva, Hotter as Pogner (though Theo Adam sang it too), Windgassen as Walther, Schmitt-Walter and Stolze as Beckmesser and David. Ludwig Weber returned to sing Kothner.

I remember the *Lohengrin* that year, both for the performance I saw, and the fact that it was one of Bayreuth's great days. On August 1, Bundespräsident Dr Heinrich Lübke made an official visit to Bayreuth, and brought with him King Bhumibol Adulyadej of Thailand, and his Queen Sirikit. Alas, rain poured down for much of the day, but there was great excitement, and the crowds watched the party arrive at the Festspielhaus to see Wieland Wagner's lovely fairy-tale realization of *Lohengrin*.

Lorin Maazel (musical director of Bayreuth's 1968 *Ring*) was the conductor. He obtained superb playing from the orchestra, and it was a beautiful and thrilling performance. Windgassen sang Lohengrin on this occasion with beauty and dignity, though he has never had Kónya's especial flair for this part. Aase Nordmo-Loevberg was a new and lovely Elsa, and she sang gloriously.

CHAPTER XI

1961—Béjart's Bacchanale

TRAVELLERS from England who come via the Hook of Holland and the route I described in Chapter II normally leave the Rheingold/ Rheinpfeil Express at Nuremberg (this train is first class only, by the way, second class passengers have to change in Frankfurt also), and from there take a local train into Bayreuth. Some years ago a friend introduced me to a variation on the same theme: if one leaves the Rheingold earlier at Wurzburg (in 1968 at 14.43) there is another train from there direct to Bayreuth arriving one and a quarter hours earlier than the connection from Nuremberg. It comes by a different route: to the north of the Franconian Switzerland through Bamberg instead of to the south, and you reach Bayreuth just after 18.30. I recommend prospective travellers to enquire specially about this route because many travel agents are unaware of it, the reason being, I believe, that the service is put on for the festival and does not appear in the regular timetables.

I did not take this route in 1961. I am not even sure that it was then in operation, and it has crept in here simply because I am reminded of it by Bamberg, where I spent an enchanted day that year. You will see little enough of Bamberg from the railway, though beyond it—nearer to Bayreuth—the monastery of Banz and the great baroque pilgrimage church of Vierzehnheiligen are visible, Banz to the left and Vierzehnheiligen just beyond on the right of the line. Still the station's name may impress upon the newcomer where Bamberg is. For of all the expeditions which can be made from Bayreuth this ancient town is, to me, the most rewarding.

A day's visit to Bamberg by local train or bus, or of course by car, is an easy trip on "spielfrei" days. Also there are usually one or two coach excursions there during the festival.

The river Regnitz flows through the town, and along its banks timbered houses back on to the water, sharply gabled, with little windows peering out from dark woodwork and brilliant flowers. Bamberg is a town where every householder rejoices in flowers; there are window boxes when space forbids a garden. The river has two branches here, and the old part of the town lies to the west of the western stream. It rises steeply, winding streets, painfully cobbled, lead upwards among old houses and inns, steps and alleys. And up one must go, preferably on foot, for a car whirls you through before the eye can focus on many of its beauties,

Bamberg is almost a thousand years old. The first mention of the city was in 973, and from the beginning it was a great ecclesiastical centre. The saintly Emperor Henry II founded Bamberg's cathedral in 1004, and made it a bishopric a few years later. In the fourteenth and fifteenth centuries the townspeople tried to free themselves from the domination of the Church but a bishop's town it remained, and was glorified by the baroque and rococo art of the 1700s. In 1818 Bamberg became an archbishopric.

It is this blending of mediæval and baroque which gives the town its special charm. Having lost and found oneself once or twice, the broad cobbled expanse of the cathedral square is reached. Here on one side is the cathedral itself, not St Henry's building (the emperor was canonized in 1152), but a magnificent Romanesque-Gothic church consecrated in 1237. There is a choir and altar at each end, and the tomb of Henry II and his wife Kunigunde in the centre. But by far the most famous treasure of the cathedral is the anonymous Bamberg Rider, a mounted knight carved in stone which dates from about 1240, and is one of the finest examples of mediæval sculpture in Germany.

Outside is the old bishops' palace, a timbered, galleried building with a superb gateway and picturesque courtyard, beloved by photographers. Across the square is the much larger "new" bishops' palace. The old one was built in the 1570s. Little more than a hundred years later (1695-1704), the then prince-bishop had this handsome neo-classical pile designed by Johann Leonhard Dientzenhofer. It stands high above the heart of the town, and is built round three sides of a terrace rose garden.

I have known rainy days in Bamberg, but my memories of this terrace, to which I have returned many times through the years, are always sunlit ones. Warm air carrying the scent of a thousand roses, the sound of bees, busy among the many-coloured blooms, and the placidity of history in repose. There is a café in the rose garden which serves light lunches, drinks, coffee, tea, and delicious cakes. Their Schokoladetorte is some of the best I know. I am very fond of chocolate cake, and I come back to this terrace to find it, and the roses and the old stonework, with a dreamy sort of gratitude to those bishops of the past.

Between the two palaces a street leads on and upwards. Thence by devious ways, down as well as up for the town is said to stand like Rome on seven hills, you may reach the Michaelsberg. This is a hill crowned by St. Michael's church, which was built in the first half of the twelfth century for a Benedictine abbey originally founded in the reign of Henry II. Its simple, lofty form was decorated with baroque elaboration in the seventeenth century. A curious and possibly unique feature dating from the early 1600s is the ceiling paintings. On the vaulting of the nave are depicted more than six hundred medicinal plants, taken from all over the known world at that time.

Outside is a quadrangle formed by the old abbey buildings, part of which are occupied by a brewery. Beyond is another terrace shaded by an avenue of lime trees. Here too there is a café. It has not the patrician grace of the bishops' rose garden, but the scent of the limes is as lovely in its own way, and the view is even better, since the Michaelsberg is higher than the cathedral square. Below, the roofs of Bamberg are piled together with the unconscious beauty of many centuries: red and brown and all the intermediate colours which weather and lichen lay upon the handiwork of man. Here is a city of kings and prelates, knights and unnumbered, forgotten burghers, resting gently in the sunshine.

For the opening of the 1961 festival Wieland Wagner had provided a new *Tannhäuser*. The general principles of the production were much the same as those of his 1954 staging, but the designs were new, and there was a different emphasis on the story. In place of the formalized chessboard pattern of design and grouping the new production concentrated on the two feminine influences between which Tannhäuser—a sensualist who could perceive the strength and beauty of chastity—yearned and faltered. On the whole the lusts of the Venusberg succeeded better than the pure ideals of the Wartburg.

This was almost wholly due to the Venusberg ballet. Wieland had designed another of his strange symbolic backgrounds for Venus' domain. Instead of the concentric elliptical caverns of seven years before he gave us a strange honeycomb mass hung above the stage which, for no definable reason, gave the effect of snakeskin, scaly, treacherous. (Plate 44). But below this the dancers made eroticism real, fiercely passionate, dangerously seductive. The choreographer was Maurice Béjart, artistic director of Twentieth Century Ballet at the Théâtre Royal de la Monnaie in Brussels. His supreme *coup de théâtre* was a net lowered to cover the back of the stage. On this the nymphs hung, spreadeagled, and the male dancers climbed to them, each pair of figures fusing into one in the dim, evocative lighting and under the pulsing spell of Wagner's music.

It was quite a bacchanale, and not unnaturally a good many people thought it went a good deal too far. I disagree. If you are going to match the music at this point, or even to provide a visual accompaniment to it, then the choreographer has got to suggest the sexual act and suggest it pretty strongly, and in a setting of absolute licence. A few legs waving rhythmically in the air simply will not do. On the other hand, lust portrayed on stage can be, and very often is, coarsely offensive. Béjart succeeded brilliantly because this bacchanale, daring as it was, remained a work of art and a dance form.

While all this was going on Venus remained completely static throughout the scene. Sheathed in a stiff gold costume from head to foot, with a massive coiffure, she stood in front of the dancers, motionless, arms outstretched. Voice alone was allowed to give life to Tannhäuser's temptress, and a very splendid voice it was—that of Grace Bumbry, one of America's leading Negro operatic artists. Madame Bumbry had a great success in the role, and the "black Venus" made newspaper headlines.

The Minstrels' Hall was all gold. The final scene was very dark, and again the Venusberg dancers spun an illusion of physical abandon round the tormented Tannhäuser and the staunch Wolfram. There was no funeral procession bearing Elisabeth's body to an earthly grave, only an angelic tableau in the sky.

Wolfgang Sawallisch conducted a performance that was orchestrally exciting but vocally uneven. On the first night Wolfgang Windgassen as Tannhäuser was not in good voice. His singing was heavy and his acting phlegmatic in the early scenes. His performance gained in vitality during the evening, but he was far from being at his best.

Elisabeth, the opposite pole to Venus, was Victoria de los Angeles, dressed in a nun-like costume of Madonna blue. This was a lovely performance vocally, but nonetheless a piece of miscasting. Victoria de los Angeles has a glorious voice, warm, tender and powerful. Elisabeth's music sounded exquisite, even heavenly, but the characterization was not right.

As many operagoers have reason to know, gratefully, this artist has an enchantingly warm, human personality. She is at her best when portraying winsome, loving, womanhood. But Elisabeth's love is of another kind, spiritual, self-sacrificing. She is such stuff as saints and martyrs are made of; one who loves God first, and her man in relation to that holy dedication. She is the kind of woman a sensualist may worship but will never really enjoy. If this had not been so Tannhäuser would not have been such a ready victim to the wiles of Venus. Elisabeth, quite unconsciously for a saint's love is rooted in humility, would always have made Tannhäuser feel an inadequate sinner. Venus made him a physical king. The singer who plays Elisabeth has this difficult task of conveying a spiritual ideal, and Madame de los Angeles was too lovable and gentle for it.

Dietrich Fischer-Dieskau was recovering from a cold and so not in his best voice as Wolfram, though as before it was a beautifully judged performance. The other four knights were all well taken by stalwarts of the company, Gerhard Stolze, Franz Crass, Georg Paskuda, Theo Adam. Josef Greindl was a strong-voiced, wise Landgrave. The lovely little air of the shepherd boy was well sung by the Danish Else-Margrete Gardelli.

1961 was not a good festival for weather—at least not during the first ten days while I was there. I see from my diaries that the first night (*Tannhäuser*) was bitterly cold, that the *Rheingold* day (July 26) was warm and sunny, but that it poured with rain for the following two days. Such years are very disappointing for those who make Bayreuth their holiday, but as far as the operas were concerned the 1961 festival was a memorable one.

Der Fliegende Holländer was revived, Sawallisch conducting. Anja Silja repeated her outstanding Senta. She was already a dynamic stage personality, and the whole opera came more fully to life from the moment of her appearance. Rapt, obsessed by her inward vision of the suffering Holländer, she sat in a tall chair surrounded by the chattering spinning girls and yet utterly alone. It was a beautiful piece of acting on her part, and of stage direction by Wieland Wagner.

George London sang the Holländer, and it was one of the finest performances I have ever heard him give. Strong, dramatic, tragic, and vocally steady. Josef Greindl gave us his Daland, as before admirably tailored to this production. Fritz Uhl was a passionate and likeable Erik. He had sung the role in 1959, and shared it with Windgassen in 1960, and now had achieved a very complete, polished performance.

Wolfgang Wagner's *Ring* in its second year had grown to full stature. He had made some changes, particularly in the opening scene of *Rheingold* where the rocky whirlpool was now effective if not completely satisfactory. The clearly lit disc below Valhalla, and the dark cavernous Nibelheim were both excellent.

There was still a division of honours in the casting of major roles. Jerome Hines sang Wotan in both *Rheingold* and *Walküre*. In the first opera his acting was rather stiff and tentative, but in *Walküre* he had the right presence and nobility, and his singing throughout was both beautiful and impressive, though the voice proved not to be quite large enough to compass the role's full majesty.

For some reason Gerhard Stolze was made up as a dark-skinned Loge. David Ward made a good Fasolt, rich of voice and well acted. Otakar Kraus repeated his splendid Alberich.

In *Die Walküre* we had the familiar and excellent Brünnhilde of

34 Bayreuth's baroque margraves' operahouse

35   Eberhard Waechter as Amfortas, 1958

36 Sándor Kónya as Lohengrin, 1958

37 (a) *Lohengrin*, Act I, 1958

37 (b) *Der Fliegende Holländer*, Act I, 1959

38   Josef Greindl as Daland, 1959

39   Anja Silja as Senta, 1960

40   Thomas Stewart as Amfortas, 1960

41   Birgit Nilsson as Brünnhilde, 1960

42 The *Ring*, 1960–64.   (a) *Rheingold*

42 (b) *Die Walküre*, Act III

43 The *Ring*, 1960–64. (a) *Siegfried*, Act I

43 (b) *Götterdämmerung*, Act III—Siegfried's death

44 *Tannhäuser,* 1961, Act I—Venusberg

45   Grace Bumbry as Venus, 1961

46 Victoria de los Angeles as Elisabeth, 1961

47 (a)   *Tristan und Isolde*, Act I, 1962

47 (b)   David Ward as Fasolt, Peter Roth-Ehrang as Fafner, *Das Rheingold*, 1962

48 *Götterdämmerung*, Act II, 1962. Otakar Kraus as Alberich,
Gottlob Frick as Hagen

49   Jess Thomas as Lohengrin, 1962

Astrid Varnay. She and Hines made the great Brünnhilde-Wotan scenes both moving and exciting. Fritz Uhl was the new Siegmund, and sang with beauty and intelligence although his voice was rather small for the part. Régine Crespin, in a singularly unbecoming costume, sang Sieglinde magnificently. Gottlob Frick was again a memorable Hunding.

In *Siegfried* Birgit Nilsson returned as Brünnhilde, radiant of voice and bearing. Hans Hopf had improved his Siegfried enormously, emerging as a worthy partner with plenty of voice to compass the ecstatic music of the final scene. There was also a new Wotan/ Wanderer in the person of James Milligan.

For a singer possessed of a fine bass-baritone voice and a gift for acting it is not so very difficult to make a good impression with the Wanderer. Several artists have started their Wotan careers in this way, working backwards progressively to the dramatic and vocal subtleties of *Rheingold*. They do not all succeed in the earlier operas. A fine Wanderer does not always become Wotan in toto. Therefore it is dangerous to hail even an outstanding performance of the Wanderer as promise of a world Wotan. Yet there was that in Milligan's singing which made many of us throw caution to the winds and believe that we had heard one of the very great Wagnerians of the future.

James Milligan was a Canadian, born in Halifax, Nova Scotia. In 1955 he won first prize in the International Music Competition at Geneva. For five years he was a member of the Canadian National Opera. In England he sang at Glyndebourne and Covent Garden, and before his Bayreuth debut he had gone to Switzerland and joined the regular company at the Basle Opera.

He had a glorious voice of beautiful ringing quality, power and range, and he used it with real musicianship. As an actor he had that indefinable quality which we call stage presence. He moved well, and played his part with the naturalness which conceals art. He *was* the Wanderer in a way which I have never seen displayed except by singers who have had years of experience in this part. It was a thrilling occasion.

Exactly four months later James Milligan died on stage in Basle, during a rehearsal. He was thirty-four years old. The world of opera lost an artist of very great promise, but his name adds lustre to one tragically brief page in Bayreuth's history.

Götterdämmerung was, as it should be, the crown of the *Ring*. Nilsson was in superb voice as Brünnhilde. Frick's scene with the vassals was tremendously exciting. Hopf was not in such good voice as he had been in *Siegfried*, but all the lesser parts were well sung.

Above all Rudolf Kempe had found the real feeling of the Festspielhaus and of the orchestra. The playing was very fine indeed thoughout, with some wonderful climaxes.

In *Parsifal*—once again the Wieland Wagner/Knappertsbusch *Parsifal*—there were three major cast changes. The American tenor Jess Thomas sang Parsifal. For the previous three years he had been a member of the Baden State Opera at Karlsruhe and he had already made guest appearances at Munich but his international fame was yet to come. He made a very good impression in Bayreuth with a fine voice, as did another American, Irene Dalis, in the role of Kundry. Both showed promise of what were to be notable performances in these roles in later years.

Lastly there was Hans Hotter's Bayreuth debut as Gurnemanz, a part which he had already, of course, sung elsewhere. It was ideally suited to his voice, and the compassionate old knight lived there before us on the stage.

The leading singers of the 1961 festival showed clearly how international the Wagner brothers were in their casting. It is sometimes thought that Richard Wagner's operas are largely the prerogative of German and Austrian singers. In fact this is far from true and, in the post-war years especially, outstanding artists from many different countries have won laurels in the great Wagnerian roles. Wieland and Wolfgang Wagner have always been internationally minded in their choice at Bayreuth.

After the German and Austrian contingent, the United States headed the 1961 list with Grace Bumbry, Irene Dalis, Jerome Hines, Grace Hoffman, Regina Resnik, Thomas Stewart, Jess Thomas, Astrid Varnay (who came from America, though of Swedish descent). From Canada came George London and James Milligan. Great Britain sent Otakar Kraus (though he should, no doubt, be credited to the land of his birth and early singing career Czechoslovakia) and also David Ward. Victoria de los Angeles came from Spain, Régine Crespin from France, Birgit Nilsson from Sweden. Else-Margrete Gardelli was Danish.

Nor is this list exhaustive. Other singers in supporting roles came from various countries, and through the years most of Europe, west and east, and many lands beyond have been represented among the soloists, conductors, chorus, orchestra, dancers and technicians whose work combines to give life to the Festspielhaus productions. Artistic standards here are the first priority, and as far as the practical limitations of the modern world permit, they sweep away all barriers. This particular aspect of Bayreuth's work as a focal point of international co-operation and understanding on a personal level is often overlooked, but is in fact one of its great services to a troubled world.

CHAPTER XII

1962—A Turning Point in Wieland Wagner's Art

ON July 24, opening day of the 1962 festival, the weather was quite perfect. Few places are more delightful than Bayreuth when summer plays its part. The sun is hot by English standards, and the roofs and spires of the town appear insubstantial in the heat haze. The gardens are inviting. Grass looks cool, and the shade of the trees is welcome. Many seats are thoughtfully provided under the trees, where you may sit and watch the bright banks of flowers and dream of Wagner's music, or any private little dreams which the occasion inspires.

It is not difficult to find a place within sight or sound of water. The Germans are second only to the mediæval Arabs in their love of fountains and pools and the graceful sound of running water. There are several fountains in the town, and a water-lily pool in the garden on the right-hand side of the Siegfried Wagner Allee.

These two gardens to right and left of the avenue leading to the Festspielhaus are naturally popular in good weather. For one thing they are only five minutes' walk from the theatre, and before the performance there are always several men there, quietly reading a programme or libretto. Women are less ready to submit their dresses to the dust and leaves of a garden seat before the evening has begun, but they come down in the intervals, and the self-service restaurant has an enclosure which is part of the garden, and where bushy-tailed red squirrels play like kittens under the tables.

Gardens are for those who prefer shade. The sun worshippers stand on the terrace or wander round and round the Festspielhaus itself. There are always two streams of promenaders, one clockwise, one anti-clockwise. On a warm evening the most beautiful dresses appear, brilliant as flowers or jewels, elaborate or simple. Their colours are thrown into effective contrast by the dark suits of the men, though many of the latter wear white dinner jackets when the weather warrants it. Photographers mingle with the crowd, and newcomers have their photographs taken with the Festspielhaus as background.

It is really no wonder that the Bayreuthians themselves come up to watch, for it is a pretty sight. No operahouse foyer can compare with the trees and the flowers and the cornfields of Bayreuth—when the sun shines. I may have written too much of bad weather. Considering the times I have spent in Bayreuth in the last seventeen years I would say that the weather is good distinctly more often than not. But it would be wrong to pretend there have been no bad summers there.

We, that first audience for Wieland Wagner's new *Tristan und Isolde*, did not realize that we were to witness a distinct turning point in his artistic career. In any case a turning point is usually recognized only in retrospect, when the new path has been pursued further. Something highly original, another of Wieland's "shocks" was certainly foreseen. He never failed to provide matter for discussion, controversy, excitement, or even ecstasy. But this time he adopted a very different form of design.

All his earlier productions had been examples of progressive simplification. Almost a negation of scenery in the usually accepted sense. His *Ring* had gradually dispensed with many of its original solid forms. *Parsifal* was from the outset a mystic production of lighting effects. The first *Tristan*, both *Tannhäusers*, *Meistersinger* and *Lohengrin*, as Wieland staged them, had all been studies in this method of effect by simplification. Even the *Holländer* had a bare minimum of decor, and that presented in formalized, symmetrical stage pictures.

Now in this *Tristan* he adopted massive, self-assertive forms. True, it was immensely simple. Each scene had one or at the most two huge pieces of scenery. They were the complete opposite of realistic sets. They looked quite unlike the scene as described by Richard Wagner, but in each case they were symbolic of the place, the mood, and also of the psychological forces at work in the story and even in its creation. The great difference as far as the audience was concerned lay in the fact that instead of being subtly unobtrusive, of making a visual frame for the music in the manner of Wieland's early work, these odd monolithic shapes forced themselves on the consciousness. Half one's mind played with what particular symbolism each was supposed to represent, and perhaps invested them with more Rabelaisian or phallic significance than was really intended.

For the first act a vast curved shape was reared upwards at the back of the stage on the right-hand side. We were told it represented the stern of a ship, though it looked more like a strange beast—or other things. Downstage to the left a semicircular screen sheltered a low seat. This area, bathed in red light, formed Isolde's cabin. Each merely served to suggest the setting. The ship's stern was seen from the side, so Tristan and Kurwenal standing in front of it would have been in the water, or on a quay. When the lovers drank Brangäne's potion the whole stage was used for the scene, not just the corner within the screen. (Plate 47a.)

The second act was completely bare save for a huge monolith with two holes at the top. These holes looked down, owlishly, on the seat where Tristan and Isolde sang the great love duet. In the third act Tristan lay on the stone courtyard of his castle, and the castle was represented by one strange segment of masonry: a triangle which was not a triangle, for one side was straight and another curved. It too had a large round hole at the apex.

All this was new, even for New Bayreuth. And to be honest it was distracting. But this staging had one great virtue: it was spacious and uncluttered, and Wieland's production—that is the direction of the artists, their moves and grouping—as distinct from the sets, was magnificent. Having seen this *Tristan* many times since I have almost ceased to notice the scenery. This is not really a reaction calculated to please a designer, but as far as I am concerned it was a magnificent production, but with inappropriate sets.

Musically this *Tristan* was a triumph from the start. Karl Böhm was the conductor, and his interpretation was inspired with a loving insight. All the glories of the score were there—spiritual, sensual, tragic, ecstatic.

Birgit Nilsson sang divinely, well partnered by Windgassen. They have made this production especially their own, returning many times since to sing in it. Wieland Wagner had introduced several alterations in the stage directions. In the first act, after drinking the potion Tristan and Isolde, expecting death, rush straight into each other's arms instead of waiting until the love philtre has done its work. At the very end after singing the Liebestod Isolde does not sink down upon Tristan's body but dies standing, upheld by the glorious realization of love in death. There were other innovations, such as the appearance of King Marke on stage at the end of Act I, but these two were the major ones. At first they came as a surprise, but the acting of these two great artists proved Wieland's idea to have been inspired.

Josef Greindl, in beautiful voice, was a really moving King Marke. Eberhard Waechter was the Kurwenal. It is a part which often tempts the singer into roughness, even unsteadiness of voice. Waechter succeeded in singing the music with beauty and yet suggesting the toughness which provides a devoted, down-to-earth balance when everyone else is carried away by emotion. There was a new Brangäne in the person of the Swedish Kerstin Meyer. She sang and acted well, and gave a thoroughly exciting performance. Perhaps a little too exciting, for the vocal line suffered at times from the vehemence of her characterization.

Lohengrin returned with its former beauty, and a completely new set of leading singers with the exception of Franz Crass as King Heinrich. He had shared this role with Theo Adam in 1959. The Lohengrin was Jess Thomas, tall, young and knightly with a fine heroic tenor voice. He was an extremely good Lohengrin, though he lacked Kónya's particular mystic quality in this role.

Anja Silja was Elsa. The part does not suit her as ideally as does Senta, but she is an excellent actress, and it was a real and complete performance. It was distressing, however, to find that her voice had already developed signs of wear. Many of the top notes sounded shrill and ugly when she put pressure on her voice, though the mezza voce remained full and lovely.

Ortrud was excitingly sung by Irene Dalis. The historic event of this production, however, was Ramon Vinay's return as a baritone to the scene of his tenor triumphs of a few years before. As Telramund his singing was not memorable, but as always his performance as a whole was brilliantly conceived and acted: his second act scene with Ortrud was electrifying, and the most dramatic part of the evening. Crass was an outstanding King Heinrich, and Sawallisch, who was this year's *Lohengrin* conductor, got the orchestra to give of their best.

He also returned to conduct the 1961 *Tannhäuser* which had lost none of its visual or musical impact. Most of the leading artists were the same as in the previous year: Windgassen as Tannhäuser, Victoria de los Angeles as Elisabeth (Anja Silja also sang the part at some performances, but I did not hear her in it that year), Grace Bumbry as Venus, Greindl as the Landgrave. The one completely new performance was Eberhard Waechter's Wolfram von Eschenbach, and it was a magnificent one both musically and dramatically.

Parsifal, conducted by Knappertsbusch, provided one of the season's greatest musical experiences. Hotter's Gurnemanz had the complete mastery of the part which his Wotan had always possessed, and yet was of course utterly unlike the erring god. An unforgettable experience "even by his own standards", as one critic wrote.

Jess Thomas was a very well sung and intelligently played Parsifal. George London and Gustav Neidlinger appeared again in their familiar roles of Amfortas and Klingsor, and did great credit to both. At the performance I saw Irene Dalis was suffering from a throat infection and had to be replaced as Kundry before the second act by Astrid Varnay, who as usual saved the situation.

The one important change in Wolfgang Wagner's *Ring* was the introduction of a new Wotan. This was Otto Wiener, and he sang the part right through the three operas. This continuity in casting is, as I have said earlier, very much to be desired in any *Ring*. Unfortunately

Otto Wiener is not a Wotan. Excellent singer as he is in some other parts, such as Hans Sachs, he has not a Wotan voice nor does he project this complex character in a way which can command the stage and form the pivot of the whole cycle.

The first *Rheingold* never came fully to life. Wiener went through it like a sleepwalker, and the other gods seemed equally somnolent. The one wholly satisfying performance was Otakar Kraus' brilliant Alberich, though Gerhard Stolze's Loge had effective life and bite.

After the unaccountable dullness of *Rheingold*, Rudolph Kempe conducted a *Ring* which was orchestrally beautiful. His vision of the whole work is supremely artistic: majestic, tender, inspired with all the elements of love, fear, triumph, and at the last peace. Yet he weaves this tremendous tapestry in such a way that the texture is never clogged with the weight of sound, never blankets his singers' voices. There is less danger of this in the perfect acoustic balance of the Festspiel-haus, but it does happen from time to time. Kempe is never guilty of it.

The *Walküre* performance had many virtues. Wiener's Wotan came to life here, and he gave a cleanly sung, straightforward performance, though it lacked any real inspiration. He was at his best in *Siegfried* where his Wanderer had dignity and his voice showed to advantage in some noble singing.

Astrid Varnay gave a beautifully integrated performance as Brün-hilde in *Walküre*, though it lacked vocal brilliance. Birgit Nilsson continued the role in *Siegfried* and *Götterdämerung*, but was not at her best in this particular cycle.

Most of the other chief parts were cast as before, but Grace Hoffman was a beautifully sung new Fricka, Eric Klaus a promising Mime, and Jutta Meyfarth made a very effective Sieglinde. She was less successful with Gutrune. Marcel Cordes, the new Donner and Gunther, was not very happily cast in these roles.

How often criticism sounds carping and ungrateful to artists who work extremely hard to give pleasure to their public, and whose standard of performance must of necessity vary from time to time for many reasons. The professional critic is often taken to task for his brutal assessment of this or that singer. In fact many members of the opergoing public are just as caustic. In the restaurants and cafés of Bayreuth condemnation as well as praise is bandied about with the greatest enthusiasm. Everyone is a critic in his own right. And why not, having paid for his seat may not the humblest member of the audience air his views?

Why not indeed, but there is something which we should all learn in operagoing, and that is to differentiate between judgement on a particular performance by a singer, and assessment of that singer's art in general. This sounds so obvious a fact as not to need stating, yet there are many people who get the two inextricably muddled.

Every great artist from time to time falls below their highest standard. Every good average singer will occasionally give a bad performance. There are all sorts of reasons for this. A particular role may not suit them vocally or temperamentally. A new production may differ widely from their habitual interpretation of a part, and they are unable to fit themselves into the new conception. More often it is simply a matter of health.

Very few people who have no direct contact with the singing profession realize how disastrously delicate an instrument the human voice is, and how easily affected by infection, physical weariness, weather, or a dozen other trivial circumstances. A common cold can cause operatic havoc. Where ordinary people take a couple of aspirins and snuffle their way through the day's work without question the singer is virtually paralyzed. Nor can the strongest willpower or experience compel a voice to service.

Short of acute laryngitis, the straight actor can usually get through his part, with the help of a doctor's drugs, without the audience being aware that anything is wrong. Not so the singer. The medical profession can help tremendously and no operahouse is without a throat specialist who can be called in, but the best of them cannot guarantee that the affected voice will not fail at a crucial moment. Even the ordinary drugs which most people take to combat a mild infection may themselves adversely affect a voice. Some singers fear to take them for this reason.

If the illness is not serious there is always the problem of whether to attempt the performance or not. If the artist refuses the public, especially his or her devoted followers, will be disappointed. If they sing, consciously well below form, the audience will criticize the quality of the singing unless an announcement is made that the artist is suffering from a throat infection. Even this is not proof against misunderstanding. Somewhere a voice will probably be heard to suggest that the singer is not ill at all, and the announcement was merely an excuse to cover the shortcomings of an ageing voice.

Let a singer appear three times with a cold, and someone will certainly declare that the voice is "finished". I have heard this sort of thing said—in Bayreuth—years ago about more than one great singer whose full vocal glory came later. Such snap judgments often prove laughable, but they can also be very brutal at the time.

CHAPTER XIII

1963—The Explosive *Meistersinger*

1963 marked the one hundred and fiftieth anniversary of Richard Wagner's birth. Centenaries and the like are fashionable in these days, and since there was another twenty years to wait for the centenary of the composer's death in 1983, operahouses all over the world seized this opportunity for a Wagner celebration.

On July 23 Bayreuth started the festival calmly, not with an opera production but another performance of Beethoven's Ninth Symphony to which, following the lead of Richard Wagner himself, they turn for great ceremonial occasions. It was a fine, if not a great performance. Karl Böhm conducted, and the soloists were Gundula Janowitz, Grace Bumbry, Jess Thomas and George London. The chief laurels went to the Bayreuth chorus trained by Wilhelm Pitz.

The weather celebrated the event with Bayreuth's most perfect summer conditions—perfect, that is, if you enjoy intense heat. For the first few days of the festival the temperature veered between 80° and 90° Fahrenheit (27°–33° C.) and the gardens round the Festspielhaus shimmered in the heat haze.

For two days the public had to wait for the season's novelty, and speculation ran high. Then on July 25 it came with Wieland Wagner's new *Die Meistersinger von Nürnberg*.

If sensation, innovation, shock, public reaction spell success, then this was a triumph. Nothing that Wieland had done before, nothing that he did in his brief remaining three years of life afterwards had the controversial impact of this production. His 1965 *Ring* was revolutionary in a comparable way, but it was not so complete a transformation as this *Meistersinger*, which tore down and trampled underfoot all accepted ideas of the opera, the story and its philosophy.

Much has been said and written by Wieland Wagner himself and others on the subject of his ideas, inspirations and the sources on which his theories were based. They provide a fascinating if complicated study, and much more conjecture and deduction will continue to be written about them for many years to come. This book, however, is not the place for that particular kind of discussion.

There is, almost always, a wide difference between an artist's intentions and his achievements: that is, how far he has been able to transmit those intentions to his public, and to create the particular effect he intended. Personally I believe that no artist, be he painter, writer, composer, actor or producer should ever have to explain his work. If explanation is needed that is in itself an admission of failure. Whatever the art form it must be judged by the direct effect it makes on its public. I do not for a moment suggest that Wieland Wagner had such a failure here. I am prepared to accept that the effect of this production was exactly what he intended—it was, like most Bayreuth productions, admirably professional. But it may be that some readers will feel that parts of this production took on a different aspect after they had talked personally to Wieland Wagner, read interviews with him, or articles on the subject. Such considerations are of immense importance in a critical analysis of the artist. Here they are irrelevant because we are concerned with the results not the intentions. The result was the impact upon that first audience of elegantly dressed Wagnerites who filled every seat in the Festspielhaus that blazing July afternoon.

The staging was strange and new in conception for this opera, but it was the production, the dramatic approach rather than the visual side, which constituted the real revolution. Richard Wagner had created a story of, on the whole, kindly folk: stupid and narrowminded at times, but capable of recognizing wisdom. The people of Nuremberg as sketched in *Die Meistersinger* have their standards of right and wrong in behaviour and in art, even though they may confuse the letter with the spirit of their laws. They may be smug but they are not rotten. They honour Hans Sachs, and the whole spirit of the opera shows that Wagner honoured him too.

Now, by a clever twist of production Wieland Wagner threw down the whole of this concept like a house of cards. The mastersingers were a set of boorish artisans. The apprentices became hooligans. Pogner was little more than a figure of fun. No one took any notice of Hans Sachs. The lovers Eva and Walther were a modern couple who understandably had little time for the uncouth burghers.

The crowd scenes were so handled as to convey the impression of a mob easily aroused to dangerous excesses. At the end of Act II the usual cheery rumpus of awakened neighbours and youths delighted with the excuse for a scrum, became something altogether different: a crowd of drunkards and lechers who collapsed on the stage instead of melting away at the sound of the approaching nightwatchman. The watchman himself was a comic figure who picked his way among the prostrate bodies intentionally blind to the evidence of disorder. It was little better in the great festive scene of St John's Day on the banks of the Pegnitz. An unruly crowd jostled and danced while decorated floats were trundled in, the guilds brought their emblems and devices, and the atmosphere was anything but one which would honour Sachs or listen to any song contest.

Now all this might well form a clever parody on the modern world. Riots and noise and contempt of law and order are commonplace today; more so than they were in 1963, but even then this stage representation had contemporary force. It was apt in the context of the outside world, but it had nothing to do with Richard Wagner's opera. Sachs may soliloquize on the world's madness, but Wagner did not write either the words or music of *Meistersinger* as simply an elaboration of the follies which the shoemaker considers in the Wahn-monolog. Moreover he made Sachs at the end triumph in the cause of wisdom and understanding. As Wieland showed the story to us it is questionable whether Sachs' praise of sacred German art would have meant anything to his hearers, and even more doubtful whether Sachs, as he had to be played in this production, would have possessed the inspiration and understanding embodied in it and in the Wahnmonolog.

At almost every point the production was contrary to the music. One could not absorb both, as they were foreign to each other. I found that if I wanted to hear the orchestra and singers I must shut my eyes. Thus eyes and ears had to take turns that day to assimilate this celebration production of Wagner's most popular opera. It is a sad comment on the development in the artistic career of Wieland Wagner; he who had won his early fame with productions which seemed to make the music itself visible, which achieved that marriage of sight and sound which is the perfection of the operatic producer's art.

For scenery he used a permanent set based on the form of the sixteenth-century Elizabethan stage. This galleried set served tolerably well for the church in Act I (plate 51), but was quite as inappropriate for the streets of Nuremberg as was his 1956 midsummer dream (and lacked the beauty of that picture). For the final scene it meant that once again the Johannistag celebrations took place in a kind of pavilion which, with the elaborately decorated wagons of the guilds, gave it the character of a masque—though a very uncourtly one. (Plate 54a.) Sachs' workshop in which so many important developments take place was no more than a shed in the middle of the stage. The backdrop which filled the rest of the stage was covered with drawings symbolic of Nuremberg and its feast day, including a grotesque representation of St John's baptism of Christ in Jordan. (Plate 53b.) This was happily replaced by a plain curtain the following year.

The conductor faced with the care of the score in this production was Thomas Schippers. It was an unenviable task, and he succeeded as well as could be expected. The singers were likewise presented with grave difficulties. Otto Wiener was a dramatically colourless Sachs, most of his authority being denied him. Jess Thomas sang Walther von Stolzing most beautifully, and looked handsome and romantic. Anja Silja was an attractive and very modern Eva, and Kurt Böhme played Pogner all out for farce. Carlos Alexander's Beckmesser fared better than most, for in this production Beckmesser should have won the day, and was a much stronger, cleverer character than is usual. Alexander's performance was a brilliant one in its own way.

Writing about this *Meistersinger* at the time, I described it as a nineteenth-century work in a sixteenth-century frame with seventeenth-century trimmings and the mood of a twentieth-century anti-opera. I think most people felt this clash of influences. There were violent reactions against it among both Press and public, and the performance was booed long and heartily.

Yet it is no less true that some people were thrilled by it, captivated by the new approach, completely carried away by the sheer professionalism of the whole thing. I remember one keen Wagner lover, on his first visit to Bayreuth, telling me in all sincerity that its beauty had moved him to tears. Thus Wieland Wagner once again divided Bayreuth audiences, but as before both factions were hypnotized by his work.

To accommodate the Wagner pilgrims who came to Bayreuth in this special year there were three cycles of Wolfgang Wagner's *Ring*. On the production side this was undoubtedly its best year since this staging was launched in 1960. The lighting was far better, and it therefore had greater visual beauty since one could see the effects of Wolfgang's Scheibe and its symbolic forms. Dramatically, too, there was much greater impact. Rudolf Kempe's conducting had not only his own special gifts of tenderness and translucent orchestral clarity, but a new fire and majesty.

Das Rheingold was now really dramatic, and a worthy opening to the mighty *Ring* epic. *Walküre* provided the greatest emotional experience. Only *Parsifal* and *Tristan* can equal a fine *Walküre* in this respect. *Siegfried* and *Götterdämmerung* were both impressive with some great moments.

Once more there were three different Wotans and two Brünnhildes in each cycle, and this inevitably means that one tends to regard each opera as a separate entity rather than a part of one complete work.

One of the most interesting events of this 1963 *Ring*, especially in retrospect, was that Theo Adam made his first Bayreuth appearance as Wotan. Now Adam is one of the international Wotans, then he appeared only in *Rheingold*. This is, as discussed several times here, the most difficult of the three operas from Wotan's point of view, and the hardest in which to make an initial success.

It would be an exaggeration to say that Adam made a spectacular debut in the part. In any case he is not a spectacular type of artist. Having come to Bayreuth first in 1952, he had quietly graduated to successively more important roles, which is the real way to learn operatic stagecraft, and also both to develop and to conserve the singer's most precious possession—his voice. In that first *Rheingold* Adam was dramatically unremarkable, but he sang nobly and showed that here was the vocal colour, range and quality which constitute a Wotan voice. The rest came with time, as succeeding years have shown.

Hans Hotter sang the *Walküre* Wotan in the first cycle, and was in splendid voice. So was Otto Wiener as the Wanderer in *Siegfried*, where he proved again that this is the aspect of Wotan best suited to him.

In *Walküre* there was a new Brünnhilde—the Finnish soprano Anita Välkki, already known in this part to London *Ring* audiences. Her voice was warm and powerful, and she made a touching Brünnhilde, affectionate and girlish. In *Siegfried* and *Götterdämmerung* Astrid Varnay returned to what had been one of her greatest roles. At the beginning of the 1963 festival she was recovering from an attack of laryngitis and therefore was not in good form vocally, but despite singing which was considerably substandard her total performance as Brünnhilde in both operas triumphed by sheer artistry.

There was a new Loge this year in the person of Ken Neate. Unfortunately the voice was dry and lacked adequate power, but from the acting point of view Neate was one of the very best Loges New Bayreuth has had. He moved gracefully and with assurance, and his acting reflected, very subtly, every mood and reaction of the cynical spirit of fire. It was a performance which I shall remember for a long time.

Otakar Kraus as Alberich proved once again how much this production owed to his performance. *Rheingold* basically needs a strong triangle—Wotan, Loge, Alberich. On this occasion the Wotan, Adam, was well sung but dramatically tentative; Neate's Loge had these qualities in reverse—vocally light-weight but brilliantly acted. Kraus' gifts and experience were admirably balanced, and so—a great Alberich.

The same was true of Gottlob Frick as Hunding and Hagen: the blend of artistic gifts with practised musicianship which makes a great singer capable of great performances.

Hans Hopf had become progressively a better Siegfried, and his performances in both *Siegfried* and *Götterdämmerung* were strongly sung and likeable. Fritz Uhl as Siegmund sang most beautifully in the first act of *Walküre* but was less successful in the second. Jutta Meyfarth sang Freia, Sieglinde and Gutrune. As the goddess she was disappointing, but her Sieglinde was well sung, and she managed to make a person of Gutrune.

Tristan und Isolde returned with the same outstanding team as before: Karl Böhm conducting, Birgit Nilsson (Astrid Varnay also sang Isolde during the season), Wolfgang Windgassen, Kerstin Meyer as Brangäne, and Greindl's King Marke. Gustav Neidlinger returned as Kurwenal.

Nilsson's voice sounded a little tired; there was an edge to some of her top notes, a hardness to which this brilliant type of voice is sometimes prone. To me, Birgit Nilsson's singing has always possessed a diamond-like quality: pure, flawless, thrilling, shining in ensemble, cutting through the heaviest orchestrations as a diamond cuts glass. Its beauty is as great, but entirely different from some other great dramatic sopranos; Kirsten Flagstad for example, whose voice has the rounded glory of pearls. On this occasion the diamond had a little two much cutting edge at times.

But what a glorious Isolde Nilsson had created: her anger, her passion, her complete single-mindedness, all were here, yes and her soaring ecstasy in the Liebestod, the triumphant joy of love fulfilled in death.

It is much more difficult to consider in detail Wagner's leading women characters than the men. Interpretations of Siegfried, Wotan, Tannhäuser, Tristan himself, differ far more widely than do different Brünnhildes and Isoldes. The great singers of Wagner's heroine roles each bring their own qualities of voice to the music, and excel in their own way in portraying the personality, but there is much less scope for a different reading of the parts, for there are fewer complexities. Rudyard Kipling once wrote in a very different context that a maid was created for one purpose only by blind Nature, but man for several. Wagner's approach to his women characters bears out this principle, and in addition neither Isolde nor Brünnhilde have free will in the pattern of their love and fate; Isolde being under the influence of the love potion, and Brünnhilde the edicts of Wotan. But within the framework of Isolde's nature Birgit Nilsson has created a wonderfully vivid portrait.

Hans Knappertsbusch, celebrating his seventy-fifth year, conducted *Parsifal* with his own love and reverence and joy in the music. One spoke of Knappertsbusch's *Parsifal*, and yet it was always Wagner's *Parsifal* that he gave us, not the personal exploitation of an opera with which some virtuoso conductors dazzle their public. He possessed a real musical humility in this respect, and therein lay his particular greatness.

Windgassen's deeply felt Parsifal, George London's Amfortas, Irene Dalis' Kundry, Neidlinger's Klingsor, all were inspired by the mystic quality of this master, who served the music nobly with his own art.

And there was Hans Hotter's Gurnemanz. This role is the complete opposite to the Isoldes and Brünnhildes whose characterization allows for little deviation from the accepted one. Partly because he takes small part in the action of the opera, and also because Wagner made him a thinker, Gurnemanz can be played in various different ways. New Bayreuth has been blessed in several notable portrayals of the part, each quite distinct.

Hotter's has, in voice and bearing, the infinite compassion of a saint, the wisdom, the human understanding, and—after his disappointed outburst dismissing the unperceiving Parsifal—the hard-won patience of a man disciplined by life and his own vows. The increased age and spiritual strength which have come to Gurnemanz between the first and third acts are most beautifuly realized, never by a hair's breadth overplayed. Hotter's voice is a wonderful instrument for this part, and his singing of the old knight's holy joy when Parsifal returns to fulfil his mission of absolution is in itself a benediction.

CHAPTER XIV

1964—*Tannhäuser* Redecorated

THE 1964 production was new and not new. Wieland Wagner presented his *Tannhäuser* of three years before with a number of changes, more than the year-to-year variations which had kept all his other works alive when they were revived. It was, therefore, virtually new without being a completely fresh conception of the opera. The sets and costumes had certain alterations of colour or decoration, and they were not for the better. (Plate 54b.) Temporarily at least Wieland seemed to have lost his sense of colour: the chorus were dressed in violet and a strident blue which effectively killed the softer colour. The scenery and lighting had lost clarity in the second act, the effect was tarnished, muddy.

More important was the change in the Venusberg bacchanale. Maurice Béjart's daringly inspired ballet was replaced by new choreography devised by Gertrud Wagner. It was exciting, impressively erotic, and perhaps wholly satisfactory to those who had not seen Béjart's more brilliant version. To those who had, it was a very poor substitute.

Altogether there was a sense of anticlimax. There were, of course, practical reasons why a new full scale production was not to be expected from either of the brothers. In 1965 Wieland was to launch a completely new *Ring*. In 1959, the year before Wolfgang's *Ring*, Wieland had produced his *Holländer*, and Wolfgang had only one revival of his own *Tristan und Isolde*. Now, when the positions were reversed, Wolfgang had the four operas of his *Ring* to rehearse in addition to all his administrative commitments, and Wieland with the preliminary *Ring* thinking to be done was also responsible for *Parsifal*, *Tristan*, *Meistersinger*—plus this *Tannhäuser*. No blame could attach to either that there was nothing really new, but one could have wished that Wieland had been content to revive the 1961 *Tannhäuser* as it was.

Otmar Suitner conducted the opera, and orchestrally achieved a fine stirring performance. Wolfgang Windgassen repeated his Tannhäuser and provided the chief delight of the evening. Finely sung, and impeccably acted, here was the man of passion and perplexity in very truth. Strongly masculine, weak in moments of temptation, this

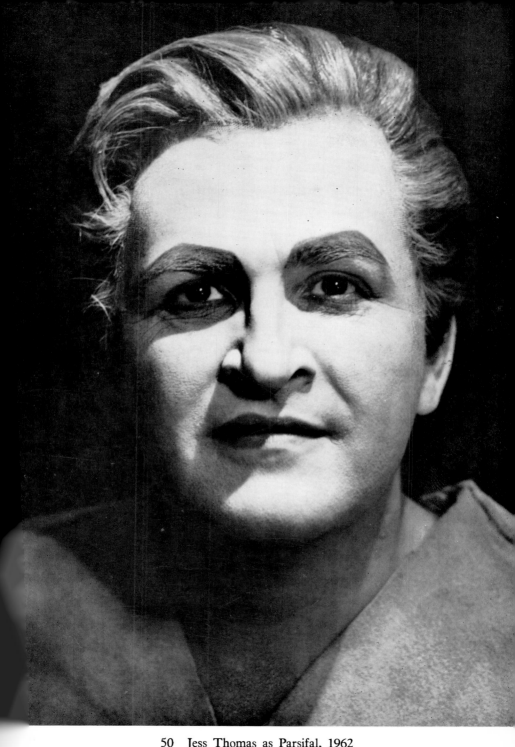

50   Jess Thomas as Parsifal, 1962

51 *Die Meistersinger von Nürnberg*, Act I, 1963

52   Jess Thomas as Walther von Stolzing, Anja Silja as Eva, 1963

53 *Die Meistersinger*, 1963. (a) Act I

53 (b) Act III Scene 1

54 (a)   *Die Meistersinger,* Act III Scene 2

54 (b)   *Tannhäuser,* Act II, 1964

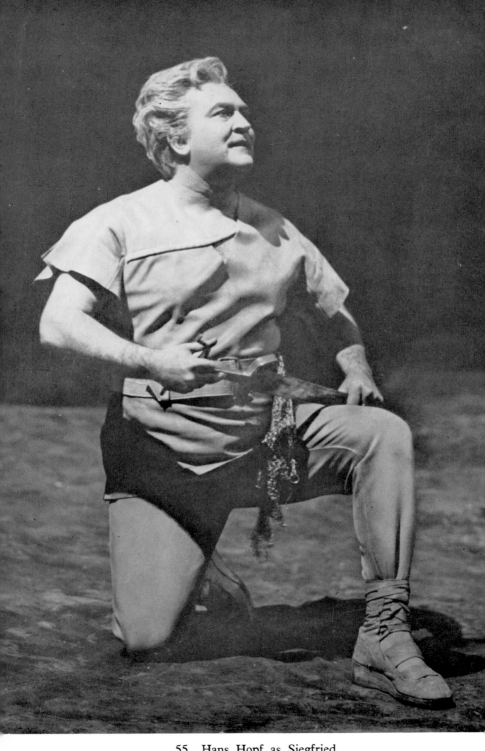

55   Hans Hopf as Siegfried

56 Otakar Kraus as Alberich, 1963

57 Birgit Nilsson as Isolde, 1964

58　Sándor Kónya as Walther von Stolzing, 1964

59　Fountains at the Eremitage

60   Hans Knappertsbusch

61 *Parsifal*, Act III Scene 1, 1965. Hans Hotter as Gurnemanz,
Jess Thomas as Parsifal, Astrid Varnay as Kundry

62 *Tannhäuser*, 1965. Ludmila Dvorakova as Venus

63   The *Ring*, 1965. *Das Rheingold*

64   The *Ring*, 1965. *Die Walküre*, Act II

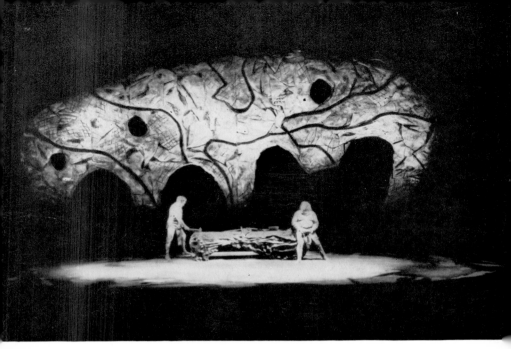

65 The *Ring*, 1965. (a) *Siegfried*, Act I

65 (b) *Siegfried*, Act II

Tannhäuser had the spiritual vision of the artist which made him love and worship the saintly Elisabeth and also succumb to the sheer physical delights of Venus. The allure of practised love-making, of sensual art would have a very special charm. He was capable of bitter repentance, of passionate purpose of amendment, of black despair. Minstrel knight, Tannhäuser is, unlike any of Wagner's other heroes, essentially an artist (Walther von Stolzing is a patrician dilettante). Every emotion sways, enchants, torments him. This is what Windgassen had developed in his performance. He is a complete Tannhäuser, alive, tragic, fascinating—and always musicianly.

Unfortunately his performance had something of solitary grandeur on this occasion, as neither of the two feminine leads amounted to anything like a full characterization. Leonie Rysanek was Elisabeth, and after a very insecure start she sang well, but for some reason her Elisabeth never came over to the audience as a person—let alone a very remarkable person—at all. Strange that this should have been so, for Madame Rysanek is a gifted actress as well as singer, and it is rare indeed for her to give a colourless performance.

The new Venus was the Swedish singer Barbro Ericson. Once again Wieland Wagner gave her small scope for acting, the completely static pose remained, but her costume was changed. In place of the straight metallic gown which had made Grace Bumbry look like a goddess cast in gold, Venus was now visually the Earth Mother, her robe parted to reveal bare breasts covered only by a tunic of net—or was it an openwork form of chain-mail?! In its way this was very effective, but the trouble with this performance was a vocal one. Barbro Ericson's voice seemed to be a full contralto, and much of the role lay uncomfortably high for her.

Eberhard Waechter was the Wolfram, as in 1962, and it was a moving if rather light-weight performance. Else-Margrete Gardelli repeated her beautifully sung young shepherd. Finally there was a singer who was to become one of Bayreuth's important names of the future—Martti Talvela. He had been heard but not seen in 1962—as Titurel. Now his tremendous height and noble stage presence no less than a very rich and beautiful bass voice made him a notable Landgrave.

1964 was another year when the festival opened in blazing summer weather. The sun beat down upon the town and the Festspielhaus, and audiences rejoiced or moaned about the heat according to their climatic tastes. No one pretends it is easy to work hard when the thermometer on the western wall of the Festspielhaus is registering 32°C., but on the continent people are more accustomed to hot weather than we are in England. They seldom complain about it with the pained surprise

H

of the British when they are swept by a heat wave. Still it must have been very hard on the singers, members of the orchestra and all the others who work behind the scenes at Bayreuth.

Perhaps the weather was one reason why several of the singers were vocally below par in the *Tristan* performance which opened the festival on July 18. This was not true, however, of Birgit Nilsson, whose Isolde was in superb form and gloriously sung. Nor of the Brangäne, Kerstin Meyer, though she was a little inclined to overact. This Brangäne cringed before the disasters which overtook her mistress.

It was the men whose singing fell below the best of which each had so often given proof. Windgassen's Tristan was as always a fine performance, but not so musical as usual. The same was true of Gustav Neidlinger's Kurwenal. Hans Hotter was singing King Marke for the first time in Bayreuth. He gave a deeply moving performance, one which touched the heart and made the tragedy of the unfortunate king the real and poignant part of the story which it should be. But Hotter was already suffering from the slipped disc trouble which affected him later that year during a London *Ring* season, and his voice showed it.

Karl Böhm and the orchestra gave a beautiful account of the score.

It was Karl Böhm who took over *Die Meistersinger* this year. As happened in the case of the 1956 *Meistersinger,* the second year witnessed a number of modifications. The production settled down to some extent, though of course its basic revolutionary conception remained unchanged. Still Richard Wagner's music was allowed to triumph over all the eccentricities on the stage, and that was the most vital need. Whether this was due to Böhm's particular gifts coupled with considerable Bayreuth experience (it was hard indeed to expect Thomas Schippers to conduct successfully such a controversial production as his first Bayreuth assignment), or to a change of heart on Wieland's part, I do not know. Perhaps he had never intended the stage to drive the music out of mind. Anyhow the balance was restored.

There were several cast changes, notably the impersonator of Hans Sachs. In place of Otto Wiener we had Josef Greindl who had, in fact, shared the role with Wiener the previous year. Now Wiener, when in good voice, is an excellent Sachs, reliable and musical, but in this production he had been swamped, and the customary authority which the role carries had been denied him by the producer. Josef Greindl is a really outstanding actor, quite apart from singing, and herein lay the difference. No production, however bizarre, can eclipse Greindl. His mere presence on the stage will focus attention, not by drawing it away from other singers on the stage, he is far too good an artist for that, but simply because he is so completely the character he happens to be portraying at that moment. Therefore his Sachs was a live, human person, a humorous, kindly philosopher, and the story like the music regained something of its normal balance. Vocally he was not at his best; his voice sounded tired and rather worn, but his performance as a whole went far towards saving this *Meistersinger*.

Sándor Kónya was the new Walther von Stolzing. Graceful, handsome, and finely sung in both the lyrical and heroic passages, Kónya's Stolzing ought to have been ideal. Unfortunately his performance did not really belong to this turbulent new Nuremberg. Therefore it was never fully alive, inspired by and identified with the production in the way of his Lohengrin.

Apart from these two most of the leading singers were the same as in 1963. Anja Silja repeated her eager, unpoetic twentieth-century Eva. Kurt Böhme was her obtuse, comic father (could this indeed be Veit Pogner, the much respected goldsmith?). Carlos Alexander had polished still further his keen, clever, ambitious Beckmesser. David was excellently sung, and played according to Wieland Wagner's plan, by Erwin Wohlfahrt, also for the second year.

We did not know that the 1964 *Parsifals* would be the last performances that Hans Knappertsbusch would conduct at Bayreuth. Illness overtook him that autumn, and he died a year later, on October 25, 1965, at the age of seventy-seven. To those of us who had known those wonderful years from the early 1950s there will always be something missing from Bayreuth without the familiar figure of "Kna", both about the town and in the orchestra pit where he had created so many noble performances of his beloved Wagner operas.

It was a very beautiful *Parsifal* that I saw and heard that year. Hans Hotter as Gurnemanz was singing under obvious difficulties because of the trouble with his back, but although not vocally at his best the performance was in some ways even more moving than before.

Then we had a new and memorable Parsifal in Jon Vickers—whose name, by the way, is always spelled Wickers in German-speaking countries. Vickers is a very complete and dedicated artist, and his 1958 Siegmund was vividly remembered by many Bayreuth festivalgoers. As Parsifal he had another role well suited to his particular gifts—a beautiful tenor voice which combines lyrical and dramatic qualities, and acting of great sensitivity and insight. His Parsifal progressed from the unthinking boy to the man who has acquired self-command by tribulation, and the transition was beautifuly conveyed by an artist to whom acting is a personal talent not an artificially applied veneer.

George London's Amfortas and Neidlinger's Klingsor were both familiar and in good form. Barbro Ericson appeared as Kundry, but here as in *Tannhäuser* the part did not lie well for her voice, and much of her singing sounded strained.

One of the 1964 production changes in *Parsifal* was that we had a new ballet for Klingsor's flower maidens. The choreographic part of the opera had had its ups and downs through the years. Sometimes it had been enchanting; sometimes the display of seduction had been sterile or even absurd. In 1964 Gertrud Wagner devised a new and very lovely ballet which was wholly successful—dreamy, tantalizing, graceful. It is arguable that the form of the flower maidens' enticement should be designed to suit the specific interpretation of Parsifal, for Parsifals differ surprisingly and varying types of temptation belong to different readings of the part. However that may be, this was a very effective flower maidens scene, and seemed exactly right for Vickers' Parsifal.

Wolfgang Wagner's *Ring* was making its last appearance. Wieland's *Ring* had survived eight seasons, his brother's only five, for with the ever-growing fame of Bayreuth and its reputation for all things new there was a call for constant rethinking and innovation. But from difficult beginnings Wolfgang's production of the great cycle had progressed to a very fine maturity. The decor was original, effective and spacious. It had enshrined some magnificent performances, including Birgit Nilsson's Brünnhilde. I, for one, very much regretted its passing.

For health reasons Rudolf Kempe was unable to conduct the *Ring* at Bayreuth in 1964. Instead we had Berislav Klobucar, and he was to be congratulated on a fine rendering of the score, exciting, powerful and tender.

This time Theo Adam sang Wotan in both *Rheingold* and *Walküre*. In the first opera he had developed his understanding of the part, though his singing was rather lacking in vocal colour, but he was wholly successful in *Walküre*, singing and acting with nobility and real command. In *Siegfried* the part was taken by Hubert Hofmann, whose Wanderer was adequate but far from outstanding.

Anita Välkki returned to sing the *Walküre* Brünnhilde. Her interpretation had changed somewhat. It was less girlish and in some ways too mature—the ageless Brünnhilde who is neither young nor old which some singers can achieve escaped her, and her top notes were sometimes shrill. Still, she was a convincing warrior maid, especially in the second act with Fritz Uhl's excellent Siegmund.

In *Siegfried* and *Götterdämmerung* Astrid Varnay was Brünnhilde. The years had taken toll of her voice, for she has not spared herself in the singing of many of the heaviest and most exacting soprano roles at operahouses all over the world. The vocal bloom was damaged, and under pressure the voice was sometimes harsh. But so great an artist is she that her performance overcame all vocal limitations. She was inspired, dynamic, truly the daughter of a god, bride for a hero, victorious in death. Among all the fine singers and beautiful voices who have essayed the role Astrid Varney remains one of the very few real Brünnhildes we have heard in post-war years.

Gottlob Frick repeated his splendidly powerful, implacable Hunding and Hagen. Hans Hopf was not in good voice as Siegfried on this occasion, but Jutta Meyfarth had made great strides in her singing of Freia, Sieglinde and Gutrune. The new Alberich, Zoltan Kelemen, showed promise.

After the first six days of that tropical festival there was a thunderstorm (it followed *Parsifal* not *Götterdämmerung* in this case) and the temperature fell for a couple of days. But it soared again. Many Bayreuth visitors must remember that year for its idyllic festival weather. Most of the time it was too hot to go out for any of the longer expeditions. The gardens and the fountains had charm enough, though to find these on a larger scale it was worthwhile to take a bus from the market place in Maximilianstrasse to the Eremitage. This takes about fifteen minutes, and the energetic—of whom I am not one—walk it in an hour.

The Eremitage, or hermitage, was the eighteenth-century home of the Margraves of Bayreuth. Margrave Georg Wilhelm had the Altes Schloss or old château built in 1715-18, and twenty years later it was enlarged for that Margravine Wilhelmine who had the Bibiena Operahouse built. She wrote her memoirs here and her brother Frederick the Great visited her several times. The second château was added in the middle of the eighteenth century.

Today it is peaceful, except when too many people are tempted by its attractions. There are pools and fountains and a great deal of opulent baroque statuary; the miniature palaces themselves are too ornate for beauty, but the grass and the trees and the cool arcades of summer green are restful and timeless, and one can eat and drink pleasantly at the Eremitage gasthof. (Plate 59.)

Oddly enough there is a link with England. The last Margrave resigned his rights to Prussia in 1791, and when he left Bayreuth it was to England that he retired.

CHAPTER XV

1965—Wieland Wagner's Second *Ring*

WHAT now? was the general feeling before Wieland Wagner's new *Ring*. Having set for himself a standard of daring innovation, of what seemed to be a policy of originality at all costs, the answer was unpredictable, and the public naturally flocked to see the result.

For some years there had been a strong group of Wieland devotees who applauded everything he did with as much fervour as the more fanatical followers of Richard Wagner himself. But there was also a body of festival-goers who felt that, with the last *Meistersinger* at least, he had gone too far. Between the two, and forming the largest part of regular Bayreuth audiences, were those Wagner lovers who owed a deep loyalty to the festivals, honoured Wieland Wagner for the supremely artistic work that he had done, and watched with a kind of personal anxiety lest his quest for sensational effect should betray his own past achievements.

To some extent both the hopes and fears of all these people were realized. The new *Ring* was brilliant and startling. It threw overboard most of the few remaining traditional concepts. It largely rejected character and replaced this with symbolism. And because Wieland Wagner's undeniable genius was accompanied by an ever-growing experience and command of stage techniques, the whole was carried out with masterly professionalism.

Depending upon whether the operagoer found this a vital new interpretation of the saga or a travesty and betrayal of Richard Wagner's greatest work, this production was good or bad. If the verdict was the latter it could not be excused as any form of ineptitude.

In other operahouses one sees, from time to time, productions which are bad because they are slack, amateurish, uninspired; where the aim was right but the company failed to achieve it. This has never been the case at New Bayreuth. Both brothers have always been commendably professional. Neither in the Festspielhaus nor amongst the audience is there the cosy feeling of an amateur coterie, of a holiday fit-up organization such as exists in some small festivals. Bayreuth's achievement is such that it must be judged by the highest standards. It is never mediocre, though its productions naturally include some substandard performances. But the productions themselves have always been positive: positively right, or positively wrong.

For me, Wieland's fundamental approach to this *Ring* and many of the details of staging which stemmed from it were wrong, being at variance both with Richard Wagner's conception of the story and his music. But the whole thing was brilliantly executed.

He had combined here the two contrasting methods he had used in his 1962 *Tristan* and his 1963 *Meistersinger* and fused them into one style. Following *Tristan* he used huge isolated pieces of scenery which were heavily symbolic. Symbolism was far more extensively developed here than in *Tristan* (where you could ignore it if you wished), and it sprang from the *Meistersinger* treatment of the plot. This was to change the whole balance of the story. The gods were no longer godlike. They moved—Wotan included—and behaved like pawns in the game of primeval instinct and lust.

It is easy to say that the dwellers in Valhalla are a poor lot; that Wagner's *Ring* itself is about the decline of their might, and the greater nobility of love exemplified by Siegfried and Brünnhilde. True, but if they are not shown to have been mighty, there is no fall, no drama. This is especially true of Wotan whose action and remorse and suffering form the thread upon which the whole cycle is strung.

Richard Wagner, like the mediæval storytellers, was fond of introducing magic potions and spells to account for certain otherwise inexplicable changes of heart or behaviour. From the modern audience's point of view they are rather a pity, because free will is what gives life to any drama. The real impact of a play or opera, its power to achieve comedy or tragedy, depends upon its ability to convince us of the free will of the characters, that they might have acted differently under the same circumstances. Despite his use of magic Richard Wagner gave the power of decision to many of his characters, and therein lies the poignancy of the operas. Wieland virtually removed the gift in this *Ring,* giving it the heavy sense of fate which belongs to classical Greek drama. Certainly there is justification for the comparison, and Wieland Wagner and various writers have studied it in detail, but the *Ring* in performance did not gain by this treatment.

Das Rheingold's opening scene had the gold itself in a strange erotic form—presumably the mouth of the womb of avarice. Following the same symbolism, when the gold was piled to hide the desirable eternal youth and beauty of Freia the blocks formed a grotesque woman's figure. (Plate 63.) Valhalla was a vast claustrophobic wall with narrow windows, seamed with black lines like bars. One critic likened it to a penitentiary. It was certainly a grim, bleak fortress which suggested stagnant water and rats rather than a palace for gods and the heroic dead.

In *Walküre* Hunding's dwelling, with its distorted tree, and the stratified rocks of the second act intentionally dwarfed the singers' figures. (Plate 64.) In *Siegfried*'s first act Mime lived under the belly of a weird beast. (Plate 65a.) Even the forest scene was played against a background of twisted, fossilized tree trunks, though the lighting here was often very beautiful. (Plate 65b.)

Götterdämmerung's Gibichung Hall was stark and barbaric. The broad pillar-like blocks and crosspieces which suggested its walls were gnarled with pockmarks like miniature craters, and hung with the skulls of animals. (Plate 66.) The altars to Fricka, Wotan and Donner which form the background for the second act gave Wieland an opportunity to design three of his mighty monoliths.

It was quite surprising to find that the costumes followed the accepted pattern of Wagnerian dress. That is to say they were simple, dignified and without date. But in one respect Wieland introduced symbolism here too. In the manner of his Venus costume for *Tannhäuser* Erda and the Norns, usually swathed to the chin in heavy garments, wore their draperies open to reveal apparent bare flesh to the waist. Here was the Earth Mother and her daughters with a vengeance. Unfortunately the effect was absurd rather than voluptuous.

This, then, was the framework in which the *Ring* was presented to the excited public in 1965. It did not disappoint them as regarded matter for comment, and there was no lack of that.

From the point of view of performance the *Ring* I saw was a fine one, allowing for the restricted characterization which the production permitted, and as it was the second cycle the new presentation had already had the advantage of one complete series of public performances. This was the first time in fourteen years that I had not seen the first *Ring* at Bayreuth. The reason was one of timing. The first *Ring* was given in six days, followed by a break of four days with no performances before the rest of the festival got under way. Wishing to see all the productions in a minimum of time, I chose the second cycle which, as usual, was given between performances of the other operas.

Karl Böhm was the *Ring* conductor and a very fine reading his was, both passionate and noble. In the cast Wieland Wagner had combined forces from his own first *Ring* with others from his brother's, and brought in some new singers as well. Theo Adam sang the *Rheingold* and *Walküre* Wotan. He brought to it admirable vocal gifts, the singing was beautiful, but the changed dramatic balance affected him. On the acting side he was noticeably less good than he had been in Wolfgang's *Ring* the year before.

Birgit Nilsson was in superb form as Brünnhilde. One was tempted to think she had never sung it better, especially in *Walküre*.

Wolfgang Windgassen returned to the role of Siegfried and brought
to it even greater artistry and understanding than before. A beautiful
performance. He also appeared as Loge, and gave a well-sung and
most interesting study of the fire spirit, refuting all the predictions
that he has too tall and heroic a figure for this part.

Josef Greindl was once again a superb Hagen, and this time he
also sang the Wanderer. Being a bass rather than a bass-baritone
some of the tremendous vocal range of this part lay rather high for
his voice, but it was a splendidly sung performance nonetheless, and
he brought to the *Siegfried* Wotan a noble stage presence. As I said
before, no production can turn Greindl into an automaton. The same
was true of Gustav Neidlinger who returned to the role of Alberich.
Another experienced and excellent performance was Leonie Rysanek's
Sieglinde.

Outstanding among the *Ring* newcomers was Erwin Wohlfahrt's
Mime. This was a real characterization, brilliantly acted without
sacrificing the music; so many Mimes distort their singing to gain
dramatic effect. James King was a well-sung and promising Siegmund.
Martti Talvela used his splendid bass voice to great effect as Fasolt
and Hunding. Ursula Boese sang the self-righteous Fricka admirably;
from the dramatic point of view she was less successful.

Thomas Stewart's Gunther was hampered by the production and
less effective than before. Kerstin Meyer was disappointing as
Waltraute—too intense. Ludmila Dvorakova was more successful with
Gutrune, although her solo at the beginning of the last scene was
cut (restored the following year), thereby allowing even less scope
in this difficult part. There were good trios of Rhinemaidens (Dorothea
Siebert, Helga Dernesch, Kerstin Meyer) and Norns (Lili Chookasian,
Ursula Boese, Anja Silja), although the former did not appear in
Rheingold, where their parts were mimed by ballet dancers who did
not even open their mouths to simulate singing.

Of the four operas the most wholly successful was *Siegfried,* which
was carried by the performances of Windgassen, Wohlfahrt and
Greindl, and the radiant awakening of Nilsson's Brünnhilde. *Götterdämmerung* suffered from production experiments or omissions. The
dead Siegfried was left lying on the ground while the orchestra,
playing the funeral march, called for the tragic drama of his exit on
the bearers' shoulders. Gutrune was denied her nervous vigil.
Brünnhilde was not seen to cast herself into the funeral pyre. Finally
the general annihilation at the end was a very tame affair of projections.

This was an all-Wieland year. Not since 1952 had there been a
Bayreuth festival without the special interest of comparison between

the two brothers' styles. Now Wolfgang's *Ring* having had its day, there was no production of his in the repertory. In fact we were not to see another Wolfgang production, until 1967.

The rest of the programme was made up with revivals of Wieland's *Holländer, Tannhäuser* and *Parsifal*.

In 1965 the Holländer himself was played by Thomas Stewart (Hotter at some performances). It was surprising that Stewart proved a disappointing Vanderdecken. He was already a very good Amfortas, and a good Amfortas is often a good Holländer. He is an intelligent, dramatic actor and a sound musician. Yet this performance lacked the vital spark, there was no mastery of the other-worldly quality of the character—the sinner cursed but still seeking redemption in a woman's faith. The anguish came across as vocal strain, and when Stewart's singing is strained his voice develops an unfortunate vibrato.

Anja Silja was the Senta, and proved again that this is one of her very best roles. She also proved what I have discussed before—the problem of human variation between one performance and another. I saw *Der Fliegende Holländer* twice in 1965. On the first occasion Anja Silja sang with all the fresh beauty of her first performances five years before. She was a glorious, radiant, inspired Senta. The second time the voice was not under full control and inclined to screech. Which showed only too clearly how widely judgments of a singer may vary in a single season.

Josef Greindl repeated his sound, earthy Daland. As the steersman and Erik, Hermann Winkler and William Olvis were not more than adequate. Otmar Suitner was the conductor, and made this *Holländer* exciting.

Wieland Wagner had transformed his *Tannhäuser* once more, not as regarded staging or costume, but in various subtleties of production which gave it far greater effect. And there was another new bacchanale. This time the choreographer was Birgit Cullberg from Sweden, and she created a magnificently erotic Venusberg ballet in which almost literally no holds were barred. It was, too, an extremely artistic piece of work, and rivalled Béjart's in this combination of sex and artistry.

Wolfgang Windgassen was in wonderful form, vocally and dramatically, as Tannhäuser. Leonie Rysanek had "found" the character of Elisabeth; moving and saintly, this was a lovely performance and beautifully sung. Ludmila Dvorakova was the new Venus, and her fine, seductive singing added greatly to the effect of the performance as a whole. Martti Talvela was again a dignified, noble Landgrave. There was a new Wolfram von Eschenbach—Hermann Prey. As was to be expected Prey sang the part with a melting beauty of tone, but his performance as a whole was lightweight, a little too sweet and gentle, and lacked the strength which is essential to this character. André Cluytens conducted, and gave the whole opera a touch of magic. It was a splendid occasion on stage and off (August 21), for the President of the German Federal Republic was paying one of his visits to Bayreuth, and with Dr Lübke in the audience the Festspielhaus was at its most festive.

It had been hoped that Knappertsbusch would have conducted *Parsifal* again in 1965, but he suffered a broken hip shortly before the festival, and André Cluytens took his place. He gave us a performance which was not, perhaps, so deeply religious, but in its own way no less spiritual and very beautiful.

Hans Hotter's Gurnemanz was not less than superb. He was in glorious voice,. and his performance revealed every facet of the character, gave life and infinite understanding to every phrase of the music. Jess Thomas had developed his Parsifal greatly; it was now acted with an impressive sincerity and dignity as well as nobly sung. Theo Adam brought beauty and feeling to the singing of Amfortas. Astrid Varnay's Kundry was admirably acted, but even her artistry could not compensate for limited vocal resources.

It was in 1965 that I took the opportunity of a "spielfrei" day to make my first visit to Coburg. Why I had waited thirteen years to do so I do not know, except that Bayreuth is essentially a place of habit, and for some reason Coburg is not one of the festival visitor's regular places of excursion. In fact I should not have gone there at all if an old friend had not made it sound so easy—which it is.

Knowing my lethargic habits at festivals, he pointed out that there was a train about half-past ten in the morning which took one to Coburg in comfortable time for lunch, and one back in the afternoon which got the traveller to Bayreuth well before dinner time. All of which is perfectly true. The train journey, with one change at Lichtenfels, takes just under two hours in each direction.

Coburg has a special interest for Britons because it was a childhood home not only of Queen Victoria's mother but also of her beloved consort Prince Albert of Saxe-Coburg-Gotha. If modern visitors from England think this counts for little in their lives, let them go to Coburg and see. For there they will have greatness thrust upon them, and be welcomed like cousins still. I and the friends with whom I made the expedition were driven up to the castle and the adjacent hotel where we lunched (it is a forty-five-minute walk, and a steepish hill) by a taxi driver who greets the English with delight. His knowledge of the British royal family tree put us to shame, and whoever we met in the town seemed to share the same spontaneous friendliness.

Coburg, now of some fifty thousand inhabitants, is built beside the little river Itz, but has been dominated for eight hundred years by the great castle called the Veste, standing on the hill above. There Prince Albert's forebears welcomed Martin Luther for a six-month sojourn during the Diet of Augsburg. Later they had another and more luxurious palace in the town below—the Ehrenburg—which is part Renaissance and part Baroque. Between the two are parks and gardens, and a natural history museum started by Prince Albert and his ducal brother.

In the town square you can buy the local *bratwurst*, sausages roasted over burning pine cones. There are old houses and churches and the whole place has a gentle charm and an almost forgotten peace.

CHAPTER XVI

1966—Year of Tragedy

A SHADOW hung over the festival of 1966, and I think it was sensed by many people who did not even know exactly what was the cloud that caused it.

Travelling across Germany in the train, I had a chance conversation with a German who was bound for Munich but interested to hear that I was going to Bayreuth. "Did you know", he asked, "that Wieland Wagner is very ill?" I did not, but on arrival I found the town oppressed by rumour and counter-rumour.

Bayreuth is a place where news travels fast. The town is small enough for everyone to know every event of importance, and the lives of the Wagner family are, like royalty, the personal concern of every inhabitant. During the festivals the same is true among the visitors as well as the artists and all the Festspielhaus personnel. Rumour and gossip fly round, becoming more highly coloured as they are relayed from group to group.

In this case the news was only too true. Wieland Wagner had been taken ill some weeks before the festival opened. Details were uncertain. Some said that he was in a Munich clinic, others that he had left the clinic and was recuperating, but not well enough to return to Bayreuth during the maelstrom period of the festival itself.

It was known that he was being kept closely informed of every facet of the production work. His influence was strong in this festival, but for the first time it had to be exercised from a distance.

I believe it was Wieland Wagner's own wish that no official announcement of his illness should be made, and in general the Press respected this wish with great loyalty. In such critiques as I saw no mention was made of the fact that Wieland Wagner was too ill even to be in Bayreuth.

The reason for this reticence is understandable. A festival should have a happy holiday atmosphere. It is an old and praiseworthy principle of the theatre that the public shall know nothing of whatever strains and troubles may go to the making of a performance. Theirs but to enjoy the finished product. Moreover it can well be said that illness is a part of the artist's personal life where he or she ought to have the right of privacy. In this publicity-avid age celebrities of all kinds are permitted less and less of this human privacy. Curiosity tears down the respect for trouble which is still accorded to most ordinary individuals. To be famous means that the world expects to share those details which normally are discussed only between a patient's doctor and family.

Small wonder, then, if Wieland Wagner wished to keep his illness out of the newspapers. But whether it was wise to maintain such a complete official silence in this case, is another matter. For one thing there were a great many devoted admirers of Wieland Wagner's work, and loyal supporters of the Bayreuth festivals, who were deeply and sincerely concerned for his wellbeing; who felt the anxiety of friends, although they might never have met either of the Wagner grandsons in person. For another, rumour thrives in a vacuum.

This atmosphere of personal anxiety was the background to a festival which had no new production, but some beautiful revivals of earlier ones.

There was another glorious *Tristan und Isolde*. Press and public alike acclaimed the splendour of Karl Böhm's conducting which, like the art of great singers, grows ever deeper in understanding and more inspired in its realization of ecstatic love. Birgit Nilsson at her finest. Windgassen endowing Tristan with all the dignity and anguish as well as the passion of the ill-starred knight. Christa Ludwig was the new Brangäne, a lovely performance, warm of voice and feeling. Martti Talvela's King Marke was beautifully sung. Only Eberhard Waechter as Kurwenal was, this time, rather too lightweight dramatically to match the heroic qualities of the other performances. The two small tenor parts of the seaman and the shepherd were beautifully sung by Peter Schreier and Erwin Wohlfahrt.

This was the second time that New Bayreuth gave three cycles of the *Ring* in one season. I saw the second, which was conducted by Otmar Suitner: a good if not great orchestral interpretation.

This time we had a new Brünnhilde in *Walküre* and *Siegfried*: Ludmila Dvorakova (Nilsson sang in the other cycles). It was as yet a tentative performance, very uncertain at the beginning, but Dvorakova showed that she possessed a rich and lovely voice for the part and a rare gift for acting, qualities which have later proved her to be a very fine Brünnhilde indeed, both in Bayreuth and elsewhere. Tall and graceful with an ethereal type of beauty, she looks a perfect Brünnhilde: daughter of a god, a princess among women. The voice is more mezzo than soprano and therefore lacks some power at the top, but it is most beautifully used. Very, very rarely does she press her voice to the detriment of its tonal quality. Few Brünnhildes sustain so much really beautiful singing throughout this role, and beauty combined with understanding and feeling for the character. Astrid Varnay took over for the great, challenging demands of the *Götterdämmerung* Brünnhilde, and once more triumphed dramatically, though hardly vocally.

Hans Hotter sang Wotan throughout this *Ring*, Theo Adam appearing in the other two cycles. Again the majesty and insight of Hotter's interpretation held the stage, giving meaning, indeed revelation of the whole mighty tragedy. The production could make no puppet-god of him. In *Rheingold* he was in beautiful voice. *Walküre* found him vocally off-colour, the voice sounding tired and strained, but in *Siegfried* he sang magnificently.

Windgassen's Siegfried was in fine form in both operas. It is his sympathy which is so striking in this part. Siegfried can be a most irritating, bumptious young man, or simply stupid. Windgassen's Siegfried has charm and gaiety and youth—a far more positive youth, in fact, than many younger singers are able to convey. As Hagen's plot and the shadows of death close round him, this Siegfried shines out, the hero pure in heart.

Josef Greindl was a tower of evil strength as Hunding and Hagen. Erwin Wohlfahrt repeated his brilliant Mime. Neidlinger was again Alberich.

There was a new pair of Volsung twins. Claude Heater made little impression as Siegmund, but Gwyneth Jones created one of the chief sensations of the season with her Sieglinde. Lovely to look at, radiantly feminine, with a big and thrilling voice, she gave an outstanding performance. Her Sieglinde, already famous in London, took Bayreuth by storm.

As a whole, Wieland's *Ring* remained virtually unaltered. Its symbols and change of dramatic balance were there very much as in 1965. But there was less feeling of automation since the more experienced singers had been able to establish the characters of their parts more fully, despite the production.

Tannhäuser came back with considerable success. This time the opera was conducted by Carl Melles, a Hungarian and newcomer to the ranks of Bayreuth *dirigenten,* and he gave us an exciting performance. The other important change was a new Tannhäuser in the person of Jess Thomas. His fine ringing tenor gave excitement to the role. He looked young and handsome and unstable, which is a fair outline for one interpretation of this character. But the performance was superficial, lacking the depth of experience.

Anja Silja was Elisabeth (she also sang Venus at some performances). Her gift for dedicated womanhood (e.g. Senta) came to the fore here. She was a moving, effective Elisabeth, even though there was a little too much theatricality in her saintliness, and she sang well when she did not press her voice too hard. Venus in the performance I saw was again Ludmila Dvorakova, beutifully sung and most effective. Hermann Prey repeated his Wolfram and Martti Talvela his Landgrave.

Parsifal brought another new conductor to Bayreuth, Pierre Boulez. It would be hard to imagine a greater contrast to Bayreuth's beloved Knappertsbusch *Parsifals*. This was swift, light—in comparison with the traditional dignity—and compelling. According to the records of timing which are kept at Bayreuth, the slowest *Parsifal* was conducted by Toscanini in 1931: 5 hours 5 minutes, excluding intervals. Knappertsbusch took 4 hours and 40 minutes. Now Boulez got through the opera in 3 hours 49 minutes. (Boulez' timing is without the overture, but it would be under 4 hours all told, about the same as Clemens Krauss.) These wide variations in timing are staggering, and yet Boulez gave us a beautiful performance. Despite his identification with modern music Boulez has a real love and feeling for *Parsifal*, seeing in it a turning point not only in Wagner's work but in the whole course of operatic composition. His reading is one which sets *Parsifal* firmly in the world of the moderns, and yet does not outrage the feelings of the Wagnerian traditionalists.

Hotter repeated his profound and beautifully sung Gurnemanz. Astrid Varnay was Kundry, and Gustav Neidlinger Klingsor. At the performance I saw there were two last-minute changes of cast. Owing to the illness of Sándor Kónya, Hans Hopf sang Parsifal, and brought to the role dignity and understanding. Thomas Stewart replaced Eberhard Waechter as Amfortas.

This is one of Stewart's finest roles. As is the way of a real artist, each time he sings Amfortas he adds to his portrayal new insight and deeper feeling. Moreover he sings the part with growing beauty. Some singers concentrate first on the vocal quality of their performance and develop the characterization later. Stewart appears to work from the other end. He has a quick appreciation of the dramatic outline of a part, an outline which he fills in and colours as he continues to sing it, but at the beginning his actual singing is often monotonous, lacking smoothness of line and memorable phrasing. Later this is achieved too, and by 1966 he had full mastery of Amfortas. It was superbly acted and beautifully sung.

One little incident at that performance has stayed in my mind. I was talking to a small American from Chicago; one of the chance acquaintances which one is continually making in Bayreuth. This was his first return visit to Europe since he had served there as a G.I., and he came now as a Wagner pilgrim. "I told my friends I must not die until after *Parsifal*. I have waited so many years for this."

66　The *Ring*, 1965. *Götterdämmerung*, Act I, Gibichungs' Hall

67   Wolfgang Windgassen as Siegfried, 1965

68   Erwin Wohlfahrt as Mime, 1965

69　Ludmila Dvorakova as Brünnhilde, 1966

70   Thomas Stewart as Wotan, 1967

71 Heather Harper as Elsa, 1967

72 Donald McIntyre as Telramund, 1967

73 *Lohengrin,* 1967. (a) Act I

73 (b) Act II

74 (a) *Lohengrin*, Act III, 1967

74 (b) *Die Meistersinger*, Act I, 1968

75　*Die Meistersinger von Nürnberg*, 1968　(a)　Act II

75 (b)　Act III Scene 2

76　Theo Adam as Hans Sachs, 1968

77 Gwyneth Jones as Eva, 1968

78   Berit Lindholm as Brünnhilde, 1968

79 (a) Wieland Wagner rehearsing Martha Mödl as Isolde, 1952

79 (b) *Tristan und Isolde,* 1962. Wieland Wagner, Birgit Nilsson,
Wolfgang Windgassen, Josef Greindl

80 (a) Wolfgang Wagner rehearsing *Die Meistersinger*, 1968,
with Janis Martin (Magdalene) and Hermin Esser (David)

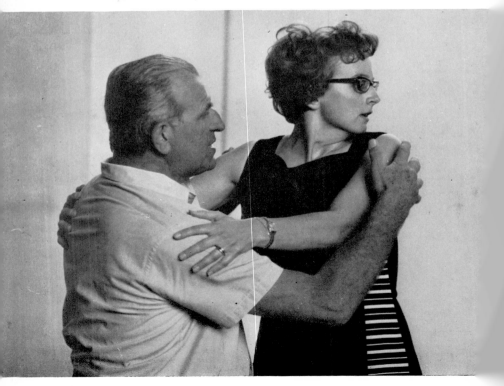

80 (b) Hans Hotter directs Berit Lindholm as Brünnhilde in
the *Ring*, 1968

81 Sixtus Beckmesser as Thomas Hemsley
Hans Sachs as Norman Bailey

82 (a)   Der Fliengende Holländer. Act III 1969–70

82 (b)   Das Rheingold 1970. Scene 4

The fanfare sounded for the last act: the theme of the Good Friday music calling us through the evening shadows. "Now I can die", he said with a laugh in which there was no trace of mockery. This was a year of mixed weather in Bayreuth. When I arrived after the season had run for its first ten days the weather was cool and damp. Not the penetrating cold and continuous rain which constitutes Bayreuth at its very worst, but all too English for my taste. There are some energetic people who dislike heat and actually prefer these cool days. They say they can do their sightseeing and concentrate better on the music in such conditions. I admire the excellent philosophy of this point of view, but cannot share it. When the sun fails to shine and the air to welcome one with kindly warmth I pull my coat around me and hurry about the town bemoaning the fact that I cannot sit in the gardens and dream. I ought to know the fickleness of the Bayreuth climate by now—after all it is in hill country where the elements are usually changeable—but I have never outgrown a childish hope that the festival will always live up to its climatic best.

Finally, before I left, the weather did relent, summer burst out and it got hotter and hotter, building up to a heavy thundery atmosphere by the time I left. But it came too late for the "spielfrei" days during my visit. With grey skies and the possibility of rain it did not seem worthwhile to make any long expeditions, so on the second free day I went, with friends, to Bad Berneck. When the weather is uncertain, or one is too idle to go farther, the choice nearly always falls on Berneck.

This is a little spa with Kneipp baths 10 miles (16 km.) due north of Bayreuth. It is, with the exception of the even more local Eremitage, the easiest of all excursions. A bus outside the main post office (which is almost opposite the railway station) will take you there in about half an hour. Take the 12.40 and you arrive in time for lunch. The 17.55 brings you home by a different route, through harvest fields and sleepy villages, and delivers you back in Bayreuth at 18.30. There is quite a choice of other buses, but these appeal to my leisurely sense of time in Bayreuth.

Berneck is built at the mouth of one of the steep narrow valleys of the Fichtelgebirge, a region of mountain and forest which lies in the north-eastern corner of Bavaria. There is nothing very much to see except an attractive little typical German resort. Bayreuth as a whole is typical of nothing but itself, and so this contrast makes a pleasant interlude in the musical life of the festival. A few Bayreuth visitors are always to be found here on "spielfrei" days, but the regular Berneck holidaymakers are of a very different type: cheerful

I

German families who sit in the cafés and the pretty gardens where a band plays enthusiastically. There are one or two hotels and a number of *gasthäuser*. Lunch and an afternoon coffee can be taken at various places. Between meals one walks up the valley of the little Ölschnitz, or climbs into the woods which clothe the valley sides. The Germans are great walkers. "Shall we walk a little?" is the courteous phrase with which they counter the English tendency to stand or sit about, whether it be on an outing or during the intervals of an opera performance. In Berneck one does walk a little, and with pleasure, along the paths which lead into the town's enfolding hills. It is a gentle, kindly place.

On August 28 the 1966 Bayreuth season ended with the third *Götterdämmerung*. September is always the holiday month for those whose work is bound up in the festival. October sees them back again, already planning for the following year.

But this time that month of rebirth saw the fulfilment of the tragedy which had shadowed Bayreuth's summer. Wieland Wagner died in a Munich hospital on October 17, 1966. The news carried shock and sorrow all over the world. Shock to those who knew nothing of his months of illness, and even to the others who did know, but had heard that he was making progress. Sorrow to his personal friends and admirers, and to many thousands who followed his work only by hearsay, but regarded him as the leading creative figure in opera production throughout the world. Which he was.

Whatever personal critical views might be held of his productions, Wieland Wagner's artistic stature and the debt owed to him by post-war styles of operatic staging are indisputable. Although Bayreuth was the scene of the largest number—and the most famous—of his productions, he had also produced at a number of other leading European operahouses, notably Stuttgart (seven different operas), Hamburg, Frankfurt, Munich and Vienna. Certain of these productions, and Bayreuth ones, were taken to other countries by their original companies, and by this means Wieland's work was seen in London, Edinburgh, Naples, Venice, Brussels, Copenhagen. Nor was his work restricted to the Wagner canon. His range extended from Gluck's *Orfeo* and Beethoven's *Fidelio* to *Lulu* by Alban Berg.

The most spectacular "export" of Wieland Wagner's Bayreuth actually took place after his death, though the plans were of course made long before. This was the visit of a full Bayreuth company to the Osaka Festival in Japan in April 1967. Performances of *Tristan und Isolde* were conducted by Pierre Boulez, with Birgit Nilsson, Wolfgang Windgassen, Hans Hotter, Herta Töpper, Frans Andersson. In *Die Walküre* were Anja Silja, Theo Adam, Helga Dernesch, Jess

Thomas, Grace Hoffman and Gerd Nienstedt; the conductor was Thomas Schippers, and at one performance Wolfgang Rennert.

At the time of his death Wieland Wager was forty-nine years of age, young indeed in an artistic career of this kind. Most of those who had followed his development through the previous fifteen years were, I think, conscious that he had reached a crucial stage. Interest, excitement, anxiety, centred round his next step. What that would have been, into what paths of production his restless artistic spirit would have led, are questions which must now forever remain unanswered. But from the world of opera rose a spontaneous tribute to one who had accomplished so much in so short a time.

CHAPTER XVII

1967—Bayreuth Under One Helmsman

THOSE who had been faithful to Bayreuth throughout many years came back in 1967 with sorrow and some uncertainty. How great would be the change without Wieland?
Superficially there was no change at all. Bayreuth's festival organization is, as I have said, a highly professional one. Wolfgang Wagner had always been in charge of the administrative side and continued his work in the same practised tradition of New Bayreuth. Under a contract between Wieland and Wolfgang Wagner it was agreed that on the death of one the surviving brother would continue in control, and despite some unfortunate controversy and publicity on the subject Wolfgang therefore remains the rightful sole director.
Almost a year had elapsed since the shock of Wieland's death; and all the work on the 1967 season had been carried out after the tragedy. In a way the revivals of Wieland's productions seemed to run more smoothly than they had done the previous year under the anxiety of his illness. His absence certainly affected these productions in ways which I shall consider later, but in general there was little difference, save that one vital personality has passed from the scene. It was an interim year. Important changes were bound to come, but they still lay in the future.
Nonetheless there was one great if indefinable change which affected the regular public: the fact of Wieland Wagner's death brought us face to face with the realization that this was the end of an era. Most regular operahouses and long-established festivals continue their artistic life for many years, perhaps several generations, without perceptible alterations. Directors, conductors, singers come and go, often leaving an irreparable gap for certain members of the audience, yet the whole goes on, for artistic generations are intermingled in the whole ensemble.
Bayreuth is one of the oldest of music festivals, yet the creation of New Bayreuth was so revolutionary that it had been born again in 1951. The two Wagner brothers were the centre of this young festival's life, and round them they had gathered a nucleus of artists who came back year after year, and no less a nucleus of public. We had all grown up together.

At forty-nine Wieland Wagner died young. Fifteen years is not long for a producer's career, and his few earlier productions had been overshadowed by war. But fifteen years is a long time in the life of most singers; few have longer than this at the height of their fame, for most need a number of years to develop their voices and reputations. It is also an appreciable span in the life of an operagoer. With Wieland's death the scales fell from our eyes. We looked at each other and saw the marks of time, saw too our own grey hairs. Some of those great singers who had delighted us were now past their prime, others had retired already. All this would have happened in exactly the same way had Wieland lived, but his death brought recognition of the changes sharply to our minds. There were certain glories of Bayreuth which we should never see and hear again in exactly the form we had once known them.

The sense of loss was therefore wider and deeper even than that for a great artist such as Wieland Wagner. It left us sad and touched with a chill of general bereavement.

Very probably this rude awakening was good for us. Perhaps we had become too much a family. It is not unnatural that the public should develop this close-knit feeling, in a place like Bayreuth. They watched the Wagner family themselves, until they seemed personal friends: Frau Winifred Wagner mother of the two famous sons, Friedelind Wagner their sister from America who came every year with a group of students for whom she held master classes; the brothers' wives and sons and daughters, and above all, of course, Wieland and Wolfgang. We had seen them all for so long, felt a part of the circle which had not greatly altered since 1951, despite the constantly changing pattern on the stage. Now Wieland was gone, and we others—Wagners, artists, public—must go forward and not allow the merits of the past to befog enthusiasm for the future. It is readily understandable that this readjustment must be hard for many of those concerned in the Bayreuth organization. Because of the personal devotion which many operagoers bestowed on Bayreuth as they knew it, the problem of readjustment is almost as great for them. But it is very necessary. Even now, more than two years after Wieland's death, there are still too many of the public whose eyes and thoughts are turned backwards. Strange paradox that this should happen in a place and among people who so wholeheartedly embraced the Wagner brothers' creed of all things new!

The 1967 season opened with Wolfgang's new *Lohengrin,* his first new production since his *Ring* in 1960, and one which was scheduled before his brother's death. His own style, which had always existed but was sometimes overshadowed by Wieland's more startling ideas, was fully expressed here: Clear, simple staging, a fairy-tale quality, but one which was firmly rooted in mediæval times. In the first act the meadow by the Scheldt was flanked by trees but they were formal ones of silver filigree, framing the brightly clad figures till the whole —very lovely—picture looked like an illustration in some illuminated missal. The swan had no substance, it was a shining bird spirit on the cyclorama. (Plate 73a.)

For the second act the fortress and minster at Antwerp were represented by towering stone walls on which, at the back, were traced a row of Romanesque arches—a clever touch which gave this effective, claustrophobic set a place in time. (Plate 73b.) The bridal chamber was a formal pavilion. Here poor Elsa's faith fails, and she asks Lohengrin the fatal question. This is the very heart of the opera, and symbolically and effectively the setting suggested that they were for that brief spell set apart from the rest of the world.

Silver trees and ethereal swan returned for the last act, framing the splendidly dressed principals and chorus. (Plate 74a.) There was nothing very new or different about the staging of this *Lohengrin*, but it was beautifully lit, never jarred or distracted one from the music or the story, and to me was one of the most wholly successful productions I have seen at Bayreuth.

Rudolf Kempe was the conductor, and spun a magic veil of sound from the orchestra. His gift for exquisite string tone was paramount. There was knightly chivalry, a spiritual quality too delicate for tragedy—*Lohengrin* is never quite real enough to touch the deeper chords of tragedy. It was orchestrally a very lovely performance, for this opera is particularly suited to Kempe's gifts and sense of style. And yet there was just something lacking. The whole thing was a little too ethereal. *Lohengrin* is one of Wagner's early operas. In it he was still writing "tunes", and had not yet developed the great musical fabrics woven of *Leitmotive* which came later. A stronger rhythm was needed to display the simpler beauty of the *Lohengrin* melodies.

There were no less than four different Lohengrins in 1967. Sándor Kónya had been scheduled to sing in all performances, but he became ill and was unable to sing after the premiere. I saw Jean Cox in the part, and a dignified even moving knightly hero he made, singing with power and beauty and a real appreciation of character.

Two British singers won laurels in this production. Heather Harper sang Elsa. Her voice is not really quite large enough for the role, but it is pure and true—essential qualities for Elsa—and she sang with real artistry. Her innocent, feminine Elsa, all feeling and no intellect, was a perfectly justifiable reading of the part, and no doubt the one Wolfgang wanted. Donald McIntyre, on the other hand, was an unusually intelligent forceful Telramund: dark-voiced, well sung and dramatic. Grace Hoffman partnered him with an effective Ortrud. Karl Ridderbusch was said to have been an excellent King Heinrich at other performances. He was below par when I heard him, but I believe he was suffering from a hand injury.

All the other six operas were rehearsed by Peter Lehmann, Wieland Wagner's personal assistant who had worked with him at Bayreuth for some years. Faced with the unenviable task of reviving productions virtually unchanged which would, in Wieland's hands, have known a hundred minor variations, he did a remarkably good job. Peter Lehmann has real feeling for Wieland's inspiration.

There were, too, some interesting new performances: In the *Ring* (conducted for this second cycle by Otmar Suitner) Thomas Stewart sang Wotan in *Rheingold* and *Walküre*. His dramatic gifts served him and the part well; this was no wooden Wotan, but a proud and suffering man. Man still, rather than god, but impressive and affecting, and in the main well sung though lacking vocal colour. In *Siegfried* Greindl sang the Wanderer.

The same balance of casting existed for Brünnhilde, Ludmila Dvorakova singing in *Walküre* and *Siegfried* and giving a really beautiful performance, which had progressed tremendously beyond that of the previous year. For the final dramatic challenge of *Götterdämmerung* the role was taken over by Astrid Varnay.

Wolfgang Windgassen's Siegfried, Greindl's Hunding and Hagen, Neidlinger's Alberich and Wohlfahrt's Mime were all towers of strength. And James King and Leonie Rysanek were again an exciting, well matched Siegmund and Sieglinde.

Pierre Boulez did not seem so successful with *Parsifal* this year; there was a lack of musical inspiration in the first act, and though both second and third acts had the authentic spirit, as a whole it lacked the compelling beauty of 1966. This may have been partly because several of the chief protagonists were new in this production, and their performances were still rather embryonic. Franz Crass brought his very beautiful voice to the service of Gurnemanz, singing and acting carefully. There was considerable promise here, but scarcely a complete performance. Much the same might be said of James King's Parsifal, though a well-sung and moving study. Gerd Nienstedt was a thoroughly effective Klingsor, but the memorable artists that evening were Christa Ludwig as a wonderfully persuasive Kundry, and Thomas Stewart's superb Amfortas.

Tannhäuser, at least the performance I saw, was the season's failure, and the less said about it the better. It is seldom, however, that any opera performance is without some saving grace. This had two: the admirable conducting of Berislav Klobucar, and a well-sung Wolfram von Eschenbach by Thomas Tipton.

There was one other special excitement during the festival. For a number of years the International Youth Festival Meeting, Bayreuth (Internationales Jugend-Festspieltreffen Bayreuth) had gathered together students from all parts of the world during the second half of the Bayreuth Festival. (It has, by the way, nothing to do with Friede-lind Wagner's master classes.) In 1967 nineteen different countries were represented. The students—some of them young professionals—are singers, instrumentalists, production assistants, and so on. Apart from attending Festspielhaus performances they work together and give one or two public performances—a concert or an opera.

For this year they had chosen Wagner's first opera, written when he was twenty—*Die Feen*. Very few Wagnerites have ever had the chance to see it, and once this production was announced Wagner "collectors" rushed to Bayreuth to attend one of the two performances which were given in the modern Stadthalle in the old town. Enthusiasm got somewhat out of proportion, and in some quarters this student production received more attention than the whole set of Bayreuth festival performances. But it was extraordinarily interesting: a remark-ably good performance by student standards, and one which proved *Die Feen* to be true early Wagner, and an opera well worth reviving in its own right.

CHAPTER XVIII

1968—And the Future

1968 was a crucial festival in the history of New Bayreuth. Inevitably the previous year had been a bridge between the first famous period when the two brothers worked together and the new phase when Wolfgang Wagner alone carries the weight of responsibility. It is far too early still to judge or even assess how the future will develop, but 1968 provided certain indications of what Wolfgang has in mind and some evidence of his views on future policy.

As far as the public is concerned two major questions had been in every Bayreuth-goer's mind, and on their lips, since the news of Wieland Wagner's death: would his brother continue Wieland's avant-garde policy of presenting the operas in startlingly original ways, and would the actual productions cease to be restricted to the Wagner family?

Both questions have been answered verbally by Wolfgang Wagner in discussion with many critics and reporters, and his statements have been confirmed in the 1968 festival.

"There will be no sensationalism", he said to me, quietly but firmly, when we were discussing the form that future productions might be expected to take. This is not of course a rejection of his brother's art; it is bound up with the question of new producers. For very soon after Wieland's death Wolfgang announced that, from time to time, outside producers would be invited to work at Bayreuth.

Here then we have the perspective in which Wolfgang Wagner views the future, practical and wise. And quietly as it has been stated, this is a turning point in the history of New Bayreuth. Apart from Hartmann's *Meistersinger* given in 1951 and 1952 only productions designed and directed by one of the two brothers had been seen on the Festspielhaus stage in all those years. It had for some time been a matter of debate among the public as to whether they would or could continue indefinitely to produce new variations on the theme of staging the same ten operas. Wieland's death settled the question. What already appeared to be something of a test of ingenuity for two men was manifestly impossible for one.

There remained the corollary of what type of producer Wolfgang Wagner was likely to invite to Bayreuth. Wieland having established a reputation for the unexpected and revolutionary it might have been thought that originality would be the first qualification, and this is where Wolfgang has shown not only wisdom but, under the circumstances, no little courage. *There will be no sensationalism.* Wieland Wagner was a genius. However opinions might differ about his productions his artistic gifts were beyond question, but every highly individual creative artist of this type is followed by those who try to copy them. This is common in all forms of art, and the result is something which is merely different or startling in form without the spirit which illuminated—and probably justified—the same kind of audacity when employed by the greater artist.

From this kind of neo-Wielandism Wolfgang Wagner will fortunately defend Bayreuth. Otherwise the festivals might follow the Gadarene swine to self-destruction. I am sure that we shall see new approaches to the staging of Wagner's operas and plenty of originality in the years to come, but if we can believe Wolfgang Wagner's intention—and I for one think that we can—these will be the work of producers who understand the operas and have something worthwhile to contribute to them, rather than those who capture the transient notoriety of newspaper headlines and gossip columnists.

First practical evidence of Wolfgang's policy was the mood of his own new *Die Meistersinger von Nürnberg*. *Meistersinger* seems to have been the test piece for changing styles at Bayreuth in the past eighteeen years. Hartmann's 1951 version was the last traditional production to be seen here. Wieland's 1956 and 1963 *Meistersingers* were two of his most controversial works. In giving us his own conception of this opera Wolfgang chose to show the public quite clearly that he personally has no ideas of using stunts and gimmicks to gain publicity for Bayreuth. The production, which I shall discuss in detail later, restores the true balance of Richard Wagner's opera. Wolfgang is not afraid to bring back traditional touches, and yet it is essentially a modern production, simplified, suggestive rather than explicit of his grandfather's stage directions.

More than any statement of policy or intentions this is a sign of what we may expect in the future. It is a natural outcome of his own style as shown at Bayreuth since 1953 and it is of course only a further stage of what will continue to develop and take different forms with changing operatic life. But it is an answer to the questioners, and an answer given where any theatrical statement must be made— on the stage. To me it is one of the most encouraging signs of the continuing life and artistic integrity of New Bayreuth.

The other major step taken by Wolfgang Wagner was to invite Hans Hotter to take over the stage direction of the *Ring* in Wieland's settings. Hotter therefore became the first "outside" producer to have worked here since 1952, for Peter Lehmann, who had revived all Wieland's productions in 1967 and was responsible for *Tristan* and *Parsifal* in 1968, was, as Wieland's former assistant, really an integral part of the Wagner production organization.

That Wolfgang Wagner should turn to Hans Hotter at this point seems, at first sight, a natural choice. Hotter had sung at Bayreuth nearly every year since 1952, and during that time had appeared in very many of the leading bass-baritone and bass roles. He was a well-known international artist from the beginning, and his gifts and experience did much to add lustre to Bayreuth's fame. He had taken up producing some years before, and already had an international reputation in this field also. He is on all counts a Wagnerian *par excellence*.

All this is true, and yet—Hotter's style of producing as he has shown it at operahouses in London, Vienna, Munich, Hamburg, Zurich and other places, is far removed from modern Bayreuth methods.

It would be ridiculous to suggest that there are only two kinds of stage producer. This is a highly individual art and there are very many variations of style and personality among the men and women who make it their career. There is, however, a very marked difference in result between two main groups of producers. One consists of young men—or women—who become producers very early in their lives, probably after some theatrical experience at a university and perhaps as part of the production staff in a theatre. Wieland and Wolfgang Wagner were themselves of this category. Only a few of them are, like the Wagners, designers as well as producers, but all start with a great many personal ideas and probably the need, in the current phrase, to express themselves. If they are gifted their work may be brilliant, and it will nearly always bear a personal imprint. If the production is a classical play or opera which is familiar to everyone, the producer who has no other outlet for his artistic expression will almost certainly try to give it a new or even controversial presentation. The reason is not really that the audience will be bored by the old masterpiece, but that the producer wants to show his inventiveness.

The other group of producers of whom I am thinking are those who were first actors or singers, and Hans Hotter is one of these. Several other singers are now moving into the production field, and of course a great many leading actors combine the two stage arts. In England Sir John Gielgud is an outstanding example of a great actor who is also a very fine producer, and it is interesting that he and Hotter are producers of the same kind.

Both were at the summit of their own branches of acting and singing before they turned to production, and I suspect that neither was directed by a further need to express himself. Their productions always suggest that they approach each play or opera not from the standpoint of giving a new look, but of revealing more fully what the playwright, composer, librettist, has entrusted to those who must breathe life into their works. Being great actors and wise actors, these two men have the gift of drawing remarkable qualities of acting from members of their casts, of showing us live performances from those one had thought incapable of anything more than the simplest histrionics. They work as a conductor does, by calling out the best in every player and co-ordinating it into one whole living work which is much greater than the sum of the parts.

This is a self-effacing way of producing. It does not attract publicity. But at its best it can be very, very exciting because it often reveals unsuspected heights or depths, humour or pathos, in some work which seemed as familiar as one's own daily life. There is a limit to the number of ways in which a standard work can be reoriented and redecorated without becoming ridiculous. There is really no limit to the fascination which comes from interplay of character, the unfolding of drama.

This then is the kind of producer, in the person of Hans Hotter, whom Wolfgang Wagner invited to help with the existing *Ring*. Prophecy and guesswork have no place in this book. I have neither inside information nor a crystal ball in which to read Bayreuth's future, but I wonder—and I hope. Is it possible that Wolfgang Wagner has a new path in mind for Bayreuth? A style—psychological if we must give it a label—where music and acting are paramount, where the mood comes not from the setting, however beautiful, nor from symbolism, but from personalities. Will the day come when we shall say that Bayreuth is not only the place to see and hear Wagner's operas but also to *know* them by the magic of stage revelation?

Naturally 1968 was a season full of interest, questioning, vitality, both inside the Festspielhaus and out of it. Only the weather really failed the visitor. Rain, cold winds, grey skies, more rain. It was one of the very worst Bayreuth summers I can remember. Occasionally a warm sunny day smiled on us, but usually it fled in the night, and dawn broke whimpering and tearful again.

Still this did not deter the festival guests, and the struggle to get seats was greater than ever. There is always a determined group of people, young and old, who stand round the box office door hoping to obtain returned tickets. They hurry towards everyone who walks that way, often waving money. Those who speak no German are of course at a disadvantage; the articulate can complete a purchase while the foreigner is still fumbling for words.

One student, French-speaking I think, found an ingenious solution. Walking up the Siegfried Wagner Allee one day in pouring rain I saw a solitary figure standing at the point where the road divides in front of the Festspielhaus terrace. Very sombre, even pathetic it looked, in funereal black: black suit, black raincoat, black-rimmed spectacles, black hair and over all the shelter of a vast black mushroom-like umbrella. Round his neck hung a large white card bearing the words "Bitte! Karte für Heute!" (Please—ticket for today!) Whether this ruse succeeded I do not know, but he collected sympathetic grins from all the other damp passers-by.

Every seat was filled, and there were more of them too. The new, harder, narrow seating installed for 1968 provides for an audience of 1,916 people, in place of the former 1,833, but still the problem remains.

When I saw the student I was walking up from the bus stop. 1968 provided a good deal of bus weather when there was no particular joy or virtue in walking. As I have said earlier, Bayreuth has an excellent town bus service. One, number 7, runs from the old market place in Maximilianstrasse to the foot of the Siegfried Wagner Allee by way of the station and various circuitous routes. After this point, where I get out, it goes off to the right of the Festspielhaus and presumably to the hospital, since it is marked "Krankenhaus". These buses run about every twenty minutes, and at the same intervals a bus comes down the same road and will take you back to Maximilianstrasse.

One day I was about to board a bus going to the town, and then noticed it was number 4. This, I thought, is heading somewhere quite different. I asked, but was assured that it was going to Maximilianstrasse, which it did. After some time I realized that all the buses on this route were number 4's. I wanted to know which way the number 7's came back. They did not; no number 7 ever came back. I had a mental vision of them all driving round and round the world like so many fliegende Holländers. It seemed rather a waste of buses. Then the explanation was given to me, and it is delightfully Wagnerian. Somewhere round the hospital corner all the number 7's turn into number 4's. I believe the system may be even more confusing. I came back from the Eremitage on a bus which I am pretty certain was a number 2. I expected to change at Maximilianstrasse or the station. Not so, it took me to my own Siegried Wagner Allee stop. It must have turned into a number 7. Five minutes later it would become a number 4. Tarnhelms are clearly part of local transport equipment.

The primary reason for a new production of *Die Meistersinger von Nürnberg* was that 1968 marked the centenary of the opera's first performance, and there was a really happy festival spirit in Wolfgang Wagner's production. The first act setting of St. Katharine's Church is simplified but realistic: dark stone walls with a silvery glint, pillars and gallery, a corner of the church where we see first the worshippers, then the frolicking apprentices, then the mastersingers, good-natured, self-important, very much at home. (Plate 74b.) The street scene of the second act is truly Nuremberg; here are the houses, the elder and the lime tree, the winding street leading away to a crowded world of huddled roofs and gables—and yet the artist's touch is light, for the panels between the timbering are semi-transparent. (Plate 75a.) This is an impressionist's vision of a completely human reality. The same is true of Sachs' house, and the festival meadows by the Pegnitz where there are trees and seats and a real sense of the open air. (Plate 75b.) Twenty years ago this production would probably have been condemned as unbearably modern; today there are people who call it conservative. In fact it is a stage of operatic evolution rather than revolution, for none of the essential background of the story is omitted, yet it is unmistakably a production of today.

Karl Böhm had conducted the first performances, but when I saw this *Meistersinger* the baton had been taken over by Berislav Klobucar, who gave us a warm, gay, human reading. It may not have been a great performance, but it was a very delightful one.

The same was true of most of the singing. Walter Berry was to have sung Hans Sachs at a number of the performances. Owing to a nervous crisis he withdrew on the day of the dress rehearsal, and Theo Adam who was scheduled to share the role had to take over all eight performances. This proved to be one of the very best of Adam's parts. He sang beautifully, giving colour, tenderness, humour to the music. He looked right: a sturdy, handsome, middle-aged Sachs. Moreover he acted with real understanding and conviction. This was indeed a Hans Sachs, and he well deserved the ovation he received.

Karl Ridderbusch was an excellent and beautifully sung Pogner, dignified and moving. As Walther von Stolzing Waldemar Kmentt was elegant and knightly, though the voice was not round and free enough to give full beauty to the music. Thomas Hemsley was a subtle Beckmesser, well sung and acted "straight" without most of the funny business which usually goes with the part. Janis Martin was one of the best Magdalenes I can remember: young, lively and admirably sung. Her David was Hermin Esser who also sang well. The master-singers were a well sung and acted band of townsmen, all individuals, and they brought their wives with them to the festival—a nice touch. Kurt Moll sang the nightwatchman with haunting beauty. There remains the Eva of Gwyneth Jones. She looked lovely, though her acting was at times a little too knowing and coy. Unfortunately her voice proved rather too large for the part, or to be more accurate she had not acquired the knack of adjusting her singing to the lyric requirements of Eva. At times there was too much sheer sound, and this unbalanced the quintet.

Wolfgang Wagner's *Lohengrin* did not fare quite so well as in the previous year, though Alberto Erede, the new conductor, wove a delicate gossamer string tone from the orchestra. James King seemed curiously unawakened in the name part. His singing was unremarkable, and in his acting there was no feeling of the mystic knight. Heather Harper repeated her pure-voiced, pathetically innocent Elsa, and Donald McIntyre his dark-voiced, sinister Telramund. Ludmila Dvorakova was a thrilling Ortrud.

For the *Ring* Hans Hotter was in charge on the stage and Lorin Maazel in the pit, thus forming a completely new team. Nonetheless Wieland Wagner's *Ring* it remained; his overall conception, his symbolism, his stage directions were adhered to religiously, together with his decor. It could not be otherwise, for so individual an approach to the work allows of no compromise. Yet there was a very subtle difference, typical of Hotter's particular gifts as producer: the characters took on a new importance. They were still as Wieland saw them, but nearly all of them had a new life in themselves—there was a vivid sense of drama on the stage which formerly had been shown only by a few of the very experienced artists.

Lorin Maazel was distinctly less successful with the orchestra. After his beautiful *Lohengrin* in 1960 it was disappointing to find this *Ring* orchestrally so pedestrian. There was some really bad playing in the second cycle which I saw, especially at the opening of *Rheingold,* and though there were also some glorious passages—notably in the last act of *Götterdämmerung*—the whole lacked a command of broad phrasing. The musical side of all four operas was subdued and tentative. Maazel is a sensitive musician, and these difficulties probably stem from the fact that he has not regained his former feeling for the unusual acoustics of the Festspielhaus. One hopes that in 1969 he will have found this command and confidence and will let his orchestra ride the glories of the score.

Berit Lindholm was a new and promising Brünnhilde in *Walküre* and *Siegfried*—young, graceful, with a fine voice. Gladys Kuchta sang the role in *Götterdämmerung,* giving it the dramatic intensity of experience, if less vocal beauty. Thomas Stewart took over Wotan in

Rheingold and *Walküre* in the second cycle to release Adam for extra *Meistersingers*. Stewart had developed his portrait of the chief god still farther since 1967, making him more intense and troubled. It was an impressive if slightly too irascible performance, but unfortunately he forced his voice almost continuously. There was little beauty in his singing and far too much vibrato.

Ticho Parly was a subdued Siegfried in the opera of that name, but Wolfgang Windgassen, who had not been in his best voice as Loge, sang and acted the *Götterdämmerung* Siegfried magnificently. Here again was Wagner's *Ring* hero, gay, strong with youth's egoism which comes from innocence and not the baser springs of selfishness.

Josef Greindl's Hagen was superb as ever, also his menacing Hunding. The Wanderer which he also sang now poses too many problems of range for his voice. Gustav Neidlinger repeated his very fine Alberich. Janis Martin was a new and impressive Fricka. Owing to the illness of Erwin Wohlfahrt* Gerhard Stolze returned to sing Mime. Leonie Rysanek was Sieglinde. Richard Martell looked handsome and sang well as a new Siegmund.

Peter Lehmann guided the revivals of Wieland Wagner's *Tristan* and *Parsifal* with skill and mastery. Owing to the indisposition of Karl Böhm, Berislav Klobucar conducted the *Tristan* which I saw, and it was a really inspired performance. "He makes the music a carpet for Nilsson's voice", as a fellow-critic said to me. Both she and Windgassen sung superbly. Grace Hoffman was the excellent Brangäne. Martti Talvela sang King Marke's music most beautifully, but failed to touch the heart. The only newcomer was the Kurwenal, Gerd Feldhoff, of whom I expect to see and hear much more at Bayreuth in the future. He has a fine voice, a good stage presence, and a real gift for acting a Wagnerian role.

Pierre Boulez had found all his original inspiration for *Parsifal* and perhaps more. Swift and light-winged it might be, but the performance I saw on August 15 was one of the great ones. Josef Greindl sang Gurnemanz with wonderful feeling; this was the work of a great artist, one who wholly understands the role. Jean Cox was Parsifal and will one day make a fine one, he already shows great promise. Gerd Feldhoff's Amfortas was more than promising—a most beautifully sung and moving assumption of the role. Gerd Nienstedt was an excellent Klingsor. Amy Shuard, after a very uncertain start, proved a most musicianly Kundry. The music suits her voice.

How long, one wonders, shall we continue to have this beautiful 1951 *Parsifal*? In 1969 anyway, but plans for a new one were under

---

*Wohlfahrt's death followed in November 1968; a very real loss to Bayreuth and opera in general. He was only 36 years of age.

discussion before Wieland Wagner's death. That tragedy cancelled the idea. But however well other producers may keep Wieland's work alive no one pretends that this is the same thing as his own inventive, developing ideas. His influence on production has set its mark deep on operatic staging the world over; it will not be erased, but the days of his actual productions are numbered. Those who would see them as they remain will have to go to Bayreuth soon.

Altogether, 1968 was an interesting festival, full of promise for the future. One particularly poignant memory is that of a group of Czech festival *mitwirkenden* gathered outside the stage door at noon on August 21. The Warsaw Pact invasion of Czechoslovakia had taken place the day before, and in the lunch hour these artists crowded round transistor radios, listening for news of their country and their home towns. One woman was in tears. Tragedy shadowed the international comradeship of music.

K

CHAPTER XIX

1969—The Outsiders' Production

THERE was a very definite sense of purpose in the 1969 festival, a feeling of moving into the future. Inevitably, some people regretted this, but for those who care for Bayreuth it was encouraging to find that the difficult transition period which succeeded Wieland's death had passed.

The first outward and visible sign was a new self-service restaurant superseding the system described in Chapter II. Formerly there had been the large main restaurant on the right-hand side of the Festspielhaus, a small self-service one on the left, and the artists' canteen at the rear, behind the stage. This last was intended for festival personnel only, but it was also used by critics and a very large number of the public. As a result there was often delay in serving the rightful clientele.

All this was swept away firmly in 1969. The old main restaurant remains unaltered, but beyond it a massive new self-service one has arisen, facing the east side of the Festspielhaus. This replaces the old small self-service and the public use of the canteen. Underneath it is the new canteen which is reached by underground passage from inside the stage door, thereby effectually excluding gate crashers.

We blinked with surprise at this change in our accustomed haunts, condemned it, and finally became used to it. But despite the size of the new restaurant, queues were long. It seems likely that more restaurant facilities will be needed. Food and drink are very necessary accompaniments to Wagner's operas.

The weather excelled itself during the first half of the festival. I cannot remember a season when we had such intense heat for so long. Later the weather broke, but for two weeks and more the day temperatures seemed to maintain a fairly steady 30°C, and were often higher.

July 25, the opening night, was a historic occasion: the new *Der Fliegende Holländer*, first production by an outside producer/designer team since 1951, and a test for Wolfgang Wagner's judgment in their selection.

To me the result was almost wholly successful. It is possible to find faults in any production: an effect which has no real justification, a mixture of styles, a lack of real characterization. Nothing is without flaw in an imperfect world. But this production by August Everding, designed by Josef Svoboda, is true to Wagner's music, reveals the elemental drama of the story, and is consistently fresh and exciting. Everding is the director of the Kammerspiele theatre in Munich. Svoboda (who has designed a number of productions in London) is chief of scene design at the National Theatre in Prague. On this occasion it was decided to play the *Holländer* right through without intervals, as was done in Wolfgang Wagner's 1955 production. A semi-permanent set was therefore necessary, and Svoboda created an effective stern of Daland's ship which served in this way. Behind it the Holländer's vessel suddenly reared up in the first act, with the Holländer himself appearing to sing "Die Frist ist um" from the bows, high above Daland's deck. It was a difficult position for the singer, but dramatically very effective.

In the second act this set was successfully transformed into Daland's house by fishing nets hanging from above, and the spinning chorus sitting round the sides. A new and not wholly satisfactory trick was to have a tableau vivant in place of the portrait. A living figure dressed as the Holländer stood motionless in a frame throughout the first part of the scene, vanishing, accompanied by a cry from Senta, just before, in the person of Donald McIntyre, he entered through the door below.

For the last act a flight of steps and a wall adjacent to the deck created an admirable and artistic quayside. When the voices of the Holländer's crew strike terror into the Norwegians' hearts the hull of the ghostly ship becomes transparent, showing eerie lights within. A clever effect, if not altogether in keeping with the rest of this semi-realistic production.

Everding obtained excellent acting from his cast. He has not Wieland Wagner's power of conveying otherworldliness, nor Hotter's gift for making every singer a living personality, but the all-round standard of acting was remarkably good.

Musically this production was a joy. Silvio Varviso, chief conductor of the Stockholm Opera, was inspired with the excitement, tragedy and unearthly quality of the music, and the orchestra played superbly for him.

Donald McIntyre was quite an impressive Holländer, dignified and vocally secure. The spiritual and demoniacal aspects of the role will develop later. Leonie Rysanek was Senta (Gwyneth Jones also sang it), and was in glorious voice. I do not think I have ever heard a more beautifully sung Senta than this performance by Leonie Rysanek.

Martti Talvela was an ideal Daland. This proves to be one of his best roles. Jean Cox as Erik and René Kollo as the Steersman both sang well, and the chorus were—thanks to Wilhelm Pitz—at the top of their form.

Lorin Maazel had much greater success with his *Ring* conducting this year, and there was some really beautiful playing in *Walküre* and *Götterdämmerung*. Hans Hotter returned to rehearse this, the last year of Wieland's *Ring*, and again achieved a high standard of characterization and acting. The lighting, too, was especialy beautiful.

Thomas Stewart sang Wotan in the first cycle, this time with less sense of vocal stress, though he still needs to acquire a smoother line. Berit Lindholm sang Brünnhilde in *Walküre* and *Siegfried* with considerable success. Gladys Kuchta was not in good voice as the *Götterdämmerung* Brünnhilde, at least in the first cycle, nor was Wolfgang Windgassen as Loge.

Once again the Volsung pair were Leonie Rysanek and James King, and they provided some of the best singing in this *Ring*. Janis Martin's Fricka was vocally less good than in 1968. Josef Greindl repeated his superbly dramatic Hunding and Hagen, but with diminished vocal power. Gustav Neidlinger's Alberich was magnificent, his voice seems untouched by time.

Jess Thomas was the Siegfried, his first appearance in this role at Bayreuth, though he had sung the *Siegfried* part earlier in the year at Salzburg and Vienna. As yet this is an embryonic performance. He concentrates too much on vocal volume, ignoring the lyric aspects of the role, and his acting is forced. No singer can be expected to create a whole Siegfried in one year, or even in five, so Thomas may yet develop his *Ring* hero as others have done. What is disturbing is that his Siegfried is strangely mature and sophisticated, entirely lacking the youth which Windgassen so brilliantly conveys. There is real danger that Jess Thomas may adopt a facile, superficial characterization which allows no scope for development.

Wolfgang Wagner's delightful *Meistersinger* returned with a new Hans Sachs, Norman Bailey, who has already sung the role a number of times in England and Germany. His is a kindly, humorous Sachs and one which develops vocally with each performance, but he was not really quite ready to tackle this tremendous part at Bayreuth.

Helga Dernesch was the new Eva, and made a charming warmhearted heroine. The voice is, perhaps, a little heavy for the part (she is already a Brünnhilde), but she used it admirably, and did not mar the vocal balance of the quintet. Berislav Klobucar conducted a sound, if not a great performance.

True greatness was reserved for one opera only in this festival— *Tristan und Isolde*. The magical trio who have made this Wieland Wagner production their own ever since it was first given in 1962 returned, and we had the glory as of old: Karl Böhm conducting, with Birgit Nilsson and Wolfgang Windgassen as the lovers. Nilsson and

Windgassen were both in wonderful voice, and their acting grows in poignancy. Martti Talvela's beautifully sung Marke is still only two-dimensional when compared with Windgassen's Tristan, but it was a fine performance, as was Gerd Feldhoff's strong, deeply-felt Kurwenal.

Horst Stein was the *Parsifal* conductor this year, and a very beautiful performance he gave us, notable for the superb Amfortas of Thomas Stewart, and a dramatic and beautifully sung Kundry by Ludmila Dvorakova. The two chief roles, Gurnemanz and Parsifal were both sung with great beauty and feeling by Franz Crass and James King, yet their performances still lack the inner spark which constitutes greatness.

CHAPTER XX

1970—Another new *Ring*

WOLFGANG Wagner gave us another *Ring* for the 1970 season, and this is destined to hold the Bayreuth stage until the centenary year of 1976. Then we are promised a wholly different one. Speculation was rife as to whether that may be a return to Richard Wagner's own original Bayreuth staging, or at least a production in the style of a hundred years ago, or something completely modern. Naturally nothing definite was announced six years in advance, so audiences must wait—enjoying the uncertainty—to know whether the centenary will look back or to the future.

In the meantime we had this new realization of Wolfgang Wagner, and an excellent one it proved. Not wholly new. This is a development of his 1960 staging, based on the same tilted disc which is split into sections to denote the emotional and dramatic upheavals of the saga. Simple, clear-cut, this scenery provides a series of striking stage pictures which enhance the dramatic importance of the characters. For the most part the lighting was admirable: clear enough for the singers' faces to be seen, yet extremely artistic, a visual echo of the music. Only occasionally, as in the first scene of *Siegfried* Act III, were we plunged into the thick darkness of past years.

The new costumes are also mostly excellent, with a few curious exceptions. Why are Wotan's and Fricka's blue *Rheingold* costumes branded with diagonal bars of red and green? Why are the Valkyries, Brünnhilde included, dressed in bell-bottomed, baggy trousers of oriental style, cut short above the ankles? Trousers which seem to induce a pigeon-toed gait, and appear remarkably unpractical either on foot or in the saddle.

Brünnhilde is particularly unlucky about dress. Having been put to sleep in *Walküre* wearing these trousers (they are patterned with a black and white lattice design), she awakes to Siegfried's kiss in a blue trouser suit covered by a green close-fitting maxi coat. Gunther, though richly garbed himself, seems to have been mean to his bride. Brünnhilde had to wear this outfit throughout *Götterdämmerung*, even in the immolation scene.

Most of the audience, I think, hoped that Wolfgang Wagner would allow Wotan and his wife and daughters a change of wardrobe for future years.

One of the most impressive things about this *Ring* was the musical and dramatic polish of the performances in this, their first year. True, I saw the second cycle not the first, bue even so—as I have written earlier—it is very difficult to achieve such a high all-round standard when a complete new *Ring* is staged in a few weeks.

For health reasons Lorin Maazel withdrew from conducting this *Ring*, and Horst Stein took over. He gave us a sound reading, truly Wagnerian, if not altogether inspired. Some of the audience complained that his interpretation lacked the excitement of great climaxes, others that the orchestral playing was too loud. In fact it was a wise, thoughtful, overall conception, generally very considerate to the singers, and there was no lack of majesty in the great music of *Siegfried* and *Götterdämmerung*.

Singing in this, the second cycle, was good. Though only a few of the performances touched greatness a number of the younger singers showed great promise. Theo Adam's Wotan was outstanding (Thomas Stewart sang the role in the first cycle). Adam's voice has always been a most beautiful instrument for this part, though it lacks the full power for the Wanderer's great scene with Erda in *Siegfried*. Now his acting matches the singing: noble and deeply moving, especially in *Die Walküre*.

Berit Lindholm's Brünnhilde has developed. Her singing was true and stylish except for some uncertainty in her awakening scene at the end of *Siegfried*. The voice is powerful but will probably never achieve the roundness and beauty for a great Brünnhilde. Similarly her acting is good, yet she does not quite create the complete character.

Jean Cox was Bayreuth's new Siegfried. He gave us a strong, sympathetic, wholly believable hero. His acting was admirable in both operas. From the musical point of view Cox has a good Siegfried voice and his singing suggests that after another five years he may be outstanding in the role. On this occasion he made the mistake of singing too generously in the first act of *Siegfried* and therefore had little voice left for the final love duet.

Gustav Neidlinger repeated his ageless Alberich. Karl Ridderbusch was a good Hunding, and a really memorable Hagen, dramatic, and splendidly sung with true dark colour and steady as a rock. His Fasolt and Bengt Rundgren's Fafner provided the finest singing in *Rheingold*.

Hermin Esser was an adequate but uninspired Loge; neither his voice nor acting fitted the fire spirit. Janis Martin repeated her Fricka in *Rheingold*, and was an exceptionally good Gutrune. The British singer Anna Reynolds, making her Bayreuth debut, proved a notable Fricka in *Walküre*, beautifully sung, acted with threatening dignity.

Helge Brilioth was on the whole a good Siegmund. Gwyneth Jones's Sieglinde is less good than formerly, her acting has become superficial, and the voice is unsteady when she applies any pressure to it.

The new Mime was Georg Paskuda, ineffective in *Rheingold* but quite the reverse in *Siegfried*, where he gave a most interesting performance, vocally and dramatically. Norman Bailey's Gunther was disappointing, but Erda, that testing role for contraltos, was magnificently sung by Marga Höffgen.

Pierre Boulez returned to conduct *Parsifal*, giving his well known light-footed, technically brilliant reading of the score. Apart from Böhm's *Tristan* this was the conducting tour de force of the festival, and yet—one misses something. The undertones of faith seem lacking.

Franz Crass as Gurnemanz is growing in understanding of this part each year, and the same is true of James King with Parsifal. Thomas Stewart's Amfortas remains the outstanding performance in this cast, though Gerd Nienstedt is now a Klingsor to be reckoned with.

Gwyneth Jones' Kundry gave rise to considerable anxiety on behalf of this singer. Potentially this was, and still can be, one of the most beautiful dramatic soprano voices on the operatic stage today. But her 1970 performances at Bayreuth and elsewhere have all too often given evidence of over-singing. Her soft singing can still be exquisite, but the full voice spreads sadly.

This, the twentieth year of Wieland Wagner's *Parsifal* production, retains much of its old beauty, especially in the opening of the first act, and the Good Friday scene: beautiful lighting and inspired movements and grouping. Yet one becomes conscious that before long a new realization must come, be it better or worse. This production is scheduled again for 1971. Peter Lehmann has done fine work in keeping Wieland's conception alive, but the master touch is now lacking.

August Everding's *Fliegende Holländer* returned with Silvio Varviso conducting as in 1969. Again it proved one of the season's most enjoyable performances. Indeed one Bayreuth newcomer found it the most wholly satisfying of them all, though he did not see the *Tristan*. This may seem a rather heretical comment, since this *Holländer* is the only production by neither Wieland nor Wolfgang Wagner, but it is of interest.

Donald McIntyre again sang the Holländer with vocal and dramatic artistry. Martti Talvela's Daland was near perfect. René Kollo (last year's Steersman) was the Erik, and in this role gave us some of the most exquisite lyric singing of the festival, with enough dramatic timbre to fulfil the needs of the part.

Gwyneth Jones was in good voice at the performance I saw, but the romantic little girl which she now makes of Senta almost unbalanced the drama.

Wolfgang Wagner's *Meistersinger* production returned with a new conductor: Hans Wallat. He gave a sound if rather unexciting performance. Norman Bailey's Hans Sachs and Karl Ridderbusch's Pogner had grown in artistic stature. Thomas Hemsley repeated his subtle Beckmesser. Hermin Esser's David and Ernst Kozub's Stolzing were adequate but not memorable. Janis Martin, previously an excellent Magdalene, became this year's Eva: graceful, attractive, well sung, but just lacking the ideal radiance. Bengt Rundgren's beautiful voice was ideally suited to the haunting magic of the Nightwatchman's music. Here, as elsewhere throughout the operas, Wilhelm Pitz's superb training of the chorus was manifest.

A full year in advance, 1970 was announced as the last season of Wieland Wagner's 1962 *Tristan* production, with its three great protagonists from the first year: Karl Böhm conducting, Birgit Nilsson as Isolde and Wolfgang Windgassen as Tristan. There were only three performances during the festival. All tickets were sold out immediately booking opened the previous autumn, and the demand for returned tickets became hysterical. It was said that 500 DM were being offered for a single seat at the second performance which I attended. Many people haunted the box office all day for days beforehand, often with placards round their necks "Suche *Tristan*" (searching for *Tristan*). One lady at *Götterdämmerung,* the night before, wore her placard throughout the performance.

The frenzy was justified. Böhm conducted perhaps more superbly than ever before at Bayreuth. He spun the love music like ethereal silk and evoked all the anguish of the tragedy. Birgit Nilsson was in exquisite voice, with no hardness to mar the brilliance. Her acting too was magnificent, matching Wolfgang Windgassen's profoundly moving Tristan. Their supporters were all inspired too. Grace Hoffman sang Brangäne with rare beauty. Gustav Neidlinger gave one of the best Kurwenal performances I can remember, and Franz Crass, replacing the indisposed Talvela, made a really moving King Marke.

At the end I stayed for thirty-one curtain calls, and the house was still cheering and stamping when I left.

All in all it was a fine festival. Not one of the productions was even a near failure. All were scenically interesting and musically rewarding. Wolfgang Wagner had remained true to his word: there was no sensationalism.

Much the same might be said about the weather, though it did not

achieve quite the high standard of the operas. The extreme heat of
1969 was not repeated, but there were some lovely hot sunny days
and balmy nights when the audiences appeared at their colourful best,
the lights in the gardens twinkled, and the air was soft. Such a one was
my *Tristan* evening. On the other hand there were a few wet, dreary
days, and far too many when sun and rain diced with each other for
an hour's mastery, and an umbrella was one's constant companion.

On one of the lovely mornings a new Bayreuth friend led me to the
top of the Siegesturm for the first time in my nineteen years of Bayreuth festivals. This is a memorial look-out tower standing on a hilltop
swathed in woods immediately above the Festspielhaus, from which
it is little more than fifteen minutes' walk. The view from the top is
worth the climb, and the woods and field paths below might be many
miles from any town. Even the wild raspberries had not been picked.
They are most refreshing during earnest and enthusiastic discussion of
Wagner and his interpreters.

Discussion there will always be, especially at Bayreuth. At the
moment a large question mark still hangs over the future. At the 1970
press conference the Bürgermeister announced that from 1976—the
centenary of Richard Wagner's first festival and opening of the
Festspielhaus—the state will take over financial responsibility for the
festivals and for Wagner's house Wahnfried, which is to contain
Wagnerian archives. On the same occasion Wolfgang Wagner remarked
that he would not like to continue quite alone as the head of the whole
organization.

Both these statements are intentionally vague. From the first we
know that future festivals will be financially safe. Details have yet to be
worked out, but the Bürgermeister stated that the Wagner family will
remain in full control. Whether Wolfgang Wagner's remark was an
intimation of some division of administrative or artistic responsibility
in the future remains to be seen.

From the fact that the Everding/Svoboda *Holländer* is still the only
wholly "outside" production since 1951, and that there will be no
fresh production in 1971, one may infer that Wolfgang Wagner has not
yet fully decided on his future course. In the meantime we can safely
look forward to a continuation of Bayreuth festivals, whatever ideas
they may embody.

At each new operagoers will gather, old ones return. The fanfares
will sound again, calling the fathful and fortunate to Richard Wagner's
Festspielhaus. The performances they will see and hear are still unborn,
for one of the wonders of opera is that every performance is in itself a
new joint creation in which the audience is a partner. No one can
forecast exactly when and where the merely good will take wings and

soar to the sublime, or of course the reverse may happen and the performance stumble into the bog of failure. But it will be Bayreuth—New Bayreuth—where people come from all over the world to find in Wagner's music what many factions of modern life deny—the voice and beauty of eternity.

Errata

Descriptions of the festival restaurants given on pages 15 and 75 are now out of date. Details of the current restaurants are given at the beginning of Chapter XIX.

The Margraves' Operahouse is now seldom used for recitals (p. 47), the modern Stadthalle has become the normal concert venue.

Page 97.   Gutrune's solo was restored in 1967, not 1966.

Page 102.   Birgit Nilsson sang Brünnhilde only in the first *Ring* cycle.

Page 110.   Five, not four, different singers appeared as Lohengrin in 1967.

Page 111.   The *Ring* performances referred to here were the third, not the second cycle.

Page 118.   Theo Adam did not, in fact, sing Sachs in every *Meistersinger* performance in 1968. Gustav Neidlinger also appeared in the role.

Bayreuth Festivals 1951-1970

1951

(July 29—August 26)

Ninth Symphony by Ludwig van Beethoven
Conductor: Wilhelm Furtwängler
Soloists: Elisabeth Schwarzkopf, Elisabeth Höngen,
Hans Hopf, Otto Edelmann
Chorusmaster: Wilhelm Pitz

Parsifal
Conductor: Hans Knappertsbusch
Production and Decor: Wieland Wagner
Chorusmaster: Wilhelm Pitz
Choreography: Gertrud Wagner

Amfortas: George London	1st Knight: Walter Fritz
Titurel: Arnold van Mill	2nd Knight: Werner Faulhaber
Gurnemanz: Ludwig Weber	1st Esquire: Hanna Ludwig
Parsifal: Wolfgang Windgassen	2nd Esquire Elfriede Wild
Klingsor: Hermann Uhde	3rd Esquire: Günter Baldauf
Kundry: Martha Mödl	4th Esquire: Gerhard Stolze

Flowermaidens: Lore Wissmann, Erika Zimmermann, Hanna Ludwig, Paula
Brivkalne, Maria Lacorn, Elfriede Wild

Der Ring des Nibelungen
Conductor: Hans Knappertsbusch/Herbert von Karajan
Production and Decor: Wieland Wagner

Das Rheingold

Wotan: Sigurd Björling	Mime: Paul Kuën
Donner: Werner Faulhaber	Fasolt: Ludwig Weber
Froh: Wolfgang Windgassen	Fafner: Friedrich Dalberg
Loge: Walter Fritz	Erda: Ruth Siewert
Fricka: Elisabeth Höngen/	Woglinde: Elisabeth Schwarzkopf
Ira Malaniuk	Wellgunde: Lore Wissman
Freia: Paula Brivkalne	Flosshilde: Herta Töpper
Alberich: Heinrich Pflanzl	

Die Walküre

Siegmund: Günther Treptow
Hunding: Arnold van Mill
Wotan: Sigurd Björling
Sieglinde: Leonie Rysanek
Brünnhilde: Astrid Varnay
Fricka: Elisabeth Höngen
Gerhilde: Brünnhild Friedland

Ortlinde: Eleanor Lausch
Waltraute: Elfriede Wild
Schwertleite: Ruth Siewert
Helmwige: Lieselotte Thomamüller
Siegrune: Herta Töpper
Grimgerde: Ira Malaniuk
Rossweisse: Hanna Ludwig

Siegfried

Siegfried: Bernd Aldenhoff
Mime: Paul Kuën
Wanderer: Sigurd Björling
Alberich: Heinrich Pflanzl

Fafner: Friedrich Dalberg
Brünnhilde: Astrid Varnay
Erda: Ruth Siewert
Woodbird: Wilma Lipp

Götterdämmerung

Siegfried: Bernd Aldenhoff
Gunther: Hermann Uhde
Hagen: Ludwig Weber
Alberich: Heinrich Pflanzl
Brünnhilde: Astrid Varnay
Gutrune: Martha Mödl
Waltraute: Elisabeth Höngen/
    Ruth Siewert

1st Norn: Ruth Siewert
2nd Norn: Ira Malaniuk
3rd Norn: Martha Mödl
Woglinde: Elisabeth Schwarzkopf
Wellgunde: Hanna Ludwig
Flosshilde: Herta Töpper

Chorusmaster: Wilhelm Pitz

Die Meistersinger von Nürnberg
Conductor: Herbert von Karajan
Production: Rudolf Hartmann
Decor: Hans Reissinger
Chorusmaster: Wilhelm Pitz

Hans Sachs: Otto Edelmann/
    Hermann Rohrbach
Veit Pogner: Friedrich Dalberg
Sixtus Beckmesser: Erich Kunz/
    Heinrich Pflanzl
Fritz Kothner: Rudolf Grossmann
    Heinrich Pflanzl
Walther von Stolzing: Hans Hopf
David: Gerhard Unger
Eva: Elisabeth Schwarzkopf

Magdalene: Ira Malaniuk
Kunz Vogelgesang: Erich Majkut
Konrad Nachtigall: Hans Berg
Balthasar Zorn: Josef Janko
Ulrich Eisslinger: Karl Mikorey
Augustin Moser: Gerhard Stolze
Hermann Ortel: Heinz Tandler
Hans Foltz: Arnold van Mill
Nightwatchman: Werner Faulhaber

1952
(July 23—August 25)

Tristan und Isolde
Conductor: Herbert von Karajan
Production and Decor: Wieland Wagner
Chorusmaster: Wilhelm Pitz

Tristan: Ramon Vinay
Isolde: Martha Mödl/
    Astrid Varnay
King Marke: Ludwig Weber
Kurwenal: Hans Hotter/
    Gustav Neidlinger

Brangäne: Ira Malaniuk
Melot: Hermann Uhde
Shepherd: Gerhard Stolze
Steersman: Werner Faulhaber
Seaman: Gerhard Unger

Der Ring des Nibelungen
Conductor: Joseph Keilberth
Production and Decor: Wieland Wagner

Das Rheingold

Wotan: Hermann Uhde
Donner: Werner Faulhaber
Froh: Wolfgang Windgassen
Loge: Erich Witte
Fricka: Ira Malaniuk
Freia: Inge Borkh
Alberich: Gustav Neidlinger

Mime: Paul Kuën
Fasolt: Ludwig Weber
Fafner: Josef Greindl
Erda: Melanie Bugarinovic
Woglinde: Erika Zimmerman
Wellgunde: Hanna Ludwig
Flosshilde: Herta Töpper

Die Walküre

Siegmund: Günther Treptow
Hunding: Josef Greindl
Wotan: Hans Hotter
Sieglinde: Inge Borkh
Brünnhilde: Astrid Varnay
Fricka: Ruth Siewert
Gerhilde: Irmgard Meinig

Ortlinde: Paula Brivkalne
Waltraute: Hanna Ludwig
Schwertleite: Ruth Siewert
Helmwige: Liselotte Thomamüller
Siegrune: Herta Töpper
Grimgerde: Melanie Burgarinovic
Rossweisse: Trude Roesler

Siegfried

Siegfried: Bernd Aldenhoff
Mime: Paul Kuën
Wanderer: Hans Hotter
Alberich: Gustav Neidlinger

Fafner: Kurt Böhme
Erda: Melanie Bugarinovic
Brünnhilde: Astrid Varnay
Woodbird: Rita Streich

Götterdämmerung

Siegfried: Max Lorenz
Gunther: Hermann Uhde
Hagen: Josef Greindl
Alberich: Gustav Neidlinger
Brünnhilde: Astrid Varnay
Gutrune: Martha Mödl
Waltraute: Ruth Siewert

1st Norn: Ruth Siewert
2nd Norn: Melanie Bugarinovic
3rd Norn: Martha Mödl/
Herta Töpper
Woglinde: Erika Zimmermann
Wellgunde: Hanna Ludwig
Flosshilde: Herta Töpper

Chorusmaster: Wilhelm Pitz

Die Meistersinger von Nürnberg
Conductor: Hans Knappertsbusch
Production: Rudolf Hartmann
Decor: Hans Reissinger
Chorusmaster: Wilhelm Pitz

Hans Sachs: Otto Edelmann
Veit Pogner: Kurt Böhme/
Ludwig Weber
Sixtus Beckmesser: Heinrich Pflanzl
Fritz Kothner: Werner Faulhaber
Walther von Stolzing: Hans Hopf
David: Gerhard Unger
Eva: Lisa della Casa/
Trude Eipperle
Magdalene: Ira Malaniuk

Kunz Vogelgesang: Karl Terkal
Konrad Nachtigall: Walter Stoll
Balthasar Zorn: Josef Janko
Ulrich Eisslinger: Karl Mikorey
Augustin Moser: Gerhard Stolze
Hermann Ortel: Theo Adam
Hans Schwarz: Heinz Borst
Hans Foltz: Max Kohl
Nightwatchman: Gustav Neidlinger

Parsifal

Conductor: Hans Knappertsbusch
Production and Decor: Wieland Wagner
Chorusmaster: Wilhelm Pitz
Choreography: Gertrud Wagner

Amfortas: George London
Titurel: Kurt Böhme/
    Josef Greindl
Gurnemanz: Ludwig Weber
Parsifal: Wolfgang Windgassen
Klingsor: Kurt Böhme/
    Hermann Uhde

Kundry: Martha Mödl
1st Knight: Karl Terkal
2nd Knight: Werner Faulhaber
1st Esquire: Hanna Ludwig
2nd Esquire: Herta Töpper
3rd Esquire: Gerhard Unger
4th Esquire: Gerhard Stolze

Flowermaidens: Lore Wissmann, Erika Zimmermann, Hanna Ludwig, Paula Brivkalne, Maria Lacorn, Herta Töpper

1953
(July 23—August 23)

Lohengrin

Conductor: Joseph Keilberth
Production and Decor: Wolfgang Wagner
Chorusmaster: Wilhelm Pitz

King Heinrich: Josef Greindl
Lohengrin: Wolfgang Windgassen
Elsa: Eleanor Steber
Gottfried, her brother:
    Gerold Weber
Telramund: Hermann Uhde
Ortrud: Astrid Varnay
Herald: Hans Braun

Four nobles: Gerhard Stolze
Josef Janko
Alfons Herwig
Theo Adam
Four Pages: Lotte Kiefer
Gerda Grasser
Erika Eskelsen
Roswitha Burrow

Parsifal

Conductor: Clemens Krauss
Production and Decor: Wieland Wagner
Chorusmaster: Wilhelm Pitz
Choreography: Gertrud Wagner

Amfortas: George London/
    Hans Hotter
Titurel: Josef Greindl
Gurnemanz: Ludwig Weber
Parsifal: Ramon Vinay/
    Wolfgang Windgassen
Klingsor: Hermann Uhde
Kundry: Martha Mödl

1st Knight: Gene Tobin
2nd Knight: Theo Adam
1st Esquire: Hetty Plümacher
2nd Esquire: Gisela Litz
3rd Esquire: Gerhard Stolze
4th Esquire: Hugo Kratz
Alto Solo: Maria von Ilosvay

Flowermaidens: Rita Streich, Erika Zimmermann, Hetty Plümacher, Anna Tassopulos, Gerda Wismar, Gisela Litz.

Der Ring des Nibelungen
Conductor: Joseph Keilberth/Clemens Krauss
Production and Decor: Wieland Wagner

Das Rheingold

Wotan: Hans Hotter
Donner: Hermann Uhde
Froh: Gerhard Stolze
Loge: Erich Witte
Fricka: Ira Malaniuk
Freia: Bruni Falcon
Alberich: Gustav Neidlinger

Mime: Paul Küen
Fasolt: Ludwig Weber
Hunding: Josef Greindl
Erda: Maria von Ilosvay
Woglinde: Erika Zimmermann
Wellgunde: Hetty Plümacher
Flosshilde: Gisela Litz

Die Walküre

Siegmund: Ramon Vinay
Hunding: Josef Greindl
Wotan: Hans Hotter
Sieglinde: Regina Resnik
Brünnhilde: Martha Mödl/
      Astrid Varnay
Fricka: Ira Malaniuk
Gerhilde: Brünnhild Friedland

Ortlinde: Bruni Falcon
Waltraute: Ise Sorrell
Schwertleite: Maria von Ilosvay
Helmwige: Liselotte Thomamüller
Siegrune: Gisela Litz
Grimgerde: Sibylla Plate
Rossweisse: Erika Schubert

Siegfried

Siegfried: Wolfgang Windgassen
Mime: Paul Küen
Wanderer: Hans Hotter
Alberich: Gustav Neidlinger
Fafner: Josef Greindl

Erda: Maria von Ilosvay
Brünnhilde: Martha Mödl/
      Astrid Varnay
Woodbird: Rita Streich

Götterdämmerung

Siegfried: Wolfgang Windgassen
Gunther: Hermann Uhde
Hagen: Josef Greindl
Alberich: Gustav Neidlinger
Brünnhilde: Martha Mödl/
      Astrid Varnay
Gutrune: Natalie Hinsch-Gröndahl

Waltraute: Ira Malaniuk
1st Norn: Maria von Ilosvay
2nd Norn: Ira Malaniuk
3rd Norn: Regina Resnik
Woglinde: Erika Zimmermann
Wellgunde: Hetty Plümacher
Flosshilde: Gisela Litz

Chorusmaster: Wilhelm Pitz

Tristan und Isolde

Conductor: Eugen Jochum
Production and Decor: Wieland Wagner
Chorusmaster: Wilhelm Pitz

Tristan: Ramon Vinay
Isolde: Astrid Varnay/
      Martha Mödl
King Marke: Ludwig Weber
Kurwenal: Gustav Neidlinger

Melot: Hasso Eschert
Brangäne: Ira Malaniuk
Shepherd: Gerhard Stolze
Steersman: Theo Adam
Seaman: Gene Tobin

Ninth Symphony by Ludwig van Beethoven

Conductor: Paul Hindemith
Soloists: Birgit Nilsson, Ira Malaniuk,
      Anton Dermota, Ludwig Weber
Chorusmaster: Wilhelm Pitz

L

1954
(July 22—August 22)

Tannhäuser
Conductor: Joseph Keilberth/Eugen Jochum
Production and Decor: Wieland Wagner
Chorusmaster: Wilhelm Pitz
Choreography: Gertrud Wagner

Tannhäuser: Ramon Vinay
Elisabeth: Grë Brouwenstijn
Venus: Herta Wilfert
Landgrave: Josef Greindl
Wolfram von Eschenbach:
    Dietrich Fischer-Dieskau

Walther von der Vogelweide:
    Josef Traxel
Biterolf: Toni Blankenheim
Heinrich der Schreiber:
    Gerhard Stolze
Reinmar von Zweter: Theo Adam
Young shepherd: Volker Horn

Lohengrin
Conductor: Eugen Jochum/Joseph Keilberth
Production and Decor: Wolfgang Wagner
Chorusmaster: Wilhelm Pitz

King Heinrich: Josef Greindl/
    Theo Adam/
    Ludwig Weber
Lohengrin: Wolfgang Windgassen
Elsa: Birgit Nilsson
Gottfried, her brother:
    Gerold Weber
Telramund: Hermann Uhde
Ortrud: Astrid Varnay

Herald: Dietrich Fischer-Dieskau
Four nobles: Gerhard Stolze
    Gene Tobin
    Toni Blankenheim
    Theo Adam
Four pages: Lotte Kiefer
    Gerda Grasser
    Erika Eskelsen
    Roswitha Burrow

Der Ring des Nibelungen
Conductor: Joseph Keilberth
Production and Decor: Wieland Wagner

Das Rheingold
Wotan: Hans Hotter
Donner: Toni Blankenheim
Froh: Josef Traxel
Loge: Rudolf Lustig
Fricka: Georgine von Milinkovic
Freia: Herta Wilfert
Alberich: Gustav Neidlinger
Mime: Paul Kuën

Fasolt: Theo Adam/
    Ludwig Weber
Fafner: Josef Greindl
Erda: Maria von Ilosvay
Woglinde: Erika Zimmermann
Wellgunde: Hetty Plümacher
Flosshilde: Gisela Litz

Die Walküre
Siegmund: Max Lorenz
Hunding: Josef Greindl
Wotan: Hans Hotter
Sieglinde: Martha Mödl/
    Astrid Varnay
Brünnhilde: Astrid Varnay/
    Martha Mödl
Fricka: Georgine von Milinkovic
Gerhilde: Herta Wilfert

Ortlinde: Birgit Nilsson
Waltraute: Elisabeth Schärtel
Schwertleite: Maria von Ilosvay
Helmwige: Hilde Scheppan
Siegrune: Gisela Litz
Grimgerde:
    Georgine von Milinkovic
Rossweise: Hetty Plümacher

Siegfried

Siegfried: Wolfgang Windgassen
Mime: Paul Kuën
Wanderer: Hans Hotter
Alberich: Gustav Neidlinger
Fafner: Josef Greindl

Brünnhilde: Astrid Varnay/
    Martha Mödl
Erda: Maria von Ilosvay
Woodbird: Ilse Hollweg

Götterdämmerung

Siegfried: Wolfgang Windgassen
Gunther: Hermann Uhde
Hagen: Josef Greindl
Alberich: Gustav Neidlinger
Brünnhilde: Astrid Varnay/
    Martha Mödl
Gutrune: Martha Mödl/
    Astrid Varnay

Waltraute: Maria von Ilosvay
1st Norn: Maria von Ilosvay
2nd Norn: Georgine von Milinkovic
3rn Norn: Mina Bolotine
Woglinde: Erika Zimmermann
Wellgunde: Hetty Plümacher
Flosshilde: Gisela Litz

Chorusmaster: Wilhelm Pitz

Parsifal

Conductor: Hans Knappertsbusch
Production and Decor: Wieland Wagner
Chorusmaster: Wilhelm Pitz
Choreography: Gertrud Wagner

Amfortas: Hans Hotter
Titurel: Theo Adam/
    Josef Greindl
Gurnemanz: Josef Greindl/
    Ludwig Weber
Parsifal: Wolfgang Windgassen
Klingsor: Gustav Neidlinger
Kundry: Martha Mödl

1st Knight: Gene Tobin
2nd Knight: Theo Adam
1st Esquire: Hetty Plümacher
2nd Esquire Gisela Litz
3rd Esquire: Gerhard Stolze
4th Esquire: Hugo Kratz
Alto Solo: Hetty Plümacher

Flowermaidens: Ilse Hollweg, Friedl Pöltinger, Hetty Plümacher, Dorothea Siebert, Jutta Vulpius, Gisela Litz

Ninth Symphony by Ludwig van Beethoven
Conductor: Wilhelm Furtwängler
Soloists: Gré Brouwenstijn, Ira Malaniuk,
    Wolfgang Windgassen, Ludwig Weber
Chorusmaster: Wilhelm Pitz

1955
(July 22—August 21)

Der Fliegende Holländer
Conductor: Hans Knappertsbusch/Joseph Keilberth
Production and Decor: Wolfgang Wagner
Chorusmaster: Wilhelm Pitz

Daland: Ludwig Weber
Holländer: Hermann Uhde/
    Hans Hotter
Senta: Astrid Varnay

Mary: Elisabeth Schärtel
Erik: Wolfgang Windgassen/
    Rudolf Lustig
Steersman: Josef Traxel

Tannhäuser

Conductor: André Cluytens/Joseph Keilberth
Production and Decor: Wieland Wagner
Chorusmaster: Wilhelm Pitz
Choreography: Gertrud Wagner

Tannhäuser: Wolfgang Windgassen
Elisabeth: Gré Brouwenstijn
Venus: Herta Wilfert
Landgrave: Josef Greindl
Wolfram von Eschenbach:
    Dietrich Fischer-Dieskau
Walther von der Vogelweide:
    Josef Traxel

Biterolf: Toni Blankenheim
Heinrich der Schreiber:
    Gerhard Stolze
Reinmar von Zweter:
    Alfons Herwig
Young shepherd: Volker Horn

Der Ring des Nibelungen

Conductor: Joseph Keilberth
Production and Decor: Wieland Wagner

Das Rheingold

Wotan: Hans Hotter
Donner: Toni Blankenheim
Froh: Josef Traxel
Loge: Rudolf Lustig
Fricka: Georgine von Milinkovic
Freia: Herta Wilfert
Alberich: Gustav Neidlinger

Mime: Paul Kuën
Fasolt: Ludwig Weber
Fafner: Josef Greindl
Erda: Maria von Ilosvay
Woglinde: Jutta Vulpius
Wellgunde: Elisabeth Schärtel
Flosshilde: Maria Graf

Die Walküre

Siegmund: Ramon Vinay
Hunding: Josef Greindl
Wotan: Hans Hotter
Sieglinde: Gré Brouwenstijn
Brünnhilde: Astrid Varnay/
    Martha Mödl
Fricka: Georgine von Milinkovic
Gerhilde: Herta Wilfert

Ortlinde: Gerda Lammers
Waltraute: Elisabeth Schärtel
Schwertleite: Maria von Ilosvay
Helmwige: Hilde Scheppan
Siegrune: Jean Watson
Grimgerde:
    Georgine von Milinkovic
Rossweisse: Maria Graf

Siegfried

Siegfried: Wolfgang Windgassen
Mime: Paul Kuën
Wanderer: Hans Hotter
Alberich: Gustav Neidlinger
Fafner: Josef Greindl

Brünnhilde: Astrid Varnay/
    Martha Mödl
Erda: Maria von Ilosvay
Woodbird: Ilse Hollweg

Götterdämmerung

Siegfried: Wolfgang Windgassen
Gunther: Hermann Uhde/
    Hans Hotter
Hagen: Josef Greindl
Alberich: Gustav Neidlinger
Brünnhilde: Astrid Varnay/
    Martha Mödl
Gutrune: Gré Brouwenstijn

Waltraute: Maria von Ilosvay
1st Norn: Maria von Ilosvay
2nd Norn: Georgine von Milinkovic
3rd Norn: Mina Bolotine/
    Astrid Varnay
Woglinde: Jutta Meyfarth
Wellgunde: Elisabeth Schärtel
Flosshilde: Maria Graf

Chorusmaster: Wilhelm Pitz

Parsifal
Conductor: Hans Knappertsbusch
Production and Decor: Wieland Wagner
Chorusmaster: Wilhelm Pitz
Choreography: Gertrud Wagner

Amfortas:
   Dietrich Fischer-Dieskau/
   Hans Hotter
Titurel: Josef Greindl/
   Hermann Uhde/
   Ludwig Weber
Gurnemanz: Ludwig Weber
   Josef Greindl
Parsifal: Ramon Vinay

Klingsor: Gustav Neidlinger
Kundry: Martha Mödl
1st Knight: Josef Traxel
2nd Knight: Alfons Herwig
1st Esquire: Paula Lenchner
2nd Esquire: Elisabeth Schärtel
3rd Esquire: Gerhard Stolze
4th Esquire: Alfred Pfeifle

Flowermaidens: Ilse Hollweg, Friedl Pöltinger, Paula Lenchner, Dorothea Siebert, Jutta Vulpius, Elisabeth Schärtel

1956
(July 24—August 25)

Die Meistersinger von Nürnberg
Conductor: André Cluytens
Production and Decor: Wieland Wagner
Chorusmaster: Wilhelm Pitz

Hans Sachs: Hans Hotter/
   Gustav Neidlinger
Veit Pogner: Josef Greindl
Sixtus Beckmesser:
   Karl Schmitt-Walter/
   Toni Blankenheim
Fritz Kothner:
   Dietrich Fischer-Dieskau/
   Kurt Rehm
Walther von Stolzing:
   Wolfgang Windgassen
David: Gerhard Stolze
Eva: Gré Brouwenstijn/
   Lore Wissmann

Magdalene:
   Georgine von Milinkovic
Kunz Vogelgesang: Josef Traxel
Konrad Nachtigall: Egmont Koch
Balthasar Zorn:
   Heinz-Günther Zimmermann
Ulrich Eisslinger: Erich Benke
Augustin Moser: Josef Janko
Hermann Ortel: Hans Habietinek
Hans Schwarz: Alexander Fenyves
Hans Foltz: Eugen Fuchs
Nightwatchman: Alfons Herwig

Der Fliegende Holländer
Conductor: Joseph Keilberth
Production and Decor: Wolfgang Wagner
Chorusmaster: Wilhelm Pitz

Daland: Arnold van Mill/
   Ludwig Weber
Holländer: George London/
   Hermann Uhde/
   Paul Schöffler

Senta: Astrid Varnay
Mary: Elisabeth Schärtel
Erik: Josef Traxel
Steersman: Jean Cox

Parsifal

Conductor: Hans Knappertsbusch
Production and Decor: Wieland Wagner
Chorusmaster: Wilhelm Pitz
Choreography: Gertrud Wagner

Amfortas: Dietrich Fischer-Dieskau	Kundry: Martha Mödl/
Titurel: Arnold van Mill/	Astrid Varnay
Hans Hotter	1st Knight: Josef Traxel
Gurnemanz: Ludwig Weber/	2nd Knight: Alfons Herwig
Josef Greindl	1st Esquire: Paula Lenchner
Parsifal: Ramon Vinay/	2nd Esquire: Elisabeth Schärtel
Klingsor: Gustav Neidlinger/	3rd Esquire: Gerhard Stolze
Toni Blankenheim	4th Esquire: Alfred Pfeifle

Flowermaidens: Ilse Hollweg, Friedl Pöltinger, Paula Lenchner, Dorothea Siebert, Jutta Vulpius, Elisabeth Schärtel.

Der Ring des Nibelungen

Conductor: Joseph Keilberth/ Hans Knappertsbusch
Production and Decor: Wieland Wagner

Das Rheingold

Wotan: Hans Hotter	Fasolt: Josef Greindl
Donner: Alfons Herwig	Fafner: Arnold van Mill
Froh: Josef Traxel	Erda: Maria von Ilosvay/
Loge: Ludwig Suthaus	Jean Madeira
Fricka: Georgine von Milinkovic	Woglinde: Lore Wissmann
Freia: Gré Brouwenstijn	Wellgunde: Paula Lenchner
Alberich: Gustav Neidlinger	Flosshilde: Maria von Ilosvay
Mime: Paul Kuën	

Die Walküre

Siegmund: Ramon Vinay/	Ortlinde: Gerda Lammers
Wolfgang Windgassen	Waltraute: Elisabeth Schärtel
Hunding: Josef Greindl	Schwertleite: Marion von Ilosvay
Wotan: Hans Hotter	Helmwige: Hilde Scheppan
Sieglinde: Gré Brouwenstijn	Siegrune: Luisecharlotte Kamps
Brünnhilde: Martha Mödl/	Grimgerde:
Astrid Varnay	Georgine von Milinkovic
Fricka: Georgine von Milinkovic	Rossweisse: Jean Madeira
Gerhilde: Paula Lenchner	

Siegfried

Siegfried: Wolfgang Windgassen	Brünnhilde: Martha Mödl/
Mime: Paul Kuën	Astrid Varnay
Wanderer: Hans Hotter	Erda: Maria von Ilosvay/
Alberich: Gustav Neidlinger	Jean Madeira
Fafner: Arnold van Mill	Woodbird: Ilse Hollweg

Götterdämmerung

Siegfried : Wolfgang Windgassen	1st Norn: Jean Madeira
Gunther: Hermann Uhde	2nd Norn: Maria von Ilosvay
Hagen: Josef Greindl	3rd Norn: Astrid Varnay/
Alberich: Gustav Neidlinger	Martha Mödl
Brünnhilde: Martha Mödl/	Woglinde: Lore Wissmann
Astrid Varnay	Wellgunde: Paula Lenchner
Gutrune: Gré Brouwenstijn	Flosshilde: Maria von Ilosvay
Waltraute: Maria von Ilosvay/	
Jean Madeira	

Chorusmaster: Wilhelm Pitz

1957
(July 23—August 25)

Tristan und Isolde
Conductor: Wolfgang Sawallisch
Production and Decor: Wolfgang Wagner
Chorusmaster: Wilhelm Pitz

Tristan: Wolfgang Windgassen
Isolde: Birgit Nilsson
King Marke: Arnold van Mill
Kurwenal: Hans Hotter/
    Gustav Neidlinger
Brangäne: Grace Hoffman

Melot: Fritz Uhl
Shepherd: Hermann Winkler
Steersman: Egmont Koch
Seaman: Walter Geisler/
    Josef Traxel

Die Meistersinger von Nürnberg
Conductor: André Cluytens
Production and Decor: Wieland Wagner
Chorusmaster: Wilhelm Pitz

Hans Sachs: Gustav Neidlinger/
    Otto Wiener
Veit Pogner: Gottlob Frick/
    Josef Greindl
Sixtus Beckmesser:
    Karl Schmitt-Walter
Fritz Kothner: Toni Blankenheim
Walther von Stolzing:
    Walter Geisler/
    Josef Traxel/
    Wolfgang Windgassen
David: Gerhard Stolze

Eva: Elisabeth Grümmer/
    Sena Jurinac
Magdalene:
    Georgine von Milinkovic
Kunz Vogelgesang: Fritz Uhl
Konrad Nachtigall: Egmont Koch
Balthasar Zorn:
    Heinz-Günther Zimmermann
Ulrich Eisslinger: Erich Benke
Augustin Moser: Hermann Winkler
Hermann Ortel: Hans Habietinek
Hans Schwarz: Alexander Fenyves
Hans Foltz: Eugen Fuchs
Nightwatchman: Arnold van Mill

Parsifal
Conductor: André Cluytens/Hans Knappertsbusch
Production and Decor: Wieland Wagner
Chorusmaster: Wilhelm Pitz
Choreography: Gertrud Wagner

Amfortas: George London
Titurel: Arnold van Mill
Gurnemanz: Josef Greindl
Parsifal: Ramon Vinay
Klingsor: Toni Blankenheim
Kundry: Astrid Varnay/
    Martha Mödl

1st Knight: Walter Geisler
2nd Knight: Otto Wiener
1st Esquire: Paula Lenchner
2nd Esquire: Elisabeth Schärtel
3rd Esquire: Gerhard Stolze
4th Esquire: Hans Krotthammer
Alto Solo: Georgine von Milinkovic

Flowermaidens: Ilse Hollweg, Friedl Pöltinger, Paula Lenchner, Dorothea Siebert, Lotte Rysanek, Elisabeth Schärtel

Der Ring des Nibelungen
Conductor: Hans Knappertsbusch
Production and Decor: Wieland Wagner

Das Rheingold

Wotan: Hans Hotter
Donner: Toni Blankenheim
Froh: Josef Traxel
Loge: Ludwig Suthaus
Fricka: Georgine von Milinkovic
Freia: Elisabeth Grümmer
Alberich: Gustav Neidlinger

Mime: Gerhard Stolze
Fasolt: Arnold van Mill
Fafner: Josef Greindl
Erda: Maria von Ilosvay
Woglinde: Dorothea Siebert
Wellgunde: Paula Lenchner
Flosshilde: Elisabeth Schärtel

Die Walküre

Siegmund: Ludwig Suthaus/
    Ramon Vinay
Hunding: Josef Greindl
Wotan: Hans Hotter
Sieglinde: Birgit Nilsson
Brünnhilde: Astrid Varnay
Fricka: Georgine von Milinkovic
Gerhilde: Paula Lenchner

Ortlinde: Gerda Lammers
Waltraute: Elisabeth Schärtel
Schwertleite: Maria von Ilosvay
Helmwige: Hilde Scheppan
Siegrune: Helena Bader
Grimgerde:
   Georgine von Milinkovic
Rossweisse: Hetty Plümacher

Siegfried

Siegfried: Wolfgang Windgassen/
    Bernd Aldenhoff
Mime: Paul Kuën
Wanderer: Hans Hotter
Alberich: Gustav Neidlinger

Fafner: Josef Greindl
Brünnhilde: Astrid Varnay
Erda: Maria von Ilosvay
Woodbird: Ilse Hollweg

Götterdämmerung

Siegfried: Wolfgang Windgassen/
    Bernd Aldenhoff
Gunther: Hermann Uhde
Hagen: Josef Greindl
Alberich: Gustav Neidlinger
Brünnhilde: Astrid Varnay
Gutrune: Elisabeth Grümmer
Waltraute: Maria von Ilosvay

1st Norn: Maria von Ilosvay
2nd Norn:
   Georgine von Milinkovic/
    Elisabeth Schärtel
3rd Norn: Birgit Nilsson
Woglinde: Dorothea Siebert
Wellgrunde: Paula Lenchner
Flosshilde: Elizabeth Schärtel

Chorusmaster: Wilhelm Pitz

1958
(July 23—August 25)

Lohengrin

Conductor: André Cluytens
Production and Decor: Wieland Wagner
Chorusmaster: Wilhelm Pitz

King Heinrich: Kieth Engen
Lohengrin: Sándor Kónya
Elsa: Leonie Rysanek
Telramund: Ernest Blanc
Ortrud: Astrid Varnay
Herald: Erik Saedén/
   Eberhard Waechter
Four nobles: Gerhard Stolze
   Heinz-Günther
    Zimmermann

    Gotthard Kronstein
    Egmont Koch
Four pages: Elisabeth Witzmann
    Hildegard Schünemann
    Anne-Marie Ludwig
    Claudia Hellmann
      Gottfried

Die Meistersinger von Nürnberg
Conductor: André Cluytens
Production and Decor: Wieland Wagner
Chorusmaster: Wilhelm Pitz

Hans Sachs: Otto Wiener
Veit Pogner: Hans Hotter
Sixtus Beckmesser:
 Toni Blankenheim/
 Karl Schmitt-Walter
Fritz Kothner: Eberhard Waechter
Walther von Stolzing:
 Josef Traxel/
 Wolfgang Windgassen
David: Gerhard Stolze
Eva: Elisabeth Grümmer
Magdalene: Elisabeth Schärtel

Kunz Vogelgesang: Fritz Uhl
Konrad Nachtigall: Egmont Koch
Balthasar Zorn:
 Heinz-Günther Zimmermann
Ulrich Eisslinger: Erich Benke
Augustin Moser: Hermann Winkler
Hermann Ortel: Hans Habietinek
Hans Schwarz:
 Hans-Günther Nöcker
Hans Foltz: Eugen Fuchs
Nightwatchman: Donald Bell

Parsifal
Conductor: Hans Knappertsbusch
Production and Decor: Wieland Wagner
Chorusmaster: Wilhelm Pitz
Choreography: Gertrud Wagner

Amfortas: Eberhard Waechter
Titurel: Josef Greindl
Gurnemanz: Jerome Hines
Parsifal: Hans Beirer
Klingsor: Toni Blankenheim
Kundry: Régine Crespin
1st Knight: Fritz Uhl

2nd Knight: Donald Bell
1st Esquire: Claudia Hellmann
2nd Esquire: Ursula Roese
3rd Esquire: Gerhard Stolze
4th Esquire: Harald Neukirch
Alto Solo: Maria von Ilsovay

Flowermaidens: Lotte Schädle, Hildegard Schünemann, Gertraud Prenzlow,
 Dorothea Siebert, Friedl Pöltinger, Elisabeth Schärtel

Tristan und Isolde
Conductor: Wolfgang Sawallisch
Production and Decor: Wolfgang Wagner
Chorusmaster: Wilhelm Pitz

Tristan: Wolfgang Windgassen
Isolde: Birgit Nilsson
King Marke: Josef Greindl
Kurwenal: Erik Saedén
Brangäne: Grace Hoffman

Melot: Fritz Uhl
Shepherd: Hermann Winkler
Steersman: Egmont Koch
Seaman: Josef Traxel/
 Sándor Kónya

Der Ring des Nibelungen
Conductor: Hans Knappertsbusch
Production and Decor: Wieland Wagner

Das Rheingold

Wotan: Hans Hotter
Donner: Erik Saedén
Froh: Sándor Kónya
Loge: Fritz Uhl
Fricka: Rita Gorr
Freia: Elisabeth Grümmer
Alberich: Frans Andersson

Mime: Gerhard Stolze
Fasolt: Theo Adam/
 Ludwig Weber
Fafner: Josef Greindl
Erda: Maria von Ilosvay
Woglinde: Dorothea Siebert
Welgunde: Claudia Hellmann
Flosshilde: Ursula Boese

Die Walküre

Gerhilde: Marlies Siemeling
Siegmund: Jon Vickers
Hunding: Josef Greindl
Wotan: Hans Hotter
Sieglinde: Leonie Rysanek
Brünnhilde: Astrid Varnay/
      Martha Mödl
Fricka: Rita Gorr

Ortlinde: Hilde Scheppan
Waltraute: Elisabeth Schärtel
Schwertleite: Maria von Ilosvay
Helmwige: Lotte Rysanek
Siegrune: Grace Hoffman
Grimgerde: Rita Gorr
Rossweisse: Ursula Boese

Siegfried

Siegfried: Wolfgang Windgassen
Mime: Gerhard Stolze
Wanderer: Hans Hotter
Alberich: Frans Andersson
Fafner: Josef Greindl

Brünnhilde: Astrid Varnay/
      Martha Mödl
Erda: Maria von Ilosvay
Woodbird: Dorothea Siebert

Götterdämmerung

Siegfried: Wolfgang Windgassen
Gunther: Otto Wiener
Hagen: Josef Greindl
Alberich: Frans Andersson
Brünnhilde: Astrid Varnay/
      Martha Mödl
Gutrune: Elisabeth Grümmer
Waltraute: Jean Madeira

1st Norn: Jean Madeira
2nd Norn: Ursula Boese
3rd Norn: Rita Gorr/
      Astrid Varnay
Woglinde: Dorothea Siebert
Wellgunde: Claudia Hellmann
Flosshilde: Ursula Boese

Chorusmaster: Wilhelm Pitz

1959
(July 23—August 25)
Der Fliegende Holländer
Conductor: Wolfgang Sawallisch
Production and Decor: Wieland Wagner
Chorusmaster: Wilhelm Pitz

Daland: Josef Greindl
Holländer: George London/
      Otto Wiener
Senta: Leonie Rysanek

Mary: Res Fischer
Erik: Fritz Uhl
Steersman: Georg Paskuda

Lohengrin
Conductor: Lovro von Matacic/Heinz Tietjen
Production and Decor: Wieland Wagner
Chorusmaster: Wilhelm Pitz

King Heinrich: Theo Adam/
      Franz Crass
Lohengrin: Sándor Kónya
Elsa: Elisabeth Grümmer
Telramund: Ernest Blanc
Ortrud: Rita Gorr/
      Astrid Varnay
Herald: Eberhard Waechter

Four nobles: Harald Neukirch
      Herold Kraus
      Donald Bell
      Hans-Günther Nöcker
Four pages: Elisabeth Witzmann
      Hildegard
          Schünemann
      Anne-Marie Ludwig
      Claudia Hellmann

Tristan und Isolde
Conductor: Wolfgang Sawallisch
Production and Decor: Wolfgang Wagner
Chorusmaster: Wilhelm Pitz

Tristan: Hans Beirer/
    Wolfgang Windgassen
Isolde: Birgit Nilsson
King Marke: Jerome Hines
Kurwenal: Frans Andersson
Brangäne: Grace Hoffman

Melot: Hans-Günther Nöcker
    Fritz Uhl
Shepherd: Hermann Winkler
Steersman: Donald Bell
Seaman: Georg Paskuda

Die Meistersinger von Nürnberg
Conductor: Erich Leinsdorf
Production and Decor: Wieland Wagner
Chorusmaster: Wilhelm Pitz

Hans Sachs: Otto Wiener
Veit Pogner: Josef Greindl
Sixtus Beckmesser:
    Toni Blankenheim/
    Karl Schmitt-Walter
Fritz Kothner: Eberhard Waechter
Walther von Stolzing:
    Rudolf Schock
David: Gerhard Stolze
Eva: Elisabeth Grümmer
Magdalene: Elisabeth Schärtel

Kunz Vogelgesang:
    Georg Paskuda
Konrad Nachtigall: Egmont Koch
Balthasar Zorn:
    Heinz-Günther Zimmermann
Ulrich Eisslinger: Harald Neukirch
Augustin Moser: Hermann Winkler
Hermann Ortel: Hans Habietinek
Hans Schwarz:
    Hans-Günther Nöcker
Hans Foltz: Eugen Fuchs
Nightwatchman: Donald Bell

Parsifal
Conductor: Hans Knappertsbusch
Production and Decor: Wieland Wagner
Chorusmaster: Wilhelm Pitz
Choreography: Gertrud Wagner

Amfortas: Eberhard Waechter
Titurel: Theo Adam/
    Josef Greindl
Gurnemanz: Josef Greindl/
    Jerome Hines
Parsifal: Hans Beirer
Klingsor: Toni Blankenheim
Kundry: Régine Crespin/
    Martha Mödl

1st Knight: Georg Paskuda
2nd Knight: Donald Bell
1st Esquire: Claudia Hellmann
2nd Esquire: Ursula Boese
3rd Esquire: Harald Neukirch
4th Esquire: Herold Kraus
Alto Solo: Ursula Boese

Flowermaidens: Ruth-Margret Pütz, Rita Bartos, Gisela Schröter, Dorothea Siebert, Elisabeth Witzmann, Claudia Hellmann

1960
(July 23—August 25)

Der Ring des Nibelungen
Conductor: Rudolf Kempe
Production and Decor: Wolfgang Wagner

Das Rheingold

Wotan: Hermann Uhde
Donner: Thomas Stewart
Froh: Georg Paskuda
Loge: Gerhard Stolze
Fricka: Herta Töpper
Freia: Ingrid Bjoner
Alberich: Otakar Kraus

Mime: Herold Kraus
Fasolt: Arnold van Mill
Fafner: Peter Roth-Ehrang
Erda: Marga Höffgen
Woglinde: Dorothea Siebert
Wellgunde: Claudia Hellmann
Flosshilde: Sona Cervena

Die Walküre

Siegmund: Wolfgang Windgassen
Hunding: Gottlob Frick
Wotan: Jerome Hines
Sieglinde: Aase Nordmo-Loevberg
Brünnhilde: Birgit Nilsson/
    Astrid Varnay
Fricka: Herta Töpper
Gerhilde: Gertraud Hopf

Ortlinde: Frances Martin
Waltraute: Claudia Hellmann
Schwertleite: Rut Siewert
Helmwige: Ingrid Bjoner
Siegrune: Grace Hoffman
Grimgerde: Margit Kobeck-Peters
Rossweisse: Dorothea von Stein

Siegfried

Siegfried: Hans Hopf
Mime: Herold Kraus
Wanderer: Hermann Uhde
Alberich: Otakar Kraus
Fafner: Peter Roth-Ehrang

Brünnhilde: Birgit Nilsson/
    Astrid Varnay
Erda: Marga Höffgen
Woodbird: Dorothea Siebert/
    Ruth-Margret Pütz

Götterdämmerung

Siegfried: Hans Hopf
Gunther: Thomas Stewart
Hagen: Gottlob Frick
Alberich: Otakar Kraus
Brünnhilde: Birgit Nilsson
Gutrune: Ingrid Bjoner
Waltraute: Grace Hoffman

Ist Norn: Rut Siewert
2nd Norn: Grace Hoffman
3rd Norn: Aase Nordmo-Loevberg
Woglinde: Dorothea Siebert
Wellgunde: Claudia Hellmann
Flosshilde: Sona Cervena

Chorusmaster: Wilhelm Pitz

Die Meistersinger von Nürnberg
Conductor: Hans Knappertsbusch
Production and Decor: Wieland Wagner
Chorusmaster: Wilhelm Pitz

Hans Sachs: Josef Greindl/
    Gustav Neidlinger
Veit Pogner: Theo Adam/
    Hans Hotter
Sixtus Beckmesser:
    Karl Schmitt Walter/
    Toni Blankenheim
Fritz Kothner: Ludwig Weber
Walther von Stolzing:
    Wolfgang Windgassen/
    Hans Hopf
David: Gerhard Stolze
Eva: Elisabeth Grümmer

Magdalene: Elisabeth Schärtel
Kunz Vogelgesang: Wilfried Krug
Konrad Nachtigall: Egmont Koch
Balthasar Zorn:
    Heinz Günther Zimmermann
Ulrich Eisslinger: Harald Neukirch
Augustin Moser: Hermann Winkler
Hermann Ortel: Frithjof Sentpaul
Hans Schwarz:
    Hans-Günther Nöcker
Hans Foltz: Eugen Fuchs
Nightwatchman: Donald Bell

Der Fliegende Holländer
Conductor: Wolfgang Sawallisch
Production and Decor: Wieland Wagner
Chorusmaster: Wilhelm Pitz

Daland: Josef Greindl	Erik: Fritz Uhl/
Holländer: Franz Crass	Wolfgang Windgassen
Senta: Anja Silja	Steersman : Georg Paskuda
Mary: Res Fischer	

Lohengrin
Conductor: Lorin Maazel/Ferdinand Leitner
Production and Decor: Wieland Wagner
Chorusmaster: Wilhelm Pitz

King Heinrich: Theo Adam	Four nobles: Wilfried Krug
Lohengrin: Sándor Kónya/	Hermann Winkler
Wolfgang Windgassen	Hans-Günther Nöcker
Elsa: Elisabeth Grümmer/	Egmont Koch
Annelies Kupper/	Four pages: Gundula Janowitz
Aase Nordmo-Loevberg	Elisabeth Witzmann
Telramund: Gustav Neidlinger	Hildegard
Ortrud: Astrid Varnay	Schünemann
Herald: Donald Bell/	Claudia Hellmann
Eberhard Waechter	

Parsifal
Conductor: Hans Knappertsbusch
Production and Decor: Wieland Wagner
Chorusmaster: Wilhelm Pitz
Choreography: Gertrud Wagner

Amfortas: Thomas Stewart/	1st Knight: Wilfried Krug
Eberhard Waechter	2nd Knight: Theo Adam
Titurel: David Ward	1st Esquire: Claudia Hellmann
Gurnemanz: Josef Greindl/	2nd Esquire: Ruth Hesse
Hans Hotter	3rd Esquire: Harald Neukirch
Parsifal: Hans Beirer	4th Esquire: Herold Kraus
Klingsor: Gustav Neidlinger	Alto Solo: Rut Siewert
Kundry: Régine Crespin/	
Martha Mödl	

Flowermaidens: Ruth-Margret Pütz, Gundula Janowitz, Claudia Hellmann, Dorothea Siebert, Elisabeth Witzmann, Ruth Hesse

1961
(July 23—August 25)

Tannhäuser
Conductor: Wolfgang Sawallisch
Production and Decor: Wieland Wagner
Chorusmaster: Wilhelm Pitz
Choreography: Maurice Béjart

Tannhäuser: Wolfgang Windgassen	Biterolf: Franz Crass
Elisabeth: Victoria de los Angeles	Heinrich der Schreiber:
Venus: Grace Bumbry	Georg Paskuda
Landgrave: Josef Greindl	Reinmar von Zweter: Theo Adam
Wolfram von Eschenbach:	Young Shepherd:
Dietrich Fischer-Dieskau	Else-Margrete Gardelli
Walther von der Vogelweide:	
Gerhard Stolze	

Der Fliegende Holländer
Conductor: Wolfgang Sawallisch
Production and Decor: Wieland Wagner
Chorusmaster: Wilhelm Pitz

Daland: Josef Greindl   Mary: Res Fischer
Holländer: George London/   Erik: Fritz Uhl
          Franz Crass   Steersman: Georg Paskuda
Senta: Anja Silja

Parsifal
Conductor: Hans Knappertsbusch
Production and Decor: Wieland Wagner
Chorusmaster: Wilhelm Pitz
Choreography: Gertrud Wagner

Amfortas: George London/   Kundry: Irene Dalis/
         Thomas Stewart   Régine Crespin
Titural: Ludwig Weber/   1st Knight: Niels Moeller
         Josef Greindl   2nd Knight: Theo Adam/
Gurnemanz: Hans Hotter/   David Ward
           Ludwig Weber   1st Esquire: Claudia Hellmann
Parsifal: Jess Thomas/   2nd Esquire: Ruth Hesse
          Hans Beirer   3rd Esquire: Gerhard Stolze
Klingsor: Gustav Neidlinger   4th Esquire: Georg Paskuda

Flowermaidens: Gundula Janowitz, Anja Silja, Claudia Hellmann, Dorothea
Siebert, Rita Bartos, Ruth Hesse

Der Ring des Nibelungen
Conductor: Rudolf Kempe
Production and Decor: Wolfgang Wagner

Das Rheingold

Wotan: Jerome Hines   Mime: Herold Kraus
Donner: Thomas Stewart   Fasolt: David Ward
Froh: David Thaw   Fafner: Peter Roth-Ehrang
Loge: Gerhard Stolze   Erda: Marga Höffgen
Fricka: Regina Resnik   Woglinde: Ingeborg Felderer
Freia: Wilma Schmidt   Wellgunde: Elisabeth Steinér
Alberich: Otakar Kraus   Flosshilde: Elisabeth Schärtel

Die Walküre

Siegmund: Fritz Uhl   Ortlinde: Wilma Schmidt
Hunding: Gottlob Frick   Waltraute: Elisabeth Schärtel
Wotan: Jerome Hines   Schwertleite: Lilo Brockhaus
Sieglinde: Régine Crespin   Helmwige: Ingeborg Felderer
Brünnhilde: Astrid Varnay   Siegrune: Grace Hoffman
Fricka: Regina Resnik   Grimgerde: Elisabeth Steiner
Gerhilde: Gertraud Hopf   Rossweisse: Ruth Hesse

Siegfried

Siegfried: Hans Hopf
Mime: Herold Kraus
Wanderer: James Milligan
Alberich: Otakar Kraus

Fafner: Peter Roth-Ehrang
Erda: Marga Höffgen
Brünnhilde: Birgit Nilsson
Woodbird: Ingeborg Felderer

Götterdämmerung

Siegfried: Hans Hopf
Gunther: Thomas Stewart
Hagen: Gottlob Frick
Alberich: Otakar Kraus
Brünnhilde: Birgit Nilsson/
　　　　Astrid Varnay
Gutrune: Wilma Schmidt
　　Chorusmaster: Wilhelm Pitz

Waltraute: Grace Hoffman
1st Norn: Elisabeth Schärtel
2nd Norn: Grace Hoffman
3rd Norn: Régine Crespin
Woglinde: Ingeborg Felderer
Wellgunde: Elisabeth Steiner
Flosshilde: Elisabeth Schärtel

Die Meistersinger von Nürnberg

Conductor: Josef Krips
Production and Decor: Wieland Wagner
Chorusmaster: Wilhelm Pitz

Hans Sachs: Josef Greindl
Veit Pogner: Theo Adam
Sixtus Beckmesser:
　　　　Karl Schmitt-Walter
Fritz Kothner: Ludwig Weber
Walther von Stolzing
　　　　Wolfgang Windgassen
David: Gerhard Stolze
Eva: Elisabeth Grümmer
Magdalene: Elisabeth Schärtel

Kunz Vogelgesang: Georg Paskuda
Konrad Nachtigall: Egmont Koch
Balthasar Zorn:
　　Heinz-Günther Zimmermann
Ulrich Eisslinger: Harald Neukirch
Augustin Moser: Hermann Winkler
Hermann Ortel: Frithjof Sentpaul
Hans Schwarz: Hans Habietinek
Hans Foltz: Eugen Fuchs
Nightwatchman: David Ward

1962
(July 24—August 27)

Tristan und Isolde

Conductor: Karl Böhm
Production and Decor: Wieland Wagner
Chorusmaster: Wilhelm Pitz

Tristan: Wolfgang Windgassen
Isolde: Birgit Nilsson/
　　　　Martha Mödl
King Marke: Josef Greindl
Kurwenal: Eberhard Waechter

Brangäne: Kerstin Meyer
Melot: Niels Moeller
Shepherd: Gerhard Stolze
Steersman: Hanns-Hanno Daum
Seaman: Georg Paskuda

Lohengrin

Conductor: Wolfgang Sawallisch
Production and Decor: Wieland Wagner
Chorusmaster: Wilhelm Pitz

King Heinrich: Franz Crass
Lohengrin: Jess Thomas
Elsa: Anja Silja
Telramund: Ramon Vinay
Ortrud: Irene Dalis/Astrid Varnay

Herald: Tom Krause
Four nobles: Niels Moeller
　　　　Gerhard Stolze
　　　　Klaus Kirchner
　　　　Zoltan Kelemen

Tannhäuser

Conductor: Wolfgang Sawallisch
Production and Decor: Wieland Wagner
Chorusmaster: Wilhelm Pitz
Choreography: Maurice Béjart

Tannhäuser: Wolfgang Windgassen
Elisabeth: Victoria de los Angeles/
Anja Silja
Venus: Grace Bumbry
Landgrave: Josef Greindl
Wolfram von Eschenbach:
Eberhard Waechter
Walther von der Vogelweide:
Gerhard Stolze

Biterolf: Franz Crass
Heinrich der Schreiber:
Georg Paskuda
Reinmar von Zweter:
Gerd Nienstedt
Young Shepherd:
Else-Margrete Gardelli

Parsifal

Conductor: Hans Knappertsbusch
Production and Decor: Wieland Wagner
Chorusmaster: Wilhelm Pitz

Amfortas: George London/
Thomas Stewart
Titurel: Martti Talvela
Gurnemanz: Hans Hotter/
Josef Greindl
Parsifal: Jess Thomas/
Hans Beirer
Klingsor: Gustav Neidlinger

Kundry: Irene Dalis/
Astrid Varnay
1st Knight: Niels Moeller
2nd Knight: Gerd Nienstedt
1st Esquire: Sona Cervena
2nd Esquire: Ursula Boese
3rd Esquire: Gerhard Stolze
4th Esquire: Georg Paskuda
Alto Solo: Ursula Boese

Flowermaidens: Gundula Janowitz, Anja Silja, Else-Margrete Gardelli,
Dorothea Siebert, Rita Bartos, Sona Cervena

Der Ring des Nibelungen

Conductor: Rudolf Kempe
Production and Decor: Wolfgang Wagner

Das Rheingold

Wotan: Otto Wiener
Donner: Marcel Cordes
Froh: Horst Wilhelm
Loge: Gerhard Stolze
Fricka: Grace Hoffman
Freia: Jutta Meyfarth
Alberich: Otakar Kraus
Mime: Erich Klaus

Fasolt: Walter Kreppel
Fafner: Peter Roth-Ehrang
Erda: Marga Höffgen/
Elisabeth Schärtel
Woglinde: Gundula Janowitz
Wellgunde:
Elisabeth Schwarzenberg
Flosshilde: Sieglinde Wagner

Die Walküre

Siegmund: Fritz Uhl
Hunding: Gottlob Frick
Wotan: Otto Wiener
Sieglinde: Jutta Meyfarth
Brünnhilde: Astrid Varnay
Fricka: Grace Hoffman
Gerhilde: Gertraud Hopf

Ortlinde: Elisabeth Schwarzenberg
Waltraute: Anni Argy
Schwertleite: Erika Schubert
Helmwige: Ingeborg Felderer
Siegrune: Grace Hoffman
Grimgerde: Sieglinde Wagner
Rossweisse: Margarethe Bence

Siegfried

Siegfried: Hans Hopf	Brünnhilde: Birgit Nilsson/
Mime: Erich Klaus	Astrid Varnay
Wanderer: Otto Wiener	Erda: Marga Höffgen/
Alberich: Otakar Kraus	Elisabeth Schärtel
Fafner: Peter Roth-Ehrang	Woodbird: Ingeborg Felderer

Götterdämmerung

Siegfried: Hans Hopf	Waltraute: Margarethe Bence
Gunther: Marcel Cordes	1st Norn: Elisabeth Schärtel
Hagen: Gottlob Frick	2nd Norn: Grace Hoffman
Alberich: Otakar Kraus	3rd Norn: Gertraud Hopf
Brünnhilde: Birgit Nilsson/	Woglinde: Gundula Janowitz
Astrid Varnay	Wellgunde:
Gutrune: Jutta Meyfarth	Elisabeth Schwarzenberg
	Flosshilde: Sieglinde Wagner

Chorusmaster: Wilhelm Pitz

1963

(July 23—August 27)

Ninth Symphony by Ludwig van Beethoven

Conductor: Karl Böhm
Soloists: Gundula Janowitz, Grace Bumbry,
 Jess Thomas, George London
Chorusmaster: Wilhelm Pitz

Die Meistersinger von Nürnberg

Conductor: Thomas Schippers
Production and Decor: Wieland Wagner
Chorusmaster: Wilhelm Pitz
Choreography: Gertrud Wagner

Hans Sachs: Otto Wiener/	Eva: Anja Silja
Josef Greindl	Magdalene: Ruth Hesse
Veit Pogner: Kurt Böhme/	Kunz Vogelgesang: Ticho Parly
Theo Adam	Konrad Nachtigall: Gerd Nienstedt
Sixtus Beckmesser:	Balthasar Zorn: Stefan Schwer
Carlos Alexander	Ulrich Eisslinger: Günther Treptow
Fritz Kothner: Gustav Neidlinger	Augustin Moser: Hermann Winkler
Walther von Stolzing:	Hermann Ortel: Zoltan Kelemen
Jess Thomas/	Hans Schwarz: Fritz Linke
Wolfgang Windgassen	Hans Foltz: Ernst Krukowski
David: Erwin Wohlfahrt	Nightwatchman: Heinz Hagenau

M

Parsifal

Conductor: Hans Knappertsbusch
Production and Decor: Wieland Wagner
Chorusmaster: Wilhelm Pitz
Choreography: Gertrud Wagner

Amfortas: George London/
    Thomas Stewart
Titurel: Kurt Böhme/
    Ludwig Weber/
    Heinz Hagenau
Gurnemanz: Hans Hotter/
    Josef Greindl
Parsifal: Wolfgang Windgassen/
    Jess Thomas

Klingsor: Gustav Neidlinger
Kundry: Irene Dalis
1st Knight: Hermann Winkler
2nd Knight: Gerd Nienstedt
1st Esquire: Ruth Hesse
2nd Esquire: Margarethe Bence
3rd Esquire: Georg Paskuda
4th Esquire: Erwin Wohlfahrt

Flowermaidens: Sylvia Stahlmann, Dorothea Siebert, Anja Silja, Rita Bartos, Sieglinde Wagner, Sona Cervena

Tristan und Isolde

Conductor: Karl Böhm
Production and Decor: Wieland Wagner
Chorusmaster: Wilhelm Pitz

Tristan: Wolfgang Windgassen
Isolde: Birgit Nilsson/
    Astrid Varnay
King Marke: Josef Greindl
Kurwenal: Gustav Neidlinger
Brangäne: Kerstin Meyer

Melot: Richard Martell
Shepherd: Erwin Wohlfahrt
Steersman: Hanns-Hanno Daum
Seaman: Hermann Winkler/
    Georg Paskuda

Der Ring des Nibelungen

Conductor: Rudolf Kempe
Production and Decor: Wolfgang Wagner

Das Rheingold

Wotan: Theo Adam
Donner: Marcel Cordes
Froh: Horst Wilhelm
Loge : Ken Neate
Fricka: Grace Hoffman
Freia: Jutta Meyfarth
Alberich: Otakar Kraus
Mime: Erich Klaus

Fasolt: Franz Crass
Fafner: Peter Roth-Ehrang
Erda: Marga Höffen/
    Margarethe Bence
Woglinde: Barbara Holt
Wellgunde:
    Elisabeth Schwarzenberg
Flosshilde: Sieglinde Wagner

Die Walküre

Siegmund: Fritz Uhl
Hunding: Gottlob Frick
Wotan: Hans Hotter/
    Jerome Hines
Sieglinde: Jutta Meyfarth
Brünnhilde: Anita Välkki
Fricka: Grace Hoffman
Gerhilde: Gertraud Hopf

Ortlinde: Elisabeth Schwarzenberg
Waltraute: Elisabeth Schärtel
Schwertleite: Ruth Hesse
Helmwige: Ingeborg Felderer
Siegrune: Grace Hoffman
Grimgerde: Sieglinde Wagner
Rossweisse: Margarethe Bence

Siegfried

Siegfried: Hans Hopf
Mime: Erich Klaus
Wanderer: Otto Wiener
Alberich: Otakar Kraus
Fafner: Peter Roth-Ehrang

Brünnhilde: Astrid Varnay
Erda: Marga Höffgen/
    Margarethe Bence
Woodbird: Barbara Holt

Götterdämmerung

Siegfried: Hans Hopf
Gunther: Marcel Cordes
Hagen: Gottlob Frick
Alberich: Otakar Kraus
Brünnhilde: Astrid Varnay
Gutrune: Jutta Meyfarth
Waltraute: Elisabeth Schärtel/
    Margarethe Bence

1st Norn: Elisabeth Schärtel
2nd Norn: Grace Hoffman
3rd Norn: Anita Välkki
Woglinde: Barbara Holt
Wellgunde:
    Elisabeth Schwarzenberg
Flosshilde: Sieglinde Wagner

Chorusmaster: Wilhelm Pitz

1964

(July 18—August 21)

Tannhäuser

Conductor: Otmar Suitner
Production and Decor: Wieland Wagner
Chorusmaster: Wilhelm Pitz
Choreography: Gertrud Wagner

Tannhäuser: Wolfgang Windgassen
Elisabeth: Leonie Rysanek
Venus: Barbro Ericson
Landgrave: Martti Talvela
Wolfram von Eschenbach:
    Eberhard Waechter/
    Franz Crass
Walther von der Vogelweide:
    Arturo Sergi

Biterolf: Hubert Hofmann
Heinrich der Schreiber:
    Hermann Winkler
Reinmar von Zweter:
    Gerd Nienstedt
Young Shepherd:
    Else-Margrete Gardelli

Tristan und Isolde

Conductor: Karl Böhm
Production and Decor: Wieland Wagner
Chorusmaster: Wilhelm Pitz

Tristan: Wolfgang Windgassen
Isolde: Birgit Nilsson
King Marke: Hans Hotter
Kurwenal: Gustav Neidlinger
Brangäne: Kerstin Meyer

Melot: Niels Moeller
Shepherd: Erwin Wohlfahrt
Steersman: Hanns-Hanno Daum
Seaman: Hermann Winkler

Die Meistersinger von Nürnberg
Conductor: Karl Böhm/Robert Heger
Production and Decor: Wieland Wagner
Chorusmaster: Wilhelm Pitz
Choreography: Gertrud Wagner

Hans Sachs: Josef Greindl
Veit Pogner: Kurt Böhme
Sixtus Beckmesser:
    Carlos Alexander
Fritz Kothner: Gustav Neidlinger
Walther von Stolzing:
    Sándor Kónya
David: Erwin Wohlfahrt
Eva: Anja Silja
Magdalene: Ruth Hesse

Kunz Vogelgesang: Ticho Parly
Konrad Nachtigall: Gerd Nienstedt
Balthasar Zorn: Stefan Schwer
Ulrich Eisslinger:
    Günther Treptow
Augustin Moser: Hermann Winkler
Hermann Ortel: Zoltan Kelemen
Hans Schwarz: Fritz Linke
Hans Foltz: Ralph Telasko
Nightwatchman: Heinz Hagenau

Parsifal
Conductor: Hans Knappertsbusch
Production and Decor: Wieland Wagner
Chorusmaster: Wilhelm Pitz
Choreography: Gertrud Wagner

Amfortas: George London/
    Thomas Stewart
Titurel: Heinz Hagenau
Gurnemanz: Hans Hotter
Parsifal: Jon Vickers
Klingsor: Gustav Neidlinger
Kundry: Barbro Ericson
1st Knight: Hermann Winkler

2nd Knight: Gerd Nienstedt
1st Esquire: Ruth Hesse
2nd Esquire:
    Sylvia Lindenstrand/
    Elisabeth Schártel
3rd Esquire: Dieter Slembeck
4th Esquire: Erwin Wohlfahrt
Alto Solo: Ruth Hesse

Flowermaidens: Anja Silja, Liselotte Rebmann, Else-Margrete Gardelli, Dorothea Siebert, Rita Bartos, Sylvia Lindenstrand

Der Ring des Nibelungen
Conductor: Berislav Klobucar
Production and Decor: Wolfgang Wagner

Das Rheingold
Wotan: Theo Adam
Donner: Marcel Cordes
Froh: Hans Hopf
Loge: Gerhard Stolze
Fricka: Grace Hoffman
Freia: Jutta Meyfarth
Alberich: Zoltan Kelemen
Mime: Erich Klaus

Fasolt: Gottlob Frick
Fafner: Peter Roth-Ehrang
Erda: Marga Höffgen
Woglinde: Barbara Holt
Wellgunde:
    Elizabeth Schwarzenberg
Flosshilde: Sieglinde Wagner

Die Walküre
Siegmund: Fritz Uhl
Hunding: Gottlob Frick
Wotan: Theo Adam
Sieglinde: Jutta Meyfarth
Brünnhilde: Anita Välkki
Fricka: Grace Hoffman
Gerhilde: Gertraud Hopf

Ortlinde: Elisabeth Schwarzenberg
Waltraute: Ursula Freudenberg
Schwertleite: Maria von Ilosvay
Helmwige: Eva-Maria Kupczyk
Siegrune: Grace Hoffman
Grimgerde: Sieglinde Wagner
Rossweisse: Erika Schubert

Siegfried

Siegfried: Hans Hopf
Mime: Erich Klaus
Wanderer: Hubert Hofmann
Alberich: Zoltan Kelemen

Fafner: Peter Roth-Ehrang
Brünnhilde: Astrid Varnay
Erda: Marga Höffgen
Woodbird: Barbara Holt

Götterdämmerung

Siegfried: Hans Hopf
Gunther: Marcel Cordes
Hagen: Gottlob Frick
Alberich: Zoltan Kelemen
Brünnhilde: Astrid Varnay
Gutrune: Jutta Meyfarth
Waltraute: Grace Hoffman

1st Norn: Marga Höffgen
2nd Norn: Grace Hoffman
3rd Norn: Anita Välkki
Woglinde: Barbara Holt
Wellgunde:
           Elisabeth Schwarzenberg
Flosshilde: Sieglinde Wagner

Chorusmaster: Wilhelm Pitz

1965

(July 25—August 30)

Der Ring des Nibelungen

Conductor: Karl Böhm
Production and Decor: Wieland Wagner

Das Rheingold

Wotan: Theo Adam
Donner: Gerd Nienstedt
Froh: William Olvis
Loge: Wolfgang Windgassen
Fricka: Ursula Boese
Freia: Anja Silja
Alberich: Gustav Neidlinger

Mime: Erwin Wohlfahrt
Fasolt: Martti Talvela
Fafner: Kurt Böhme
Erda: Lili Chookasian
Woglinde: Dorothea Siebert
Wellgunde: Helga Dernesch
Flosshilde: Kerstin Meyer

Die Walküre

Siegmund: James King
Hunding: Martti Talvela
Wotan: Theo Adam
Sieglinde: Leonie Rysanek
Brünnhilde: Birgit Nilsson
Fricka: Ursula Boese
Gerhilde: Danica Mastilovic

Ortlinde: Isabella Doran
Waltraute: Gertraud Hopf
Schwertleite: Lili Chookasian
Helmwige: Liane Synek
Siegrune: Elisabeth Schärtel
Grimgerde: Ursula Boese
Rossweisse: Margarethe Bence

Siegfried

Siegfried: Wolfgang Windgassen
Mime: Erwin Wohlfahrt
Wanderer: Josef Greindl
Alberich: Gustav Neidlinger

Fafner: Kurt Böhme
Brünnhilde: Birgit Nilsson
Erda: Lili Chookasian
Woodbird: Erika Köth

Götterdämmerung

Siegfried: Wolfgang Windgassen
Gunther: Thomas Stewart
Hagen: Josef Greindl
Alberich: Gustav Neidlinger
Brünnhilde: Birgit Nilsson
Gutrune: Ludmila Dvorakova
Waltraute: Kerstin Meyer

1st Norn: Lili Chookasian
2nd Norn: Ursula Boese
3rd Norn: Anja Silja
Woglinde: Dorothea Siebert
Wellgunde: Helga Dernesch
Flosshilde: Kerstin Meyer

Chorusmaster: Wilhelm Pitz

Der Fliegende Holländer

Conductor: Otmar Suitner
Production and Decor: Wieland Wagner
Chorusmaster: Wilhelm Pitz

Daland: Josef Greindl
Holländer: Thomas Stewart/
    Hans Hotter
Senta: Anja Silja

Mary: Lili Chookasian/
    Ruth Hesse
Erik: William Olvis/
    Niels Moeller
Steersman: Hermann Winkler

Tannhäuser

Conductor: André Cluytens
Production and Decor: Wieland Wagner
Chorusmaster: Wilhelm Pitz
Choreography: Birgit Cullberg

Tannhäuser:
    Wolfgang Windgassen
    Hans Hopf
Elisabeth: Leonie Rysanek/
    Gré Brouwenstijn
Venus: Ludmila Dvorakova/
    Anja Silja
Landgrave: Martti Talvela
Wolfram von Eschenbach
    Hermann Prey/
    Eberhard Waechter/
    Thomas Stewart

Walther von der Vogelweide:
    Willy Hartmann
Biterolf: Gerd Nienstedt
Heinrich der Schreiber:
    Hermann Winkler
Reinmar von Zweter:
    Dieter Slembeck
Young Shepherd:
    Olivera Miljakovic

Parsifal

Conductor André Cluytens
Production and Decor: Wieland Wagner
Chorusmaster: Wilhelm Pitz
Choreography: Gertrud Wagner

Amfortas: Theo Adam/
    Thomas Stewart
Titurel: Martti Talvela
Gurnemanz: Hans Hotter
Parsifal: Jess Thomas
Klingsor: Gustav Neidlinger
Kundry: Astrid Varnay

1st Knight: Hermann Winkler
2nd Knight: Gerd Nienstedt
1st Esquire: Ruth Hesse
2nd Esquire: Elisabeth Schärtel
3rd Esquire: Dieter Slembeck
4th Esquire: Erwin Wohlfahrt
Alto Solo: Ruth Hesse

Flowermaidens: Anja Silja, Simone Mangelsdorff, Helga Dernesch, Dorothea Siebert, Rita Bartos, Elisabeth Schärtel

1966

(July 24—August 28)

Tannhäuser

Conductor: Carl Melles
Production and Decor: Wieland Wagner
Chorusmaster: Wilhelm Pitz
Choreography: Birgit Cullberg

Tannhäuser: Jess Thomas/
    Hans Hopf
Elisabeth: Leonie Rysanek/
    Anja Silja
Venus: Anja Silja/
    Ludmila Dvorakova
Landgrave: Martti Talvela/
    Josef Greindl
Wolfram von Eschenbach:
    Hermann Prey/
    Eberhard Waechter/
    Thomas Stewart

Walther von der Vogelweide:
    Willy Hartmann
Biterolf: Gerd Nienstedt
Heinrich der Schreiber:
    Hermann Winkler
Reinmar von Zweter:
    Dieter Slembeck
Young Shepherd: Lily Sauter

Parsifal

Conductor: Pierre Boulez
Production and Decor: Wieland Wagner
Chorusmaster: Wilhelm Pitz
Choreography: Gertrud Wagner

Amfortas: Thomas Stewart/
    Eberhard Waechter
Titurel: Kurt Böhme
Gurnemanz: Josef Greindl/
    Hans Hotter
Parsifal: Sándor Kónya/
    Hans Hopf
Klingsor: Gustav Neidlinger

Kundry: Astrid Varnay
1st Knight: Hermann Winkler
2nd Knight: Gerd Nienstedt
1st Esquire: Ruth Hesse
2nd Esquire: Elisabeth Schärtel
3rd Esquire: Dieter Slembeck
4th Esquire: Erwin Wohlfahrt
Alto Solo: Ruth Hesse

Flowermaidens: Anja Silja, Lily Sauter, Helga Dernesch, Dorothea Siebert,
    Rita Bartos, Sona Cervena

Der Ring des Nibelungen

Conductor: Karl Böhm/Otmar Suitner
Production and Decor: Wieland Wagner

Das Rheingold

Wotan: Theo Adam/
    Hans Hotter
Donner: Gerd Nienstedt
Froh: Hermin Esser
Loge: Wolfgang Windgassen
Fricka: Annelies Burmeister
Freia: Anja Silja
Alberich: Gustav Neidlinger

Mime: Erwin Wohlfahrt
Fasolt: Martti Talvela/
    Josef Greindl
Fafner: Kurt Böhme
Erda: Vera Soukupova
Woglinde: Dorothea Siebert
Wellgunde: Helga Dernesch
Flosshilde: Ruth Hesse

Die Walküre

Siegmund: James King/
 Claude Heater/
 Ticho Parly
Hunding: Martti Talvela
 Josef Greindl
Wotan: Theo Adam/
 Hans Hotter
Sieglinde: Leonie Rysanek/
 Gwyneth Jones
Brünnhilde: Birgit Nilsson/
 Ludmila Dvorakova

Fricka: Annelies Burmeister
Gerhilde: Danica Mastilovic
Ortlinde: Helga Dernesch
Waltraute: Gertraud Hopf
Schwertleite: Ruth Hesse
Helmwige: Liane Synek
Siegrune: Annelies Burmeister
Grimgerde: Elisabeth Schärtel
Rossweisse: Sona Cervena

Siegfried

Siegfried: Wolfgang Windgassen
Mime: Erwin Wohlfahrt
Wanderer: Theo Adam/
 Hans Hotter
Alberich: Gustav Neidlinger
Fafner: Kurt Böhme

Brünnhilde: Birgit Nilsson/
 Ludmila Dvorakova
Erda: Vera Soukupova
Woodbird: Erika Köth/
 Anja Silja

Götterdämmerung

Siegfried: Wolfgang Windgassen
Gunther: Thomas Stewart
Hagen: Josef Greindl
Alberich: Gustav Neidlinger
Brünnhilde: Birgit Nilsson/
 Astrid Varnay
Gutrune: Ludmila Dvorakova

Waltraute: Martha Mödl
1st Norn: Vera Soukupova
2nd Norn: Elsa Cavelti
3rd Norn: Anja Silja
Woglinde: Dorothea Siebert
Wellgunde: Helga Dernesch
Flosshilde: Ruth Hesse

Chorusmaster: Wilhelm Pitz

Tristan und Isolde

Conductor: Karl Böhm
Production and Decor: Wieland Wagner
Chorusmaster: Wilhelm Pitz

Tristan: Wolfgang Windgassen
Isolde: Birgit Nilsson
King Marke: Martti Talvela
Kurwenal: Eberhard Waechter
Brangäne: Christa Ludwig/
 Grace Hoffman

Melot: Claude Heater
Shepherd: Erwin Wohlfahrt
Steersman: Gerd Nienstedt
Seaman: Peter Schreier

1967

(July 21—August 24)

Lohengrin
Conductor: Rudolf Kempe/Berislav Klobucar
Production and Decor: Wolfgang Wagner
Chorusmaster: Wilhelm Pitz

King Heinrich: Karl Ridderbusch
Lohengrin: Sándor Kónya/
    James King/
    Jean Cox/
    Hermin Esser/
    Jess Thomas
Elsa: Heather Harper
Telramund: Donald McIntyre
Ortrud: Grace Hoffman/
    Astrid Varnay

Herald: Thomas Tipton
Four nobles: Horst Hoffmann
    Hermin Esser
    Dieter Slembeck
    Heinz Feldhoff
Four pages: Natsue Hanada
    Lotte Kiefer
    Elke Georg
    Margret
        Giese-Schröder

Der Ring des Nibelungen
Conductor: Karl Böhm/Otmar Suitner
Production and Decor: Wieland Wagner
Stage Direction: Peter Lehmann

Das Rheingold

Wotan: Theo Adam/
    Thomas Stewart
Donner: Gerd Nienstedt
Froh: Hermin Esser
Loge: Wolfgang Windgassen
Fricka: Annelies Burmeister/
    Martha Mödl
Freia: Anja Silja
Alberich: Gustav Neidlinger

Mime: Erwin Wohlfahrt
Fasolt: Karl Ridderbusch
Fafner: Kurt Böhme/
    Josef Greindl
Erda: Marga Höffgen/
    Jean Modeira
Woglinde: Dorothea Siebert
Wellgunde: Helga Dernesch
Flosshilde: Sieglinde Wagner

Die Walküre

Siegmund: James King
Hunding: Gerd Nienstedt/
    Josef Greindl
Wotan: Theo Adam/
    Thomas Stewart
Sieglinde: Leonie Rysanek
Brünnhilde: Birgit Nilsson/
    Ludmila Dvorakova
Fricka: Annelies Burmeister/
    Martha Mödl

Gerhilde: Danica Mastilovic
Ortlinde: Helga Dernesch
Waltraute: Gertraud Hopf
Schwertleite: Sieglinde Wagner
Helmwige: Liane Synek
Siegrune: Annelies Burmeister
Grimgerde: Elisabeth Schärtel
Rossweisse: Sona Cervena/
    Alice Oelke

Siegfried

Siegfried: Wolfgang Windgassen
Mime: Erwin Wohlfahrt
Wanderer: Theo Adam/
    Josef Greindl
Alberich: Gustav Neidlinger
Fafner: Kurt Böhme

Brünnhilde: Birgit Nilsson/
    Ludmila Dvorakova
Erda: Marga Höffgen/
    Jean Madeira
Woodbird: Erika Köth/ Anja Silja

Götterdämmerung

Siegfried: Wolfgang Windgassen
Gunther: Thomas Stewart
Hagen: Josef Greindl
Alberich: Gustav Neidlinger
Brünnhilde: Birgit Nilsson/
　　　　　　Astrid Varney
Gutrune: Ludmila Dvorokova
Waltraute: Martha Mödl

1st Norn: Marga Höffgen/
　　　　　Jean Madeira
2nd Norn: Annelies Burmeister
3rd Norn: Anja Silja
Woglinde: Dorothea Siebert
Wellgunde: Helga Dernesch
Flosshilde: Sieglinde Wagner

Chorusmaster: Wilhelm Pitz

Parsifal

Conductor: Pierre Boulez
Production and Decor: Wieland Wagner
Stage Direction: Peter Lehmann
Chorusmaster: Wilhelm Pitz
Choreography: Birgit Cullberg

Amfortas: Thomas Stewart
Titurel: Karl Ribberbusch
Gurnemanz: Franz Crass
Parsifal: James King/
　　　　　Wolfgang Windgassen
Klingsor: Gerd Nienstedt
Kundry: Christa Ludwig
1st Knight: Hermin Esser

2nd Knight: Kurt Moll
1st Esquire: Elisabeth Schärtel
2nd Esquire: Annelies Burmeister
3rd Esquire: Dieter Slembeck
4th Esquire: Horst Hoffmann
Alto Solo: Martha Mödl/
　　　　　Annelies Burmeister

Flowermaidens: Anja Silja/ Lotte Schädle, Lily Sauter, Helga Dernesch,
Dorothea Siebert, Rita Bartos, Sona Cervena

Tannhäuser

Conductor: Berislav Klobucar
Production and Decor: Wieland Wagner
Stage Direction: Peter Lehmann
Chorusmaster: Wilhelm Pitz
Choreography: Birgit Cullberg

Tannhäuser: Jess Thomas/
　　　　　　Wolfgang Windgassen
Elisabeth: Anja Silja/
　　　　　Helga Dernesch
Venus: Berit Lindholm
Landgrave: Tugomir Franc
Wolfram von Eschenbach:
　　　　　Hermann Prey/
　　　　　Thomas Stewart/
　　　　　Thomas Tipton

Walther von der Vogelweide:
　　　　　　Hermin Esser
Biterolf: Gerd Nienstedt
Heinrich der Schreiber:
　　　　　　Horst Hoffmann
Reinmar von Zweter:
　　　　　　Dieter Slembeck
Young Shepherd: Lily Sauter

1968

(July 25—August 28)

Die Meistersinger von Nürnberg

Conductor: Karl Böhm/Berislav Klobucar
Production and Decor: Wolfgang Wagner
Chorusmaster: Wilhelm Pitz

Hans Sachs: Theo Adam/
    Gustav Neidlinger
Veit Pogner: Karl Ridderbusch
Sixtus Beckmesser:
    Thomas Hemsley
Fritz Kothner: Gerd Nienstedt
Walther von Stolzing:
    Waldemar Kmentt
David: Hermin Esser
Eva: Gwyneth Jones
Magdalene: Janis Martin

Kunz Vogelgesang:
    Sebastian Feiersinger
Konrad Nachtigall:
    Dieter Slembeck
Balthasar Zorn: Günther Treptow
Ulrich Eisslinger: Erich Klaus
Augustin Moser: William Johns
Hermann Ortel: Heinz Feldhoff
Hans Schwarz: Fritz Linke
Hans Foltz: Hans Franzen
Nightwatchman: Kurt Moll

Lohengrin

Conductor: Alberto Erede
Production and Decor: Wolfgang Wagner
Chorusmaster: Wilhelm Pitz

King Heinrich: Karl Ridderbusch
Lohengrin: James King/
    Jean Cox
Elsa: Heather Harper
Telramund: Donald McIntyre
Ortrud: Ludmila Dvorakova
    Grace Hoffman
Herald: Thomas Stewart

Four nobles: Horst Hoffman
    William Johns/
    Hermin Esser
    Dieter Slembeck
    Heinz Feldhoff
Four pages: Natsue Hanada
    Lotte Kiefer
    Elke Georg
    Margret
    Giese-Schröder

Parsifal

Conductor: Pierre Boulez
Production and Decor: Wieland Wagner
Stage Direction: Peter Lehmann
Chorusmaster: Wilhelm Pitz
Choreography: Yvonne Georgi

Amfortas: Thomas Stewart/
    Gerd Feldhoff
Titurel: Karl Ridderbusch
Gurnemanz: Franz Crass/
    Josef Greindl
Parsifal: Jean Cox
Klingsor: Donald McIntyre/
    Gerd Nienstedt
Kundry: Amy Shuard

1st Knight: Hermin Esser
2nd Knight: Kurt Moll
1st Esquire:
    Elisabeth Schwarzenberg
2nd Esquire: Sieglinde Wagner
3rd Esquire: Dieter Slembeck
4th Esquire: Horst Hoffmann
Alto Solo: Unni Rugtvedt

Flowermaidens: Hannelore Bode, Lily Sauter, Helga Dernesch, Dorothea
Siebert, Ingrit Liljeberg, Sieglinde Wagner

Tristan und Isolde
Conductor: Karl Böhm/ Berislav Klobucar
Production and Decor: Wieland Wagner
Stage Direction: Peter Lehmann
Chorusmaster: Wilhelm Pitz

Tristan: Wolfgang Windgassen
Isolde: Birgit Nilsson/
    Gladys Kuchta
King Marke: Martti Talvela
Kurwenal: Gerd Feldhoff

Brangäne: Grace Hoffman
Melot: Reid Bunger
Shepherd: Hermin Esser
Steersman: Kurt Moll
Seaman: Hermin Esser

Der Ring des Nibelungen
Conductor: Lorin Maazel
Production and Decor: Wieland Wagner
Stage Direction: Hans Hotter

Das Rheingold

Wotan: Theo Adam/
    Thomas Stewart
Donner: Gerd Nienstedt
Froh: Hermin Esser
Loge: Wolfgang Windgassen
Fricka: Janis Martin
Freia: Helga Dernesch
Alberich: Gustav Neidlinger

Mime: Gerhard Stolze
Fasolt: Karl Ridderbusch
Fafner: Josef Greindl
Erda: Marga Höffgen
Woglinde: Dorothea Siebert
Wellgunde:
    Elisabeth Schwarzenberg
Flosshilde: Sieglinde Wagner

Die Walküre

Siegmund: James King/
    Richard Martell
Hunding: Josef Greindl
Wotan: Theo Adam/
    Thomas Stewart
Sieglinde: Leonie Rysanek
Brünnhilde: Berit Lindholm
Fricka: Janis Martin

Gerhilde: Elisabeth Schwarzenberg
Ortlinde: Helga Dernesch
Waltraute: Gertraud Hopf
Schwertleite: Sieglinde Wagner
Helmwige: Liane Synek
Siegrune: Inger Paustian
Grimgerde: Marie-Louise Gilles
Rossweisse: Unni Rugtvedt

Siegfried

Siegfried: Ticho Parly
Mime: Gerhard Stolze
Wanderer: Josef Greindl
Alberich: Gustav Neidlinger

Fafner: Gerd Nienstedt
Brünnhilde: Berit Lindholm
Erda: Marga Höffgen
Woodbird: Erika Köth

Götterdämmerung

Siegfried: Wolfgang Windgassen
Gunther: Thomas Stewart
Hagen: Josef Greindl
Alberich: Gustav Neidlinger
Brünnhilde: Gladys Kuchta
Gutrune: Helga Dernesch
Waltraute: Grace Hoffman

1st Norn: Marga Höffgen
2nd Norn: Janis Martin
3rd Norn: Berit Lindholm/
    Liane Synek
Woglinde: Dorothea Siebert
Wellgunde:
    Elizabeth Schwarzenberg
Flosshilde: Sieglinde Wagner

Chorusmaster: Wilhelm Pitz

1969

(July 25—August 28)

Der Fliegende Holländer

Conductor: Silvio Varviso
Production: August Everding
Decor: Josef Svoboda
Chorusmaster: Wilhelm Pitz

Daland: Martti Talvela
Holländer: Donald McIntyre/
    Theo Adam
Senta: Leonie Rysanek/
    Gwyneth Jones.

Mary: Unni Rugtvedt
Erik: Jean Cox
Steersman: René Kollo

Parsifal

Conductor: Horst Stein
Production and Decor: Wieland Wagner
Stage Direction: Peter Lehmann
Chorusmaster: Wilhelm Pitz
Choreography: Yvonne Georgi

Amfortas: Thomas Stewart/
    Gerd Feldhoff
Titurel: Karl Ridderbusch
Gurnemanz: Franz Crass/
    Josef Greindl
Parsifal: James King
Klingsor: Gerd Nienstedt
Kundry: Ludmila Dvorakova/
    Gwyneth Jones

1st Knight: Hermin Esser
2nd Knight: Bengt Rundgren
1st Esquire: Elisabeth
    Schwarzenberg
2nd Esquire: Sieglinde Wagner
3rd Esquire: Dieter Slembeck
4th Esquire: William Johns
Alto Solo: Unni Rugtvedt

Flowermaidens: Hannelore Bode, Elisabeth Schwarzenberg, Helga Dernesch, Dorothea Siebert, Ingrit Liljeberg, Sieglinde Wagner.

Die Meistersinger von Nürnberg

Conductor: Berislav Klobucar
Production and Decor: Wolfgang Wagner
Chorusmaster: Wilhelm Pitz

Hans Sachs: Norman Bailey/
    Theo Adam
Veit Pogner: Karl Ridderbusch
Sixtus Beckmesser: Thomas
    Hemsley
Fritz Kothner: Gerd Nienstedt
Walther von Stolzing:
    Waldemar Kmentt/
    Jess Thomas/
    Jean Cox
David: Hermin Esser
Eva: Helga Dernesch/
    Gwyneth Jones

Magdalene: Janis Martin
Kunz Vogelgesang: René Kollo
Konrad Nachtigall: Dieter
    Slembeck
Balthasar Zorn: Sebastian
    Feiersinger
Ulrich Eisslinger: Erich Klaus
Augustin Moser: William Johns
Hermann Ortel: Heinz Feldhoff
Hans Schwarz: Fritz Linke
Hans Foltz: Hans Franzen
Nightwatchman: Bengt Rundgren

Tristan und Isolde

Conductor: Karl Böhm
Production and Decor: Wieland Wagner
Stage Direction: Peter Lehmann
Chorusmaster: Wilhelm Pitz

Tristan: Wolfgang Windgassen
Isolde: Birgit Nilsson
King Marke: Martti Talvela
Kurwenal: Gerd Feldhoff
Brangäne: Grace Hoffman

Melot: Reid Bunger
Shepherd: Hermin Esser
Steersman: Bengt Rundgren
Seaman: Hermin Esser

Der Ring des Nibelungen

Conductor: Lorin Maazel
Production and Decor: Wieland Wagner
Stage Direction: Hans Hotter

Das Rheingold

Wotan: Thomas Stewart/
    Theo Adam
Donner: Gerd Nienstedt
Froh: Hermin Esser
Loge: Wolfgang Windgassen
Fricka: Janis Martin
Freia: Helga Dernesch
Alberich: Gustav Neidlinger

Mime: Gerhard Stolze
Fasolt: Karl Ridderbusch
Fafner: Josef Greindl
Erda: Marga Höffgen
Woglinde: Dorothea Siebert
Wellgunde: Elisabeth
                Schwarzenberg
Flosshilde: Sieglinde Wagner

Die Walküre

Siegmund: James King/
    Helge Brilioth
Hunding: Josef Greindl
Wotan: Thomas Stewart/
    Theo Adam
Sieglinde: Leonie Rysanek
Brünnhilde: Berit Lindholm
Fricka: Janis Martin

Gerhilde: Elisabeth Schwarzenberg
Ortlinde: Helga Dernesch
Waltraute: Gertraud Hopf
Schwertleite: Sieglinde Wagner
Helmwige: Liane Synek
Siegrune: Inger Paustian
Grimgerde: Marie-Louise Gilles
Rossweisse: Unni Rugtvedt

Siegfried

Siegfried: Jess Thomas
Mime: Gerhard Stolze
Wanderer: Thomas Stewart/
    Theo Adam
Alberich: Gustav Neidlinger

Fafner: Josef Greindl
Brünnhilde: Berit Lindholm
Erda: Marga Höffgen
Woodbird: Hannelore Bode

Götterdämmerung

Siegfried: Jess Thomas
Gunther: Thomas Stewart
Hagen: Josef Greindl
Alberich: Gustav Neidlinger
Brünnhilde: Gladys Kuchta
Gutrune: Helga Dernesch
Waltraute: Grace Hoffman
1st Norn: Marga Höffgen

2nd Norn: Janis Martin
3rd Norn: Berit Lindholm/
         Liane Synek
Woglinde: Dorothea Siebert
Wellgunde: Elisabeth
                Schwarzenberg
Flosshilde: Sieglinde Wagner

Chorusmaster: Wilhelm Pitz

1970
(July 24—August 27)

Der Ring des Nibelungen
Conductor: Horst Stein
Production and Decor: Wolfgang Wagner

Das Rheingold

Wotan: Thomas Stewart/	Mime: Georg Paskuda
Theo Adam	Fasolt: Karl Ridderbusch
Donner: Gerd Nienstedt	Fafner: Bengt Rundgren
Froh: René Kollo	Erda: Marga Höffgen
Loge: Hermin Esser	Woglinde: Hannelore Bode
Fricka: Janis Martin	Wellgunde: Inger Paustian
Freia: Margarita Kyriaki	Flosshilde: Sylvia Anderson/
Alberich: Gustav Neidlinger	Faith Puleston

Die Walküre

Siegmund: Helge Brilioth	Orlinde: Gildis Flossmann
Hunding: Karl Ridderbusch	Waltraute: Wendy Fine
Wotan: Thomas Stewart/	Schwertleite: Sylvia Anderson
Theo Adam	Helmwige: Liane Synek
Sieglinde: Gwyneth Jones	Siegrune: Inger Paustian
Brünnhilde: Berit Lindholm	Grimgerde: Faith Puleston
Fricka: Anna Reynolds	Rossweisse: Aili Purtonen
Gerhilde: Elisabeth Schwarzenberg	

Siegfried

Siegfried: Jean Cox	Fafner: Bengt Rundgren
Mime: Georg Paskuda	Brünnhilde: Berit Lindholm
Wanderer: Thomas Stewart/	Erda: Marga Höffgen
Theo Adam	Woodbird: Hannelore Bode
Alberich: Gustav Neidlinger	

Götterdämmerung

Siegfried: Jean Cox	1st Norn: Marga Höffgen
Gunther: Norman Bailey	2nd Norn: Anna Reynolds
Hagen: Karl Ridderbusch	3rd Norn: Liane Synek
Alberich: Gustav Neidlinger	Woglinde: Hannelore Bode
Brünnhilde: Berit Lindholm	Wellgunde: Inger Paustian
Gutrune: Janis Martin	Flosshilde: Sylvia Anderson
Waltraute: Anna Reynolds	

Chorusmaster: Wilhelm Pitz

Tristan und Isolde
Conductor: Karl Böhm
Production and Decor: Wieland Wagner
Stage Direction: Peter Lehmann
Chorusmaster: Wilhelm Pitz

Tristan: Wolfgang Windgassen	Brangäne: Grace Hoffman
Isolde: Birgit Nilsson	Melot: Reid Bunger
King Marke: Martti Talvela/	Shepherd: Hermin Esser
Franz Crass	Steersman: Bengt Rundgren
Kurwenal: Gustav Neidlinger	Seaman: Hermin Esser

Die Meistersinger von Nürnberg

Conductor: Hans Wallat
Production and Decor: Wolfgang Wagner
Chorusmaster: Wilhelm Pitz

Hans Sachs: Norman Bailey/
          Theo Adam
Veit Pogner: Karl Ridderbusch
Sixtus Beckmesser: Thomas
          Hemsley
Fritz Kothner: Gerd Nienstedt
Walther von Stolzing: Jean Cox/
          Ernst Kozub/
          Waldemar Kmentt
David: Hermin Esser/
          Heinz Zednik
Eva: Janis Martin

Magdalene: Sylvia Anderson/
          Sieglinde Wagner
Kunz Vogelgesang: Horst
          Laubenthal
Konrad Nachtigall: Dieter
          Slembeck
Balthasar Zorn: Robert Licha
Ulrich Eisslinger: Heinz Zednik
Augustin Moser: Georg Paskuda
Hermann Ortel: Heinz Feldhoff
Hans Schwarz: Fritz Linke
Hans Foltz: Hans Franzen
Nightwatchman: Bengt Rundgren

Der Fliegende Holländer

Conductor: Silvio Varviso
Production: August Everding
Decor: Josef Svoboda
Chorusmaster: Wilhelm Pitz

Daland: Martti Talvela/
          Karl Ridderbusch
Holländer: Donald McIntyre
Senta: Leonie Rysanek/
          Gwyneth Jones

Mary: Maria von Ilosvay
Erik: Hermin Esser/René Kollo
Steersman: Horst Laubenthal/
          Georg Paskuda

Parsifal

Conductor: Pierre Boulez
Production and Decor: Wieland Wagner
Stage Direction: Peter Lehmann
Chorusmaster: Wilhelm Pitz
Choreography: Yvonne Georgi

Amfortas: Thomas Stewart
Titurel: Karl Ridderbusch
Gurnemanz: Franz Crass
Parsifal: James King
Klingsor: Donald McIntyre/
          Gerd Nienstedt
Kundry: Gwyneth Jones
1st Knight: Hermin Esser

2nd Knight: Bengt Rundgren
1st Esquire: Elisabeth
          Schwarzenberg
2nd Esquire: Sieglinde Wagner
3rd Esquire: Dieter Slembeck
4th Esquire: Heinz Zednik
Alto Solo: Marga Höffgen

Flowermaidens: Hannelore Bode, Margarita Kyriaki, Inger Paustian, Dorothea
Siebert, Wendy Fine, Sieglinde Wagner.

APPENDIX B
Bayreuth Recordings

The following is a list of Bayreuth Festival Recordings made between 1951 and 1970 and which are, or have been, issued commercially. Those records which are no longer available in Great Britain are marked (*). The date on the left-hand side is the year when the recording was made.

1951 Beethoven's Ninth Symphony. c. Furtwängler. Schwarzkopf, Höngen, Hopf, Edelmann. H.M.V. Issued 1955 ALP 1286-7 (Mono only) (*).

1951 *Die Meistersinger.* c. Karajan. Edelmann, Schwarzkopf, Hopf, etc. Columbia. Issued 1951 LX 1465-1498, deleted, reissued 1952 as 33CX 1021-5 (Mono only) (*).

1951 *Die Walküre* Act III. c. Karajan. Varnay, Rysanek, Sigurd Björling. Columbia. Issued 1951 LX 1447-1454, deleted, reissued 1952 as 33CX 1005-6 (Mono only) (*).

1951 *Parsifal.* c Knappertsbusch. London, van Mill, Weber, Windgassen, Uhde, Mödl. Decca. Issued 1951 LXT 2651-6, deleted, reissued 1966 as GOM 504-8 (Mono only).

1953 *Lohengrin.* c. Keilberth. Wingassen, Steber, Uhde, Varnay, Greindl, Braun. Decca. Issued 1953. LXT 2880–4 (Mono only) (*).

1955 *Der Fliegende Holländer.* c. Keilberth. Varnay, Uhde, Weber, Schärtel, Lustig, Traxel. Decca. Issued 1956 LXT 5150-2 (Mono only) (*).

1958 Chorplatte. Selection of Wagner choruses. c. Pitz. Deutsche Grammophon. Issued 1958. 19168 (Stereo) (*).

1961 *Der Fliegende Holländer.* c. Sawallisch. Crass, Silja, Greindl, Uhl, Paskuda, Fischer. Philips. Issued 1962 SABL 218-20 (Stereo only) (*). Reissue see below.

1962 *Tannhäuser.* c. Sawallisch. Windgassen, Silja, Bumbry, Waechter, Greindl. Philips. Issued 1964 SAL 3445-7 (Stereo only) (*). Reissue see below.

1962 *Parsifal.* c. Knappertsbusch. London, Talvela, Hotter, Thomas, Neidlinger, Dalis. Philips. Issued 1964 SAL 3475-9 (Stereo); AL 3475-9 (Mono) (*). Reissue see below.

The above three recordings, *Holländer* 1961, *Tannhäuser* 1962, *Parsifal* 1962, reissued by Philips as a complete 11-record album (operas not sold separately) 1970, 6723001. (Stereo).

1966 *Tristan und Isolde.* c. Böhm. Nilsson, Windgassen, Ludwig, Talvela, Waechter. Deutsche Grammophon. Issued 1966 13922-5 (Stereo).

1967 *Die Feen.* Although not a part of the official Bayreuth festival, the student performances of *Die Feen* in 1967 aroused considerable interest. A single LP Colosseum Stereo Pandynamic record of excerpts from these performances was issued in 1968. Price 25 DM from: Account No. 1844, International Youth Festival Meeting, Städtische Sparkasse, 8580 Bayreuth, Germany.

APPENDIX C

Information for the Traveller to Bayreuth

Festival Tickets.
The programme for the following year's festival is published in October each year. Booking opens in November. Owing to the tremendous demand for seats it is usually essential to send in ticket applications when the box office opens. Programme and tickets from: Kartenbüro, Bayreuther Festspiele, Postfach 2320, 8580 Bayreuth 2, Germany. A few travel agencies in different countries also hold allocations of seats (see below).

Accommodation.
When the Bayreuth Festival box office despatches the opera tickets they also send a card on which the visitor can reserve accommodation of different types: hotels, guest houses, private rooms. Alternatively information can be had direct from the Fremdenverkehrsbüro, 8580 Bayreuth, Germany, or accommodation can be booked by a travel agency.

Travel.
Full details on travel to Bayreuth can be had from any Verkehrsbüro in Germany, or from the information offices of the German National Tourist Association in other countries. They can also supply information as to which travel agencies hold allocations of Bayreuth festival tickets, and/or organize inclusive holidays to Bayreuth.

Outside Germany the offices of the Deutsche Zentrale für Fremdenverkehr (German National Tourist Association) are:

Amsterdam: Spui 24, Amsterdam-1001, Tel. 24 12 93.
Brussels: 23, rue du Luxembourg, Bruxelles 4, Tel. 12 77 66.
Chicago: 11, South la Salle St., Chicago, Ill. 60603. Tel. Andover 3-29 58.
Copenhagen: Vesterbrogade 6 D 11. DK 1620 København V. Tel. (01) 12 70 95/96.
Johannesburg: Loveday & Plein Streets, P.O. Box 10883, Johannesburg. Tel. 838-5334.
London: 61, Conduit St., London, W.1. W1R OEN. Tel. 01-734 2600.
Madrid: San Augustin 2, Plaza de las Cortes, Madrid 14. Tel. 222 29 10/ 221 10 22.
Montreal: P.O. Box 417, 47, Fundy Place, Bonaventure, Montreal 114, P.Q. Tel. 878-98 85.
New York: 500 Fifth Avenue, New York, N.Y. 10036. Tel. Longacre 4-06 70/71.
Paris: 4, Place de l'Opéra, F 75 Paris 2e. Tel. 073 0808.
Rio de Janeiro: Av. Nilo Peçanha 155, s/514, Caixa Postal 3022-ZC 00-Rio de Janeiro. Tel. 22-8298.
Rome: Via L Bissolati 22, 1 00187 Roma. Tel. (06) 48 39 56.
San Francisco: 323 Geary Street, San Francisco, Calif. 94102. Tel. 986-0796.
Stockholm: Birger Jarlsgatan 11, Box 7086 S-10382 Stockholm 7. Tel. 10 93 90/91.
Vienna: Brandstätte 1, Stephansplatz 8, A-1010 Wien. Tel. 63 14 78.
Zürich: Talstrasse 62, CH 8001 Zürich. Tel. (051) 25 13 87.

LIST OF PRE-PUBLICATION SUBSCRIBERS

in order of booking

J. L. Turing
Air Commodore H. A. Hewat
P. M. Behrend
Roger Warren
Mrs. Claude Wilson
Mrs. K. Denholm Gillies
H. W. Preston
Mrs. D. Bonelle
Elizabeth Jenkins
Leonard Taylor
Mr. D. H. Burt
Bernard Glicksman
The Rev. Gregory Page-Turner
H. P. Smithson
Mrs. Joan Lane
Mr. Anthony S. Kind
Alan Taylor, Esq.
Claude Visinand
Mrs. E. M. Hudson
Miss E. Webb-Elliot
Frank Storey
Miss Audrey M. G. Innes
Mrs. G. M. L. Winton-Hirsh
Mr. J. Alfred Lee
Mrs. Phyllis I. Sabin
Mr. F. G. Eaton
W. G. Glover
Peter Parkhouse
German Institute Library
S. John Shelton
Countess Luciana Valentini Di Laviano
Adelphi Univ. Music Dept.

Mr. G. W. Wright
George Auble
Tom V. Mollet
Scottish German Society
Brian Lake
Mr. G. Thomson
Paul H. D. Findley
Miss L. D. Baynes
D. F. Mitchener
Mr. R. F. Codd
D. C. Scowcroft
J. A. T. Maddisson
Miss F. Edwards
H. G. Hands
Matthew Stoddart
Nicholas Braithwaithe
Mr. P. N. Cunningham
R. G. Mitchell
G. S. Feggetter
G. H. Lamb
Mrs. D. Stewart
Philip Leon
David Myerscough-Jones
A. J. N. Burden
Stephen E. Mead
Alexander Basil Tsakos
David Dempsey
R. C. Y. Naff
Michael C. Fletcher
Mrs. T. D. Harrison
Thomas E. Jeffrey
John Codner
Toronto Public Libraries
S. S. Mumford

INDEX

Italic figures indicate Plate numbers

Italic figures indicate Plate numbers

Italic figures indicate Plate numbers

Italic figures indicate Plate numbers